ACFT

by Angie Papple Johnston

ACFT For Dummies®

Published by: **John Wiley & Sons, Inc.,** 111 River Street, Hoboken, NJ 07030-5774, www.wiley.com

Copyright © 2021 by John Wiley & Sons, Inc., Hoboken, New Jersey

Published simultaneously in Canada

For general information on our other products and services, please contact our Customer Care Department within the U.S. at 877-762-2974, outside the U.S. at 317-572-3993, or fax 317-572-4002. For technical support, please visit https://hub.wiley.com/community/support/dummies.

Wiley publishes in a variety of print and electronic formats and by print-on-demand. Some material included with standard print versions of this book may not be included in e-books or in print-on-demand. If this book refers to media such as a CD or DVD that is not included in the version you purchased, you may download this material at http://booksupport.wiley.com. For more information about Wiley products, visit www.wiley.com.

Library of Congress Control Number: 2020949612

ISBN 978-1-119-70428-7 (pbk); ISBN 978-1-119-70429-4 (ebk); ISBN 978-1-119-70431-7 (ebk)

Manufactured in the United States of America

SKY10023294_121520

Contents at a Glance

Table of Contents

Introduction

The Army Combat Fitness Test (ACFT) is a hot topic in military circles right now, and if you're reading this book, you probably want to do your best on this make-or-break assessment. Sure, physical fitness is the cornerstone of combat readiness, but the Army's kept the same old physical training regimen for more than four decades. If it ain't broke, why fix it?

The problem is that the old test — the Army Physical Fitness Test, or APFT — was broken. It wasn't a good gauge of a soldier's overall fitness. How much can you really measure with push-ups, sit-ups, and a two-mile run? Not much.

Enter the ACFT, the Army's new and improved assessment that looks at a soldier's functional fitness level. The days of calling three events a test are over, and so are the days of gender- and age-specific scoring. Now, the Army has a completely neutral test that every soldier must pass. Performance is divided into three Physical Demand Categories based on military occupational specialty, or MOS: Moderate, Significant, and Heavy.

You have to pass the ACFT. If you don't, you may need to start looking for a new job — and that's the last thing you want to do, whether you're working toward retirement or you're just ready to complete your first contract.

About This Book

ACFT For Dummies is the resource you need to improve your physical fitness, train for the ACFT, and make good choices between 1130 and 1300. I explain each test event in detail, discuss the test's rules, show you exercises you can use to improve your performance on each event, and explain how to deal with injuries. I even give you guidance on maintaining a healthy diet.

This book also contains the answers to all your burning ACFT questions, such as

>> What exercises should I do to prepare for each event?

>> Is PRT really going to help me perform well on the ACFT?

>> How healthy are popular workouts, and will they help me pass the ACFT?

>> How important is recovery?

>> What happens if I'm on a profile?

>> Are there special exercises females should focus on? What about seasoned soldiers?

>> Are special diets worth the time and energy they require?

>> How can clean eating help me pass the test?

A final note about the ACFT: Its scoring is considered gender-neutral. As of this writing, the Army officially recognizes two genders — male and female — so when it says the test is gender-neutral, it's indicating that the scoring doesn't discriminate between biological males and biological females.

Foolish Assumptions

When I moved this book from my head to paper, I made a few assumptions about you. (Yes, I know what happens when you assume.) Mostly, I've taken a few things for granted about who you are and why you picked up this book:

>> You're either in the U.S. Army or you're about to join.

>> You understand the Army's basic physical fitness regimen, but you're not necessarily familiar with gym jargon or many exercises outside what you do for PT every morning.

>> You want to do your best on the ACFT, or you're struggling with certain events that you can't pass as of right now.

>> You want to continue your career in the Army without being involuntarily separated.

>> You're ready, willing, and able to do what it takes to improve your physical fitness level.

Icons Used in This Book

Throughout this book, you find icons that help you use the material in this book. Here's a rundown of what they mean:

This icon alerts you to helpful hints regarding the ACFT. Tips can help you save time and avoid frustration.

This icon reminds you of important information you should read carefully.

This icon flags actions that can cause injury or illness or points out mistakes you may make while you're preparing for or taking the ACFT. Often, this icon accompanies common mistakes or misconceptions people have about the ACFT.

This icon points out information that is interesting, enlightening, or in-depth but that isn't necessary for you to read.

This icon points out specific examples designed to help you prep for a record ACFT.

Beyond the Book

In addition to the material you're reading right now, this product also comes with a free, access-anywhere Cheat Sheet. No, it isn't something you can tape to the inside of your PT belt to help you perform better on the ACFT. Instead, this Cheat Sheet gives you quick pointers about what you need to know before taking the ACFT. It explains the events and exercises you can perform when you're short on time and covers basic things you should avoid when you're training. You can also find tips and techniques to max out your performance on each event. To get this Cheat Sheet, simply go to www.dummies.com and search for "ACFT For Dummies Cheat Sheet" in the Search box.

But wait! There's more! This book also comes with some helpful online videos that cover the exercises I explain in the book. Check them out at www.dummies.com/go/acftfd.

Where to Go from Here

You don't have to read this book from cover to cover to perform well on the ACFT. I suggest that you begin with Chapters 1 and 2 to pick up the basics, especially if you haven't yet taken a diagnostic or record ACFT. That way, you can get a feel for how the test is organized and which events you need to pour your blood, sweat, and tears into. This plan of attack helps you set up logical and effective goals to maximize your efforts with the time you have left to prepare.

When you know your weak spots, you can dig into Chapters 8 and 9, which explain exercises and stretches you can focus on for peak performance. If you're struggling with a certain event, flip directly to that event's section and get to work. You may want to skip sections you don't need (as long as you keep training the way you have been). For example, if you can run two miles in 12 minutes but you couldn't do a leg tuck to save your life, you probably don't need to learn much about sprint intervals and hill repeats. You need loaded isometric hangs and contralateral dead bugs.

If you're battling the tape measure each time you take a physical fitness test, have a peek at Part 4 of this book. I give you the rundown on hitting the drive-through, eating your veggies, and pounding energy drinks (and how they all impact your physical performance).

Not sure where to start? Grab your last bag of chips (at least until after the test), kick back, and start at the beginning.

1

Getting to Know the ACFT

Take a look at the Army's physical fitness requirements and how they've evolved over the past 250 years.

Test out the science behind the Army Combat Fitness Test and discover when and how the military evaluates physical performance.

Explore each ACFT event in detail and uncover how the Army scores soldiers.

Chapter **1**

Army Physical Fitness: The Cornerstone of Combat Readiness

The United States Army needs high-speed, low-drag soldiers manning its ranks, and until 2020, it measured physical fitness by using the Army Physical Fitness Test, or APFT. But change is inevitable in the Army, and the Army Combat Fitness Test (ACFT) is now the standard by which all soldiers, male and female, are judged. Your ACFT score can determine whether you qualify for continued service in the military, and, like the APFT, it's administered at the unit level.

So why the change?

The Army recognized the need to measure overall fitness rather than a soldier's ability to do push-ups, sit-ups, and a two-mile run. Although those exercises are good for measuring chest strength, arm strength, and cardiovascular endurance, they're not necessarily indicators of how well a soldier can perform on the battlefield. (And don't get your hopes up. That two-mile run didn't go anywhere. It's the last event on the ACFT.)

The ACFT uses six events to measure a soldier's functional fitness. Each event is linked to common warfighting tasks, such as carrying other soldiers out of harm's way and climbing out of sticky situations. The ACFT standards are outlined in a "living document," which means they can (and most likely will) change as the Army identifies new challenges and comes up with better solutions.

Saying Goodbye to the Old APFT

Fitness training has been on the Army's radar for years — but not from the *very* beginning. Seven decades after General Friedrich Von Steuben's Blue Book laid out the drill and ceremony the Army uses today, West Point implemented the first physical fitness program for its cadets. The program included gymnastics, calisthenics, swimming, and fencing. Six years later, cadets were assessed for their performance on a 15-foot wall climb, a 5-foot horse vault, a 10-foot ditch leap, an 8-minute mile run (or an 18-minute two-mile run), a 4.5-mile walk that a cadet had to complete in an hour, and a 3-mile ruck with 20 pounds of gear, arms, and equipment in under an hour.

The Army scrapped the whole physical training (PT) program in 1861 when the Civil War started, but in 1885, the Army hired a new Master of the Sword, Lt. Col. Herman John Koehler. Koehler's *Manual of Calisthenic Exercises* became the first Army-wide physical training manual. In 1920, the Army re-implemented its testing requirement. Soldiers had to successfully perform a 14-second 100-yard sprint, an 8-foot wall climb, a 12-foot running jump, and a 30-yard grenade throw as well as complete an obstacle course.

The test continued to evolve with the publication of Field Manual 21-20 in 1941. It's the same FM in use today, but the events (and the test's name) changed every few years until 1980, when the APFT you know and love became the standard.

Now that the creators of the last evolution have retired, the APFT has gone into retirement, too. (No word yet on whether it's buying a red sports car, though.) Its replacement: the ACFT. Like many past evolutions of Army physical fitness testing, the ACFT includes multiple events designed to represent how well you can perform on the battlefield.

Sculpting a Fit and Lethal Force

The Army knows that military operations have become more complex. You're not riding a horse into battle with your sword drawn. You're up, they see you, you're down. You're wearing and carrying 80-plus pounds of gear through rugged mountain terrain, setting up OE-254s, performing HAZMAT operations in Level A, or emptying truck after truck full of supplies on a remote operating base.

Push-ups, sit-ups, and a two-mile run just couldn't tell the military that you could perform under those rigorous conditions. In fact, *all* the APFT told the Army was that you could do push-ups, sit-ups, and a two-mile run. The APFT was designed to have 40 percent predictive power for performance in combat. But today, it's all about functional fitness — and assessments indicate the ACFT has 80 percent predictive power for battlefield performance.

Training servicemembers for the ACFT (and requiring the test itself) is the Army's way of improving soldiers' physical fitness, reducing preventable injuries, enhancing stamina, and contributing to enhanced unit readiness.

The ACFT is required for every soldier. Age and gender don't matter. Like my drill sergeant at "Relaxin'" Jackson told me, "You're an infantryman first." That means the Army wants assurance, whether you're an 18-year-old male private or a 55-year-old female four-star, that you have muscular strength and endurance, power, speed, agility, cardiovascular endurance, balance, flexibility, coordination, and high-speed reaction time.

Is the ACFT harder to pass for some soldiers than it is for others? Yes. Does that mean you may need to work harder than your battle buddy? Absolutely. But that's what this book is for. I can't go to the gym with you, but I can show you what you need to do to meet the Army's vision: "To deploy, fight, and win our nation's wars by providing ready, prompt, and sustained land dominance by Army forces."

The bottom line is that the Army is a standards-based institution, and those standards are in place to meet the requirements of combat operations.

HOW MUCH HOMEWORK DID THE ARMY DO?

The Army developed the ACFT over 20 years — it wasn't a fly-by-night decision. After creating physical readiness requirements for all soldiers and conducting a specific study on physical demands, the Army zeroed in on ten components of physical fitness necessary for warfighting. The military brass consulted with military fitness leaders from the United Kingdom, Canada, Australia, France, and the Netherlands, as well as fitness experts from universities and reps from government agencies to put together its latest evolution of physical fitness testing.

Picking Up Performance Basics

The ACFT challenges you to complete six events, each designed to test one or more fitness components. You need to prepare for these events to max out your ACFT score; I go into details on the fitness components in the following sections:

>> **3 Repetition Maximum Deadlift:** The 3 Repetition Maximum Deadlift (MDL) represents your ability to safely and effectively lift heavy loads from the ground, bound, jump, and land. This event tests how well-conditioned your back and legs are; the better-conditioned those muscles are, the less likely you are to become injured when you have to move long distances under heavy load.

   Fitness components: Muscular strength, balance, and flexibility

>> **Standing Power Throw:** The Standing Power Throw (SPT) represents your ability to throw equipment on or over obstacles, lift up your battle buddies, jump over obstacles, and employ progressive levels of force in hand-to-hand combat. It tests how well you can execute quick, explosive movements.

   Fitness components: Explosive power, balance, range of motion, and flexibility

>> **Hand Release Push-Up – Arm Extension:** The Hand Release Push-Up – Arm Extension (HRP) represents your ability to withstand repetitive and sustained pushing that's often necessary in combat tasks (like when your driver gets the HMMWV stuck in the mud and every vehicle in the convoy is mysteriously missing a tow bar). This modified push-up event tests your chest and core strength.

   Fitness component: Muscular endurance

>> **Sprint-Drag-Carry:** The Sprint-Drag-Carry (SDC) represents your ability to accomplish high-intensity combat tasks that last between a few seconds and a few minutes, such as building a hasty fighting position, reacting quickly in a firefight, carrying ammo from one place to another, or extracting a casualty and carrying him or her to safety. The Sprint-Drag-Carry tests your strength, endurance, and anaerobic capacity.

   Fitness components: Agility, anaerobic endurance, muscular endurance, and muscular strength

>> **Leg Tuck:** The Leg Tuck (LTK) represents your ability to carry heavy loads, climb over walls and other obstacles, and climb or descend ropes. The strength required for this event can help soldiers avoid back injuries. (**Note:** Throughout this book, I often refer to this event by its abbreviation, LTK, to help distinguish it from the plain old exercise known as the leg tuck.)

   Fitness components: Muscular strength and endurance

>> **Two-Mile Run:** The Two-Mile Run (2MR) represents your ability to conduct continuous operations and ground movements on foot, as well as your ability to recover quickly in preparation for other physically demanding tasks, like reacting to enemy contact or carrying ammo from Point A to Point B.

Fitness component: Aerobic endurance

TIP

The ACFT doesn't offer age brackets for scoring like the APFT did. That means whether you're 18 and fresh out of Basic Combat Training or you're a seasoned soldier with plenty of combat experience, you're held to the same standard. The aim of this book is to get you to meet or exceed the standard so you can enjoy a full and illustrious (and injury-free) military career.

Range of motion and flexibility

The Army uses the ACFT to test soldiers' range of motion and flexibility. Because both these things are an indicator of combat fitness — and because the Army needs combat-ready warriors on the battlefield — these test events can help determine a soldier's overall fitness. The fitness gurus behind the scenes know that having a good range of motion also helps prevent injury, so the Army wins twice: It gets the combat-ready soldiers it needs *and* keeps servicemembers fit to fight.

The Army is quick to point out that training for the ACFT doesn't put you at a higher risk for injury, provided that you train properly and don't overdo it. New training resources, like the updated Field Manual 7-22, *Holistic Health and Fitness*, include guidance on minimizing a soldier's risk for injury while preparing for the test. See Chapters 7 and 8 for exercises to help you improve your range of motion, and Chapter 9 for stretches that can improve your flexibility.

Balance

Balance is an important part of the ACFT, and you use it in the 3 Repetition Maximum Deadlift and Standing Power Throw. The Army wants to see how well you can resist forces that cause falls (like throwing a medicine ball behind your head). Your core plays a huge role in balance, so these events show the military brass how well-conditioned your back, abs, and legs really are. Strengthening your core is just good business anyway. A strong core contributes to healthy mobility later in life; just as importantly, it makes fitting into your uniform and falling into the right spot on the Army's height and weight chart easier. Wobble over to Chapter 8 for ideas on improving your balance to max out your ACFT scores.

Agility

Slow is smooth, and smooth is fast. You've probably heard that at least a dozen times throughout your military career, and it applies to your mentality as well as your body. Modern combat situations require mobility and agility, and you see these two key abilities tested on the ACFT. Technically, *mobility* is the ability to move freely and easily, and *agility* is your ability to do so quickly. The Army needs to know that you're able to move like a warrior. You don't have to be a professional athlete, but you do have to meet Army standards.

Most notably, the ACFT checks out your mobility and agility in the Sprint-Drag-Carry event, where you have to perform three distinct exercises quick, fast, and in a hurry. I cover those in Chapter 2.

Explosive power

Movements that require maximum (or near-maximum) power output in a short amount of time tap into what fitness pros call *explosive power.* You see professional sports players use explosive power every time you watch a game; a quarterback uses it when he throws the ball, an outside hitter uses it when she spikes a volleyball, and wrestlers use it when they lift an opponent. The ACFT measures your explosive power in the Standing Power Throw, but that's not the only event that requires it — you use explosive power during the Sprint-Drag-Carry, the Two-Mile Run (if you sprint to shave a few seconds off your time), and maybe even during the LTK.

Muscular strength and endurance

Remember the difference you and your family noticed in your physique after you graduated from Basic Combat Training (BCT)? When you joined the military, you may have already been strong — but you weren't "Army Strong." The ACFT measures your muscular strength and endurance in ways that you may not have trained for in BCT, and its demands are serious. It checks your muscular strength in four key areas: your legs, your core, your chest, and your upper back. You see muscular strength and endurance testing on the 3 Repetition Maximum Deadlift, Hand Release Push-Up – Arm Extension, Sprint-Drag-Carry, and LTK.

REMEMBER

Muscular strength and endurance are related, but they're not the same thing. You need endurance for tasks like lugging fuel cans around the motor pool, while strength ties into the maximum amount of weight you can lift one time. (In the gym, it's called a *one-rep max.*)

Aerobic exercise for cardiovascular endurance

The Army measures your aerobic fitness through its old standby, the Two-Mile Run. Though you're unlikely to have to run for two miles in a combat situation (and you're even more unlikely to have to do it in your PT uniform), you are likely to engage in aerobic exercise — cardio — on the battlefield. The Army needs to know you can hack it, and it figures out what your endurance is like by making you run. Getting a good picture of a soldier's aerobic fitness takes about 12 minutes of continuous exercise, and most people take longer than that to cover two miles. (Personally, I'd rather the Army just made me run for 12 minutes to see how far I get, but so far, they haven't been very receptive to the idea.)

Aerobic exercise requires your heart to pump oxygenated blood to your muscles. Your heart has to beat faster to keep up with your movement, and your body has to figure out how to balance itself out until you stop the exercise. Check out Table 1-1, which gives you a ballpark range for where your heart rate should be in beats per minute (bpm) during moderate and vigorous aerobic exercise. The American Heart Association doesn't distinguish between ages 20 and 30 (that's why you don't see a row in the table for 25-year-olds) because people in that age bracket typically fall into the same heart rate zones. Chapter 8 shows you how to take your cardio fitness up a notch or two, so if that's an area you need to improve, you can find suggestions there.

TABLE 1-1 **Heart Rate Zones**

Age	Moderate Exercise	Vigorous Exercise
20	100 to 170 bpm	200 bpm
30	95 to 162 bpm	190 bpm
35	93 to 157 bpm	185 bpm
40	90 to 153 bpm	180 bpm
45	88 to 149 bpm	175 bpm
50	85 to 145 bpm	170 bpm
55	83 to 140 bpm	165 bpm
60	80 to 136 bpm	160 bpm

Anaerobic exercise for short-term muscle strength

Anaerobic exercise is high-intensity, high-power movement that requires your body to expend a lot of energy in a short period of time. Things like weightlifting, jumping rope, sprinting, and high-intensity interval training (HIIT) are examples of anaerobic exercise; if you take these movements to the battlefield, you're looking at carrying a battle buddy to safety, running ammo cans between one truck and another, or throwing equipment over a wall so you can get cover from enemy fire. This kind of exercise pushes your body to demand more energy than you'd need for aerobic exercise, like running, and it relies on energy sources stored in your muscles.

TECHNICAL STUFF

Aerobic means "with oxygen," and anaerobic means "without oxygen." Sure, you still need oxygen to perform anaerobic exercises, but not in the same way that you do for aerobic exercises. Aerobic exercise uses oxygen to produce energy so your body can use fat and glucose for fuel, while anaerobic exercise can only use glucose for fuel. Glucose is available in your muscles for quick, short bursts of movement, and you get it through a process called *glycolysis*.

The Sprint-Drag-Carry is a prime example of how the Army tests your anaerobic fitness. Check out Chapter 8 for a wide range of exercises that can boost your anaerobic power.

PRT: Love it or Hate it, It's Here to Stay

The Army's Physical Readiness Training, or PRT, was designed to prepare soldiers for the ACFT. Many PRT drills have migrated into ATP 7-22.02, *Holistic Health and Fitness Drills and Exercises*. These drills, now called H2F (a complete revision of PRT), are all about functional fitness, which uses drills, exercises, and activities that are specific to performing certain tasks. Army Field Manual 7-22 and Chapter 7 of this book both contain all the info you need on H2F, but save it for 0630; to max out your ACFT, you probably need to go above and beyond the Army's maintenance PT plan.

H2F covers preparation drills, core exercises, conditioning drills, and a whole host of movement training exercises that can help you perform well on the ACFT. But the best way to make sure you're ready for all six events is to hit the gym for some serious training after work or on the weekends — and if you're a little nervous about passing a certain event (I'm looking at you, LTK), that's where you need to focus.

Understanding How the ACFT Fits into Your Army Role

You have to pass the ACFT. If you don't, your career is in jeopardy. That's not doomsday talk; if you fail, you pick up a flag, and a flag suspends favorable personnel actions, like promotions, awards, schools, and others. Even worse, Army Regulation 600-8-2 says that if you're flagged for ACFT failure, your permanent change of station is at your commander's discretion (and that's *really* bad news if you're excited about a PCS because you're on orders to Schofield Barracks or Stuttgart). Finally, the Army can administratively separate you from service for ACFT failure.

If you have a physical training profile from your medical provider, you get a shot at alternate events on a modified ACFT (I cover those in Chapter 2). However, you still have to pass the 3 Repetition Maximum Deadlift, the Sprint-Drag-Carry, and your alternate aerobic event. If you don't, you're facing the same consequences as soldiers who fail the regular ACFT.

Making the grade

REMEMBER

Every soldier is held to the same standards on the ACFT. The grading scale doesn't distinguish between males and females, and you don't get a break because you're older than your battle buddy. The days of knocking out a couple of dozen push-ups and sit-ups before shuffling around the track for 18 minutes are gone — now, it's all about whether you can keep up with your teammates.

Every job falls into one of three physical demand categories. For example, the infantry has the highest minimum standards. Other MOSs, like Chemical, Biological, Radiological and Nuclear Specialist have the lowest minimum standards. Some jobs, like Parachute Riggers and Water Treatment Specialists, are somewhere in the middle. See Chapter 4 to find out how the test is scored, as well as what physical demand category your MOS falls into.

Training on your own time — and helping your team

To improve your ACFT score, you have to put in the work. That means hitting the gym after COB and on weekends, or doing small-but-mighty exercises while you're at work or in the field. But there's an upside (other than passing the test, that is): Creating a PT plan for yourself and your team, squad, or platoon that results in a 100 percent pass rate makes a great counseling or evaluation report bullet. (I promise I won't tell anyone that you lifted some ideas from this book.) Check out Chapter 26 for tips on maxing out your score, and head over to Appendix A for a blank workout calendar you can use to set yourself — and your team — up for success.

The Army Performance Triad

The Army's Performance Triad, or P3 for short, includes sleep, activity, and nutrition. Your daily routine in these three areas can either increase or decrease your physical and mental performance, which ties into your unit's performance. P3 is important to the ACFT, too, in these ways:

>> **Sleep:** The Army recognizes that adequate sleep is critical to mission success, even if it's tough to implement. Getting enough rest while you're training for the ACFT and immediately prior to taking it is incredibly important — it determines how well you build strength and endurance, how quickly you recover, and even how you perform on short notice.

>> **Activity:** The ACFT measures your physical fitness level and how well you're likely to perform on the battlefield, and training for it is critical. Physical activity improves your mood, makes you live longer, and helps keep your mind clear so you can make good choices.

>> **Nutrition:** The Army isn't testing whether you're vitamin D-fortified on the ACFT, but putting the right fuel in your body can help you perform your best. The right foods can increase your energy and endurance, shorten the recovery time you need between activities, improve your focus and concentration, and help you look and feel better, too.

Chapter 2

Getting an Overview of the ACFT

The Army Combat Fitness Test (ACFT) is the official test of record for American soldiers all over the world, and like all the moving parts in the Army, it's governed by its fair share of field manuals, technical manuals, and Army regulations. When you're training for the ACFT, you need the right equipment, but don't sweat it, because your on-post fitness centers and your unit are supposed to have it on hand. Your unit needs special equipment to administer the test, too, which I cover later in this chapter.

With gender- and age-neutral scoring requirements, every soldier is required to meet the same scoring standard. The six-event ACFT covers it all: muscular strength and endurance, balance, agility, cardiovascular endurance, anaerobic endurance, and range of motion. Unlike the old APFT, you can't just show up on test day and expect to perform well. This one requires plenty of preparation because it's about functional fitness — not just push-ups, sit-ups, and a two-mile run.

REMEMBER

Your best bet? Start training early and often for the ACFT. Make it your primary focus for gym time and build in recovery periods so you get the most from your workouts. Fill in the blank workout calendar in Appendix A so you can carve out time to zero in on the training that will help you improve in your weakest events. And remember: Train as you fight. Don't forget to work in the actual event exercises so you know what to expect (and even how well you'll do) on test day.

Reading Up on the Army's Resources and Requirements for the ACFT

The Army has a variety of rules for both you and the test site on the big day. The following sections break down some of these requirements.

Checking out Army regs and training resources

Soldiers are still subject to AR 40-501, *Standards of Medical Fitness*; AR 670-1, *Wear and Appearance of Army Uniforms and Insignia* (the APFU is the only authorized uniform for the ACFT, in case you were wondering whether you can wear yoga pants), AR 350-1, *Army Training and Leader Development*; and AR 600-9, *The Army Weight Control Program*.

Field Manual 7-22, *Holistic Health and Fitness,* is the Army's newest training resource to prep soldiers for the ACFT. Additionally, CALL Publication 20-09 goes into detail about the test itself, ATP 7-22.01 regulates testing, ATP 7-22.02 covers conditioning and training drills, and the Army set up a special webpage to address ACFT basics at www.army.mil/acft.

Surveying site and equipment requirements

The Army is very specific about the type of PT field units can use to conduct the ACFT. It has to be a flat field space approximately 40 meters by 40 meters, and it should be well-maintained and cut grass or artificial turf that's generally flat and free from debris. Check out Chapter 3 for more information on the ACFT field's required setup. For the Two-Mile Run course, the start and finish point must be close to the Leg Tuck station. The Sprint-Drag-Carry can be performed on properly maintained grass or artificial turf with a standard 90-pound nylon sled, or it can be performed on wood, packed dirt, vinyl, or smooth concrete with a 180-pound nylon sled. You can't perform the SDC on unimproved dirt, gravel, rubberized floors, ice, or snow.

When the field is sorted out, units can only administer the ACFT with specific equipment. In addition to a measuring pointer, cones for marking lanes and distance, stopwatches, and an outdoor timing clock, these are the major equipment components for the ACFT, which I cover in greater detail in Chapter 3:

>> Hex bars

>> Bumper plates

- » Sled with pull strap
- » 10-pound medicine ball
- » 40-pound kettlebells
- » Metric measuring tape
- » Climbing bars or a climbing pod

Each unit should have the right equipment for modified ACFTs, too, which I cover in the "Biking, Rowing, or Swimming Your Way through the Alternate Events" section of this chapter. The stationary bike must feature adjustable handlebars and an adjustable seat, as well as an accurate odometer. The rower must be stationary and feature a seat, handles, and rail that can accommodate soldiers of different sizes. It has to have an accurate odometer that measures time, distance, and resistance level.

Getting used to gender- and age-neutral scoring requirements

No matter who you are or where you are in your military career, you're held to the same ACFT standards as every other soldier in your military occupational specialty. The ACFT has gender- and age-neutral scoring requirements, which means females and males must achieve the same minimum scores on the test (although the test does have three physical demand categories that apply to different MOSs, which I cover in Chapter 4). Whether you're an enlisted soldier, a warrant officer, or a commissioned officer, you have to meet the same standards as your peers across the board, based on your job.

WARNING

Some of the ACFT events are more difficult for some people to master than others are. Regardless of your personal opinion on whether the ACFT is biased against one gender or certain age groups, the fact remains that the Army isn't going to change its stance on grading any time soon — and it's extremely unlikely to go back to pre–ACFT standards that varied based on age and gender. That may mean that you need to work harder than your battle buddy does to score well on a certain event.

Diagnostic ACFTs versus record ACFTs: Pinning down test frequency

The Army's policies on taking the ACFT are considered "living documents," which means the higher-ups can change them as necessary. Because the test is new in the grand scheme of things — the APFT dominated physical fitness for four decades — the frequency of testing may change. As of this writing, the Army expects the administration part of the ACFT to be very similar to the APFT. That means your unit can schedule a test at any time.

WHAT ABOUT THE OPAT?

If you joined the Army within the last few years, you've probably taken an Occupational Physical Assessment Test, or OPAT. All recruits take it to see whether they're fit to fight in certain MOSs, and even some soldiers who reclass to a different MOS are required to take it. The OPAT is entirely separate from the ACFT, but it does have some similarities. The OPAT has four physical demand categories: Heavy, Significant, Moderate, and Unqualified. (Soldiers who are reclassing to an MOS with a higher physical demand category than the one they currently have must take the test.) The OPAT requires soldiers to perform a standing long jump, a seated power throw, a strength deadlift, and an interval aerobic run. So what happens if someone fails the OPAT? If the recruit or soldier can't eventually pass, recruiters and retention personnel may be able to renegotiate to allow him or her to enter an MOS with a lower physical demand category.

AR 350-1 says, "Commanders may administer the APFT as often as they wish; however, they must specify beforehand when the results are for record. The AA and Active Guard/Reserve (AGR) Soldiers will take the APFT at least twice each calendar year. A minimum of 4 months will separate record tests if only two record tests are given. The intent is for the Active Army and the AGR Soldiers to take a record APFT every 6 months. Mission requirements often prevent the even spacing of record tests. Therefore, commanders are encouraged to test Soldiers for record as close to the record test window as possible."

Breaking Down the Six Events and Their Scoring

The ACFT's six events all count toward your score. And just like the APFT, if you fail one event, you fail the whole ACFT. (No pressure, though.) You have to complete all six events, in order, on the same day, and the test can't take more than 120 minutes. That includes the Preparation Drill and the following:

>> 3 Repetition Maximum Deadlift, or MDL

>> Standing Power Throw, or SPT

>> Hand Release Push-Up – Arm Extension, or HRP

>> Sprint-Drag-Carry, or SDC

>> Leg Tuck, or LTK

>> Two-Mile Run, or 2MR

If you fail one of the events, you can't stop taking the ACFT. You have to complete the remaining events to the best of your ability.

Each event is worth 100 points, so a perfect score is 600. Every MOS falls into one of three physical demand categories: Heavy, Significant, and Moderate. Each soldier in that MOS must meet at least the minimum score for his or her physical demand category to pass. You need a minimum of 60 points in each event for the Moderate category, 65 points for the Significant category, and 70 points for the Heavy category. Table 2-1 shows the absolute minimum scores you must get in each event for each physical demand category (and you can find your MOS's physical demand category, as well as the points awarded for each score, in Chapter 4).

TABLE 2-1   ## Minimum ACFT Physical Demand Requirements

Category	MDL	SPT	HRP	SDC	LTK	2MR
Moderate (Gold)	140 pounds	4.5 meters	10	3:00	1	21:00
Significant (Gray)	180 pounds	6.5 meters	20	2:30	3	19:00
Heavy (Black)	200 pounds	8.0 meters	30	2:10	5	18:00

TIP

During fiscal year 2021, soldiers only need to meet the Gold standard, regardless of MOS. The normal standards will kick in when FY22 starts; that's when you'll have to pass the standards for your physical demand category.

Before you dive into the test, you need to know the protocols and why the Army uses them. First, you have to attempt all six events unless you have a physical profile (I cover the alternate events for profiles later in this chapter). Soldiers rotate through each lane in groups of four, but groups of fewer than four are authorized. The test has only one programmed rest period, and it's between the Leg Tuck event and the Two-Mile Run. If only one or two soldiers are testing, the Army requires the OIC and NCOIC — the commissioned and noncommissioned officers in charge — to provide those soldiers with a five-minute rest period between each event (which they'd get anyway if more soldiers were testing).

You get no restarts on the ACFT. If you perform a repetition incorrectly, it doesn't count — and your grader doesn't send you to the back of the line to retest. You sign your scorecard at the test site, and your signature says you agree with the scores your grader recorded. The OIC or NCOIC resolve any discrepancies within the test's 120-minute time limit. And although the Army allows video recording of the test, that video can only be used for training purposes. You can't use it to argue that you performed a rep correctly or that your grader made a counting mistake.

The Preparation Drill

A soldier who isn't taking the ACFT leads the Preparation Drill — the Army's dynamic warm-up. The Preparation Drill leader reads these instructions aloud:

> You are about to take the Army Combat Fitness Test, or ACFT, a test that will measure your upper and lower body muscular endurance, muscular strength, aerobic endurance, anaerobic endurance, and explosive power. The results of this test will give you and your commanders an indication of your state of physical readiness and will act as a guide in determining your physical training needs. After selecting a lane with your preferred weight for the 3 Repetition Maximum Deadlift Event, you may be assigned to a different lane for the next events. You will rest and recover while other soldiers complete their turns. After the last soldier completes the Leg Tuck event, there will be a 10-minute recovery period for all tested soldiers before the start of the 2-Mile Run. Do the best you can on each of the events.

The Preparation Drill lasts 10 minutes, and during that time, you're encouraged to perform the whole drill while in formation. You can skip exercises if you believe they may exhaust you or hurt your ability to perform well on the test. These are the Preparation Drill exercises, which are part of Holistic Health and Fitness, or H2F (and you thought that whole new PT program wasn't leading up to anything!):

>> Bend and Reach

>> Rear Lunge

>> High Jumper

>> Rower

>> Squat Bender

>> Windmill

>> Forward Lunge

>> Prone Row

>> Bent Leg Body Twist

>> Push-up

After the Preparation Drill, you get to figure out which MDL weight is right for you. You can use that time to warm up by lifting the hex bars. If you choose to do so, the Army recommends doing eight to ten reps at about 25 percent of your goal weight and then resting for two minutes, six reps at 40 percent of your goal weight and resting for three minutes, four reps at half your goal weight and resting for four minutes, or one rep at 80 percent of your goal weight and resting until the MDL begins. You know your body, though, and you know what you need to do to get warmed up — don't overdo it before the test starts because you're feeling pumped.

TIP

By the time you take the ACFT, you should know what MDL weight is right for you. The time to get familiar with what your body can handle is *now*, before you even show up for a record ACFT. You don't necessarily have to expend your energy figuring out your weight after the test has begun; if you've been practicing, you'll know how much you can lift on test day.

The test administrators hand out scorecards (if they weren't handed out before), and the OIC or NCOIC instructs everyone to fill in personal information. See Chapter 4 for a copy of the scorecard and more information on how it works. You must carry your scorecard to the first event and give it to your grader. You get it back after the MDL and hand-carry it to the SPT. From there, your grader keeps the card for the duration of the test.

The OIC or NCOIC then reads this statement:

> You will continue to observe the ACFT test area and follow instructions from the OIC or NCOIC throughout the test. During the events, you may conduct your choice of preparation activities. During the test, you may observe all events and offer appropriate verbal motivation to test takers. It is your responsibility to complete proper preparation and know the event standards prior to taking the ACFT. What are your questions about the event standards?

After you determine what MDL weight you're lifting for the test, you line up behind it with the other soldiers who are lifting the same weight. Graders ensure each MDL lane has an even distribution of soldiers, trying to keep it at five or fewer. Soldiers can assist graders with changing weight plates if necessary. When all the soldiers are lined up, the NCOIC begins the event.

3 Repetition Maximum Deadlift

The 3 Repetition Maximum Deadlift represents your ability to safely and effectively lift heavy loads from the ground. You use a 40- to 60-pound hex bar and weighted plates to demonstrate your strength through the MDL. You use a lot of muscles on this exercise — primarily those in your legs, forearms, and back. Figure 2-1 shows the muscles the MDL targets.

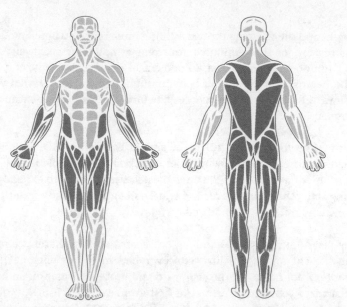

FIGURE 2-1:
Muscles used in
the 3 Repetition
Maximum
Deadlift.

© John Wiley & Sons, Inc.

The starting position for the MDL is inside the hex bar with your feet about shoulder-width apart. This event has three phases of movement:

» **Preparatory:** On the command of "Get set," step into the hex bar, bend at your knees and hips, and grasp the center of each handle. Extend your arms fully, keep your back flat, and keep your head in line with your spine. Keep your head and eyes to the front (or slightly upward) and your heels on the ground. All your reps begin from this position.

» **Upward movement:** On the command of "Go," stand up and lift the bar by extending your hips and knees. Your hips can't rise before or above your shoulders, and your back should remain straight. Stand up straight and pause slightly to reset your spine.

» **Downward movement:** After you pause at the top, flex your hips and knees slowly to lower the bar to the ground. Control your movement the entire time and keep your back straight. Don't let go of the bar! The weight plates have to touch the ground before you start the next repetition.

You have to execute three continuous reps with the same weight. If you lose control of the hex bar, you can retest at a lower weight — but you only get one additional chance. If you successfully complete three reps on your first try, you can choose to take another attempt at a higher weight. If you fail at the higher weight, no big deal; your grader counts your lower-weight score instead.

TIP

Whether to try the MDL at a higher weight after you successfully lift a lower weight is up to you. However, like the old APFT, saving some energy may be wise if you know you're going to struggle with one or more of the following five events.

Your grader can call out a safety violation. For example, if you allow your knees to move together, round your back or shoulders, or lose your balance, he or she can stop the event and tell you to go to another lane with a lower weight. If your grader sends you to another lane, it doesn't count against you.

WARNING

Stay safe when you're lifting the hex bar. Don't move your hips above your shoulders, don't round your shoulders, and keep an eye on your knees — don't let them collapse inward. Keep your movements controlled and avoid dropping the weights on the ground.

REMEMBER

The big scores to remember on the MDL: 140 pounds for 60 points, 180 pounds for 65 points, and 200 pounds for 70 points. Want to max it out? Slap 340 pounds on your bar for 100 points.

Standing Power Throw

The Standing Power Throw represents your ability to execute quick, explosive movements that you may use to move equipment or people. You use a 10-pound medicine ball for this test event, which works muscles in your legs, core, shoulders, and back. Figure 2-2 shows which muscles you use for the SPT.

The STP requires you to hold the medicine ball at hip level while you're standing with your heels at the starting line. You can prepare to throw while flexing at your trunk, knees, and hips while you lower the ball between your legs. Figure 2-3 shows the STP from start to finish.

You get two chances to show your stuff on the STP. You grasp the ball, lower it between your legs (like a kid at a bowling alley), and use your reserves of explosive power to throw it over your head and behind your back.

TIP

Drive your entire movement with power from your quadriceps. Get into a deep squat and explode upward and backward. If you only use your arms, you run the risk of sending the ball straight into the ground behind you.

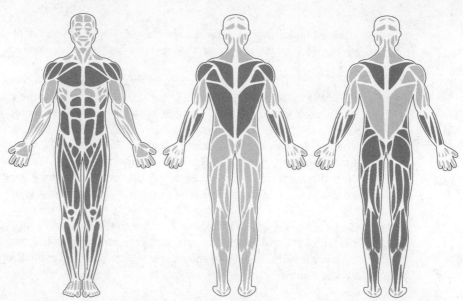

FIGURE 2-2:
Muscles used in
the Standing
Power Throw.

You can't put your heels on or over the starting line during the STP, but your feet can leave the ground when you throw. If your feet touch the line (even when you land), your grader gives you a raw score of 0.0 meters, and it counts as your first shot. If you fault on your second attempt by stepping on or over the line, you get another raw score of 0.0 meters. In that case, you get one final attempt — only because your first two were faults — and if you fault again, your event is terminated as a failure. (If you have a valid score on either the first or second throw, you don't get that third attempt.)

WARNING

If you accidentally throw your medicine ball into another lane, the distance of your throw stops where the other lane begins. For example, if you throw the ball to the right and it crosses the line at 6 meters, even if it lands at 10 meters, it's scored as a 6-meter throw.

You only get two attempts at the STP, which means you have to throw your best each time — without throwing out your back. Training is essential for the STP, and not just by throwing a medicine ball behind your head. Check out Chapter 8 for exercises that improve your performance on this event.

REMEMBER

The scores you need to pass based on your physical demand category, which I cover in Chapter 4, are 4.5 meters for 60 points, 6.5 meters for 65 points, and 8 meters for 70 points. Toss that bad boy 12.5 meters to get a perfect 100.

FIGURE 2-3: The Standing Power Throw.

Zack McCrory

Hand Release Push-Up – Arm Extension

The Hand Release Push-Up – Arm Extension measures your upper body endurance. It represents repetitive and sustained pushing you may use during wartime operations, like shoving away a combatant, moving obstacles, or pushing a disabled vehicle. This one's all about body weight, which you're already equipped with when you show up on test day. Figure 2-4 shows which muscles you put to the test during this two-minute event.

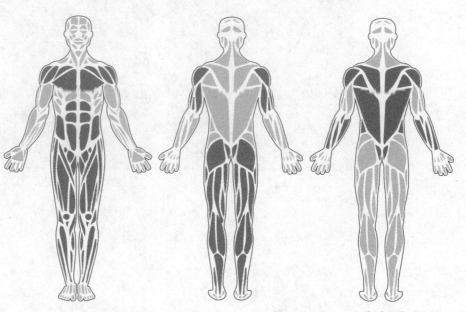

FIGURE 2-4: Muscles used in the Hand Release Push-Up – Arm Extension.

© John Wiley & Sons, Inc.

This muscular endurance event requires plenty of front and back core strength. One push-up takes four separate movements, but you do them all smoothly without pause. You start from the ground, push yourself up, bend your elbows to lower your body to the ground, pick up your hands and make a *T* with your arms, and bring your arms back to the starting position. Then (finally), you've completed one repetition. Figure 2-5 shows the HRP from beginning to end.

WARNING

The front leaning rest position is the only authorized rest position for the HRP. No more sagging in the middle or flexing your back! You can't bend or flex your knees, hips, trunk, or neck, either.

FIGURE 2-5:
The Hand Release
Push-Up – Arm
Extension.

Zack McCrory

The starting position for the HRP — where you are on the command of "Get set" — is the prone position on the ground. Your hands have to be flat, and your index fingers must be inside the outer edges of your shoulders (which makes it a lot like a tricep push-up). Your chest, hips, and thighs have to be flat on the ground, and your toes have to be on the ground with your ankles flexed. Your feet can be together or up to the grader's boot's width apart. Your head *doesn't* have to be on the ground, but if you're wiped out from the Standing Power Throw, I'm definitely not one to judge.

TIP

You can adjust your feet during the event, but you can't lift them off the ground to do it.

These are the four movements for the HRP:

>> **Movement 1:** On the command of "Go," push your body up from the ground as a single unit by fully extending your elbows. If you don't maintain a generally straight body alignment from your head to your ankles, your reps don't count. You end this movement in the front leaning rest.

>> **Movement 2:** From the front leaning rest position, bend your elbows to lower your body back to the ground. Your chest, hips, and thighs should touch the ground at the same time. You don't have to touch your face or head to the ground.

>> **Movement 3:** Move both arms out to the side, straightening your elbows until you're in the *T* position. After you extend your arms completely, bring your hands back beneath your shoulders. This is an immediate movement.

>> **Movement 4:** Place your hands flat on the ground with your index fingers inside the outer edges of your shoulders, returning to position to execute movement 1 again. When your hands are back under your shoulders, you've completed one repetition.

WARNING

If you rest on the ground, pick up your feet, fail to keep a straight body alignment, or fail to continuously move, your grader will terminate the event. The repetitions you have completed (remember, a rep isn't done until your hands are back under your shoulders) still count.

REMEMBER

You need 10 HRPs to score 60 points, 20 for 65 points, and 30 for 70 points. If you can knock out 60, you score 100 points.

Sprint-Drag-Carry

The Sprint-Drag-Carry measures four big fitness components: agility, anaerobic endurance, muscular strength, and muscular endurance. In combat, you use these skills to build a hasty fighting position, pull a casualty out of a vehicle and carry him or her to safety, react to fire, and carry ammo from Point A to Point B. Figure 2-6 shows which muscles need to spring into action to ace this event (in addition to your heart and lungs, because this one is pretty much a full-body test).

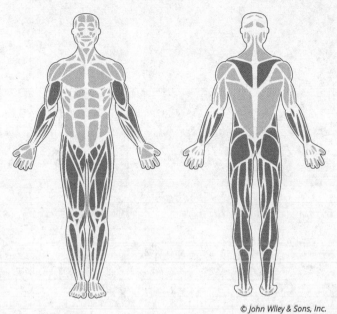

FIGURE 2-6: Muscles used in the Sprint-Drag-Carry.

The Sprint-Drag-Carry is about more than sprinting, dragging, and carrying. The SDC even has a little more sprinting than it has dragging and carrying. Here are the five parts of this event, which you start in the prone position with the top of your head behind the start line:

>> **Sprint:** On the command of "Go," jump up and sprint 25 meters in your lane. Touch the 25-meter line with your foot and hand, bust a U-turn, and sprint back to the start line.

>> **Drag:** Grab each strap handle on the sled. Pull the sled backward until you have the whole thing over the 25-meter line and then turn it around and pull it back. The entire sled has to cross the start line. Figure 2-7 shows the sled drag.

Don't jerk the straps — use a steady pull to move the sled. Remember not to sling the sled to turn it around, too.

>> **Lateral:** Face one side and perform a lateral run for 25 meters, touch the line with your foot and hand, and head back to the start line. Face the same direction on the way back. Don't cross your feet during laterals.

FIGURE 2-7:
Sled drag.

Zack McCrory

» **Carry:** Pick up your pair of 40-pound kettlebells and run to the 25-meter line. Step on or over the line with one foot, turn around, and run back to the start line.

Be careful when you turn around with the kettlebells — maintain control of your feet and the kettlebells the whole time. If you drop the kettlebells, just pick them up and keep moving.

» **Sprint:** Put your kettlebells on the ground, turn around, and sprint to the 25-meter line. Touch the line with a hand and foot and then return to the start line as fast as you can.

Your time stops when you cross the start line after your final sprint.

TIP

Set up your equipment where you want it before you start the event — that way, you don't have to mess with it during the event. Every second counts!

WARNING

In the sprints and lateral movements, you have to touch the line with your hand *and* foot. In the drag, the whole sled has to cross the line. When you're carrying kettlebells, you have to touch the line with your foot. If you fail to meet these standards, your grader calls you back. Your event isn't terminated — it's worse: Your clock keeps running, which drags down your score on this timed event.

REMEMBER

In this race against the clock, you need to complete all five events in 3 minutes flat to get 60 points. Finish in 2:30 to get 65 points, or wrap it up under 2:10 to get 70 points. Power through the whole thing in 1:33, and you max it out with 100 points.

Leg Tuck

The Leg Tuck — maybe the most infamous event on the ACFT — is how the Army measures your muscular strength and endurance. Check out Figure 2-8 for an inside look at which muscles need to work during this event. They're the same muscles that help you get over walls and obstacles as well as climb and descend ropes.

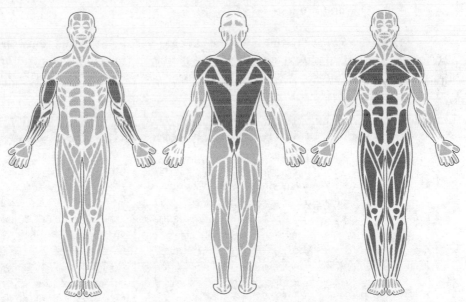

FIGURE 2-8:
Muscles used in
the Leg Tuck.

© John Wiley & Sons, Inc.

The LTK requires you to use your grip, shoulders, arm and chest muscles, abs, and even your front leg muscles. It's notoriously tough because it requires you to hang from a pull-up bar with an alternating grip, curl your body (like a shrimp) so that your knees or thighs touch your elbows or the backs of your upper arms, and return under control to the straight-arm hang — all while your body is perpendicular to the bar. Figure 2-9 shows you what the Leg Tuck looks like.

The starting position for the LTK is a straight-arm hang from the pull-up bar with an alternating grip. Ideally, your dominant hand is supposed to be closer to your head than your other hand is; for most people, that's the strategy that provides the most power. (Try it both ways when you practice, though.) Your grader can help you get up to the bar if you can't reach it, and if you're too tall to hang from the bar with straight arms, you must bend your knees, because your feet aren't allowed to touch the ground.

On the command "Go," flex at the elbows, waist, hips, and knees to bring your lower body up. Touch your knees or thighs to your elbows, and then return to the start position under control. If you keep your elbows bent, the rep doesn't count; the same goes if you swing your trunk or legs to get your knees up. You can, however, adjust your grip. Just make sure you don't touch the ground while you do it, or your grader will terminate the event.

WARNING

You only complete a repetition when you return to the straight-arm hang under control. You can't just drop from the bar on your last rep; if you do, your grader won't count it.

REMEMBER

You have to curl up to the bar once to score 60 points, three times for a score of 65, and five times if you want to earn yourself 70 points. Think you can do it 20 times? If you pull it off, you get a whopping 100 points on this event.

PREGNANCY VERSUS THE LEG TUCK

Critics of the ACFT — and there are plenty — say the Leg Tuck is invariably biased against female soldiers, who may not perform as well as their male counterparts on this event. One reason is that when a woman has a baby, she's on profile for six months. After her profile expires, her command can require her to take a record ACFT. However, for most people (males too), knocking out at least one leg tuck requires training. And what about females who have undergone C-sections? That's a major surgery, and it can lead to people having major trouble regaining abdominal strength and reactivating their core muscles. Because full recovery, and returning to your prior fitness level, can take anywhere from six months to a year, talking to your doctor about your profile after you have your child and return to work is important.

FIGURE 2-9:
The Leg Tuck.

Zack McCrory

Two-Mile Run

The Two-Mile Run, or 2MR, measures your aerobic endurance, just like it did on the APFT. The same theory is in play here: If you have higher aerobic endurance, you can recover more quickly from one task so you're ready for the next one — and you can run when you need to. In practice, performing well on the 2MR shows the Army that you'll do just fine during dismounted operations, rucking, and infiltration and extraction. Just in case you weren't sure what muscles you need to wake up to perform well on the 2MR, Figure 2-10 highlights them for you.

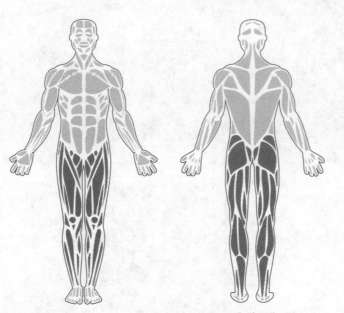

FIGURE 2-10: Muscles used in the Two-Mile Run.

© John Wiley & Sons, Inc.

Your unit chooses where you complete your Two-Mile Run. It can be on an indoor or outdoor track or on an improved surface (like a road or sidewalk). Don't worry; you're not going to be cruising down the dirt part of Perimeter Road in your favorite running shoes. The Army forbids the run from happening on unimproved terrain, which can be unsafe and potentially hurt your time.

The ACFT has a pre-programmed 10-minute rest between the LTK and the 2MR, which starts when the last soldier in your group finishes the LTK.

REMEMBER

Run times for the ACFT are a lot different from what they were on the APFT. If you only need to eke by with 60 points, you have 21 minutes to make your way through the entire course. If you need 65 points, aim for 19 minutes even, or score 70 points by running it in 18 minutes. You can max out 100 points on the 2MR by running the whole thing in 13:30.

The Recovery Drill

When everyone's finished taking the ACFT, there's one more step: the Recovery Drill. Army regs say that the Recovery Drill can be conducted in formation or individually — but that's at the OIC's and NCOIC's discretion.

The Recovery Drill includes these stretches and movements, which are all part of H2F:

>> Overhead Arm Pull

>> Rear Lunge

>> Extend and Flex

>> Thigh Stretch

>> Single Leg Over

>> Groin Stretch

>> Calf Stretch

>> Hamstring Stretch

Biking, Rowing, or Swimming Your Way through the Alternate Events

If you're on a permanent profile, the ACFT's new events don't have to spell an end to your illustrious career. You may be eligible for the modified ACFT — called the ACFT MOD — if you have clearance from your medical provider. Soldiers are required to participate in all the events they're not profiled against, but at minimum, a permanently profiled soldier has to pass the following, regardless of his or her job's physical demand category:

>> **MDL:** You have to lift a minimum of 140 pounds, which nets you a score of 60 points. Head to the earlier section "3 Repetition Maximum Deadlift" for details on this event.

>> **SDC:** Every permanently profiled soldier has to complete the SDC in under three minutes (that's the 60-point score again). You can read about the SDC in the earlier section "Sprint-Drag-Carry."

>> **An aerobic event:** Depending on your profile, you may be required to participate in a 5,000-meter row, 12,000-meter bike, or a 1,000-meter swim with a minimum time of 25 minutes for each. I cover these events in the following sections.

You still take the ACFT MOD with your unit, but you're the last in line for each event, and you take only the events your profile allows. You begin your alternate events 10 minutes after you complete your last standard event (unless you're taking the swim event, in which case you leave right away for the pool). Unlike the other ACFT events, the test supervisor reads instructions before each of these events.

The ACFT MOD is only available to soldiers who are on permanent profiles. If you have a temporary profile, the Army expects you to recondition, retrain, and pass the full six-event ACFT.

The ACFT MOD may change over time, too. The Army is serious when it says that the rules governing this test are "living documents."

Call your grader over when you're getting close to the end of your required distance on the bike or row event. He or she has to watch your odometer and clock the exact moment you cross the "finish line" to record your point score.

Bike

The bike event requires a stationary bike with an adjustable seat and handlebars so it can accommodate soldiers of different heights. The bike has to be equipped with an odometer and a stationary cycle ergometer.

You get a short warm-up period and time to adjust the seat and handlebars. Then, on the command of "Get set," grab your handlebars and get ready for the "Go" command. Your time starts on the "Go" command, and your test timer calls out the time remaining every 30 seconds during the last two minutes of allowable time and every second during the last ten seconds. You must cover 12,000 meters within 25 minutes. You must continue cycling until you reach the 12,000-meter distance, regardless of the time.

Row

If you're participating in the row event, your unit has to provide you with a stationary rowing machine. It must have mechanically adjustable resistance, and the seat, handles, and foot straps have to be adjustable, too. The rowing machine must be equipped with an odometer, and it has to be calibrated before the test.

You get a short warm-up period and some time to adjust the machine to your body size and adjust resistance. On the command of "Get set," position yourself comfortably. The clock begins when your grader says "Go." Like the bike event, your grader calls out the remaining time every 30 seconds during the last two minutes of the test and every second during the last ten seconds. You have 25 minutes to complete 5,000 meters. You must continue rowing until you reach 5,000 meters, regardless of the time.

Swim

The swim event has to take place in a pool with a 25-meter lane and a minimum depth of 1 meter. This one requires a lot of personnel: You need an event supervisor, one scorer for every three soldiers, a timer and a backup timer, and support personnel who are there to ensure safety. The event supervisor can't be a scorer, either.

You get some time to acclimate to the pool's temperature and warm up, but when you hear the command "Get set," you have to position yourself in the pool holding the wall, with your body in contact with the wall — that's the start position for this event. On the command of "Go," you can start swimming. You can use any stroke you want (including a combination of strokes). At the end of each 25-meter lap, you have to touch the pool's wall as you turn around.

You have 25 minutes to swim 1,000 meters, which in a 25-meter lane is 40 laps. Your scorer is supposed to watch you and count your laps, but counting them yourself doesn't hurt. During the event, you can walk on the bottom of the pool to recuperate if you need to.

You don't have to wear your Army Physical Fitness Uniform during this alternate event. You can wear civilian swimming attire (read: your favorite trunks or bathing suit), swimming goggles, and a swim cap if you want to. Just make sure you're sporting something that would be appropriate for you to wear in front of your sergeant major.

Chapter **3**

Understanding How the Army Administers the ACFT

You used to be able to show up to a PT test knowing that all you had to do was a handful of push-ups, sit-ups, and a two-mile run — and that you'd probably pass. The ACFT isn't like that, though. Instead, it's a challenging, six-event test that pushes your body to its limits to evaluate every possible aspect of physical fitness the Army cares about. The Army wants to know about your muscular strength and endurance, your cardiovascular fitness, your ability to perform anaerobic exercises with short bursts of power, and your balance and flexibility.

The Army has testing down to a science. So much so, in fact, that it even requires to-the-minute precision during the test. It also requires soldiers to do a little homework before the test (in addition to physical training), and it requires its graders to complete special training.

Counting Down the Minutes

Like everything else in the Army, the ACFT is heavily regulated. FM 7-22, *Holistic Health and Fitness* and ATC 7-22.02, *Holistic Health and Fitness Drills and Exercises*, have plenty of exercise prescriptions for soldiers, and the Center for Army Lessons Learned consistently pushes out new material related to the test.

Some parts of those regulations are dedicated to timing the test. The Army requires its units to complete an entire ACFT — regardless of the number of soldier taking the test — within 120 minutes. Those two hours include the warm-up drill, the practice time for the 3 Repetition Maximum Deadlift, and all the other events.

The time standard applies across the board, too, even for soldiers taking a modified ACFT. In order to pass, everyone has to finish his or her Two-Mile Run (2MR) before the time expires; the Army's 120-minute clock starts with the Preparation Drill and ends at the 21-minute mark during the 2MR or 25-minute mark for the completion of ACFT MOD events. (Not coincidentally, 21 minutes is the longest any soldier has to complete the run. If you cross the finish line after 21 minutes have elapsed, you don't get the 60 required points to pass for the moderate physical demand category.)

The Army's work-rest cycle during the test should work out like what you see in Figure 3-1. The only programmed rest period is after the Leg Tuck (LTK) and before the 2MR. The mandated 10-minute rest period begins as soon as the last soldier finishes the Leg Tuck. The other rest periods are approximate and may vary based on the number of soldiers in each lane. The only exception: When only one or two soldiers are being tested, 5-minute rest periods between the first four events are mandatory.

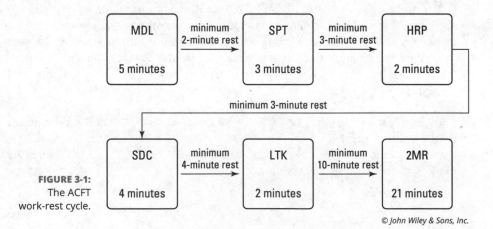

FIGURE 3-1:
The ACFT
work-rest cycle.

© John Wiley & Sons, Inc.

Doing Your Homework before the Test

During the week before you take the ACFT, you're supposed to review each test event and the standards you have to meet based on your physical demand category. In fact, just before you take the test, the OIC or NCOIC will read aloud the following statement:

> You are about to take the Army Combat Fitness Test, or ACFT, a test that will measure your upper- and lower-body muscular endurance, muscular strength, aerobic endurance, and explosive power. The results of this test will give you and your commanders an indication of your state of physical readiness and will act as a guide in determining your physical training needs. After selecting the lane with your preferred weight for the 3 Repetition Maximum Deadlift event, you may be assigned to a different lane for the next events. You will rest and recover while other soldiers complete their turns. After the last soldier completes the Leg Tuck event, there will be a ten-minute recovery period for all tested soldiers before the start of the 2-Mile Run. Do the best you can on each of the events.

Head over to Chapter 4 to read the Army's official instructions for each of the six test events.

Having the Right Tools for the Job: Required Equipment

Like everything else in the Army, you have to have the right tools for the job. In order to administer the ACFT, units must provide all the moving parts that make the test go.

The Army mandates that every battalion has one complete ACFT Equipment Set, which includes one or more

>> **Bumper plates:** Each lane must be equipped to accommodate soldiers lifting between 140 and 340 pounds of weight, and different lanes may have different weight configurations. The Army says additional 5-pound plates "may be acquired locally," which means the unit can pirate them from the fitness center or another place that's willing to share.

>> **Sled with pull strap:** Every lane requires one sled and pull strap. The sled has to be nylon and must be able to accommodate four 45-pound bumper plates. The pull strap must be 92 inches long and feature a handle on both ends.

>> **10-pound medicine ball:** The medicine ball must be approximately nine inches in diameter, made from hard rubber, and feature a textured grip surface. The Army says that the medicine ball must be weatherproof and that it has to be firm and nonmalleable.

>> **40-pound kettlebells:** Every lane needs two 40-pound kettlebells made from cast iron or cast steel, and they must have a closed, single-loop handle. Each kettlebell must be approximately 11 inches tall, have a flat base so it can stand with the handle positioned vertically, and be powder coated.

>> **Metric measuring tape:** Every lane needs a 30-meter-long, vinyl-coated fiberglass metric measuring tape. It must be in a shatter-resistant case with an "easy-to-wind, flush-folding handle."

>> **Climbing bars or a climbing pod:** Many PT fields have climbing bars, but the Army requires units to use very specific setups. See Figure 3-2 for a look at the right climbing bar measurements. A portable pull-up bar is authorized if one of the climbing pods isn't available, but it has to meet certain specifications. Whatever units use, they need one per lane.

The Army's "Supplemental ACFT Supporting Equipment List" includes artificial turf strips (for the Sprint–Drag–Carry), field cones, measuring wheels, speaker boxes, pointers, outdoor clocks, and stopwatches, which units can use at their discretion.

The PT field you use matters, too. It needs to be soft, flat, and dry and must measure at least 30 meters by 50 meters — that's a little less than half a football field. The ground has to be grass or artificial turf, and the site has to be free from significant hazards. Test administrators pick a site that has room to conduct the Preparation Drill and give briefings. The running course can be a track or any other solid, improved surface with less than a 3 percent uphill grade (with no overall decline). Figure 3-3 shows a 16-lane PT field setup.

Every test site also needs an admin table that includes grade sheets, surveys, Form DD 2977 (Deliberate Risk Assessment Worksheet), Combat Lifesaver (CLS) bags (medical kits), and ice sheets. The admin table also serves as the CLS point where the medics hang out. Though every unit's DD 2977 looks different, Figure 3-4 shows an example.

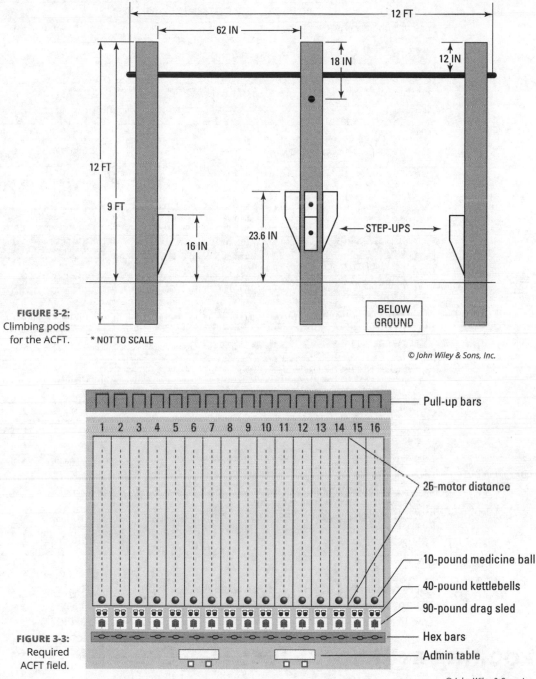

FIGURE 3-2: Climbing pods for the ACFT.

12 FT

62 IN

18 IN

12 IN

12 FT

9 FT

23.6 IN

STEP-UPS

16 IN

BELOW GROUND

* NOT TO SCALE

© John Wiley & Sons, Inc.

Pull-up bars

1 2 3 4 5 6 7 8 9 10 11 12 13 14 15 16

25-meter distance

10-pound medicine ball

40-pound kettlebells

90-pound drag sled

Hex bars

Admin table

FIGURE 3-3: Required ACFT field.

© John Wiley & Sons, Inc.

DELIBERATE RISK ASSESSMENT WORKSHEET

1. MISSION/TASK DESCRIPTION	2. DATE (YYYYMMDD)
Army Combat Fitness Test	20201101

3. PREPARED BY

a. Name (Last, First Middle Initial)	b. Rank/Grade	c. Duty Title/Position
Snuffy, Joe	SFC/E-7	ACFT NCOIC

d. Unit	e. Work Email	f. Telephone (DSN/Commercial (Include Area Code))
3BSTB	joe.snuffy.mil@mail.mil	202-456-1111

g. UIC/CIN (as required)	h. Training Support/Lesson Plan or OPORD (as required)	i. Signature of Preparer
ABCDEF		

Five steps of Risk Management: (1) Identify the hazards (2) Assess the hazards (3) Develop controls & make decisions
(4) Implement controls (5) Supervise and evaluate (Step numbers not equal to numbered items on form)

4. SUBTASK/SUBSTEP OF MISSION/TASK	5. HAZARD	6. INITIAL RISK LEVEL	7. CONTROL	8. HOW TO IMPLEMENT/ WHO WILL IMPLEMENT	9. RESIDUAL RISK LEVEL
Army Combat Fitness Test	Environmental Considerations: Hot Weather Temperature: 85 deg. F Precipitation: 0	M	Ensure water and medical personnel are available. Stress hydration. Identify prior heat casualties.	How: Identify soldiers at risk. PCCs/PCIs. Who: All support staff.	L

10. OVERALL RESIDUAL RISK LEVEL (All controls implemented):

☐ EXTREMELY HIGH ☐ HIGH ☒ MEDIUM ☐ LOW

11. OVERALL SUPERVISION PLAN AND RECOMMENDED COURSE OF ACTION

To ensure unit successfully completes record ACFT, NCOIC will brief support staff on identifying at-risk soldiers and encouraging hydration.

12. APPROVAL OR DISAPPROVAL OF MISSION OR TASK ☐ Approve ☐ Disapprove

a. Name (Last, First, Middle Initial)	b. Rank/Grade	c. Duty Title/Position	d. Signature of Approval Authority

e. Additional Guidance:

FIGURE 3-4: Sample DD 2977 for an ACFT.

© John Wiley & Sons, Inc.

Looking at Helpful Test-Day Details

If you're someone who likes to visualize every possible detail before tackling a project, this section is for you. It's where I break down some aspects of ACFT administration you may not think to, well, think about ahead of the test.

Equipment on the lanes

Graders and support staff initially set up the equipment before the test. However, test-takers can rearrange their equipment however they want — graders don't reset it between participants. That means when you arrive in your lane, you put your equipment where it's easiest for you to use (such as for the Sprint-Drag-Carry).

Soldier testing order

Soldiers rotate through each lane in groups of four, starting with the MDL. The same soldier goes first for the next four events: the Standing Power Throw (SPT), Hand Release Push-Up – Arm Extension (HRP), Sprint-Drag-Carry (SDC), and Leg Tuck (LTK). After the last soldier completes the LTK, the programmed 10-minute rest period begins, and everyone moves to the running path or track at the same time.

Card-carrying ACFT-takers: Scorecards

Test administrators can hand out scorecards prior to the test or at the testing site, after the Preparation Drill. The OIC or NCOIC instructs you to fill out your personal information on the scorecard, which includes your name, gender, unit, MOS, date, pay grade, and age. The OIC or NCOIC then reads these instructions:

> You are to carry this card with you to the first event — the Maximum Deadlift — and give it to the grader. The Maximum Deadlift grader will record your Maximum Deadlift weight and return the card to you to take to the Standing Power Throw lane grader. The Standing Power Throw lane grader will maintain control of the card for the duration of the ACFT. The grader will record your raw score and scaled score, initial the card, and return it to you after completing the ACFT. You must sign the scorecard before departing the test area to show your agreement with your score.

Because you carry your card to the MDL station and to the SPT station only, you don't see it again until you're finished with the test. Get a look at the scorecard in Chapter 4.

WARNING

The grader has the final word on your score for every event. If you don't agree with one or more of your scores, you have to talk to your grader before you sign your ACFT scorecard at the end of the test. When you sign it, you're saying that you agree with your scores.

Stylin' and profilin': What you can't use during the ACFT

The only authorized uniform for the ACFT is your Army Physical Fitness Uniform. (The only exception is if you're a permanently profiled soldier taking the ACFT MOD, which allows you to wear civilian swimming attire in the pool.) You can't use any devices or equipment that can possibly afford you an unfair advantage — so nasal strips, back braces, elastic bandages, and limb braces are completely off the table. You can wear your smart watch or fitness tracker, a heart-rate monitor, or a step counter, but no other electronic devices, such as your phone (some things never change).

TIP

You can use gloves that conform to AR 670-1 for any event, at any time of year, in any climate.

Making the Grade to Score the ACFT

Back when the Army used the Army Physical Fitness Test (APFT) as its test of record, any noncommissioned officer or officer could grade push-ups, sit-ups, and a two-mile run. But because the ACFT has six events (and because five of them are more complicated than push-ups and sit-ups), graders have to be certified. A group of ACFT Military Training Teams, or MTTs, travels Army-wide to certify new Master Fitness Instructors and mid-level supervisors; these people can then administer the ACFT and train new graders. The Army's goal is to certify all NCOs and officers as at least Level I graders, and some will go on to become Level II and Level III graders.

Graders at all levels go through intensive training. First, they must take the ACFT themselves, which builds their foundation for knowing how to properly administer the test and evaluate participants. Then, they learn how to set up ACFT lanes according to Army standards. Prospective graders learn about each event, including why it's included on the test and the muscle groups soldiers use, as well as how to properly execute the movements (so they know how to grade test-takers). When that's done, the prospective graders teach each event to the instructors and must pass assessment in order to become certified.

Level I ACFT graders

Level I ACFT graders undergo a validation training session run by an ACFT Level II or Level III grader-instructor. Level I graders can

>> Validate testing locations

>> Validate testing equipment to standard

>> Grade all six ACFT events to standard

>> Conduct ACFT familiarization training and prepare soldiers to take the test

>> Qualify for Level II training

Level II ACFT graders

Level II ACFT graders are considered Master Graders, and they're certified after validation training that comes from the U.S. Army Physical Fitness School or the U.S. Army Center for Initial Military Training (USACIMT), or from a Level III grader-instructor. (Level II graders can't train or validate other Level II graders.) Level II graders can

>> Serve as a testing OIC or NCOIC to administer a unit ACFT

>> Validate testing locations

>> Validate testing equipment to standard

>> Grade all six ACFT events to standard

>> Administer a 90-day record ACFT

>> Train Level I graders

>> Become Level III graders, but only if they're already Master Fitness Trainers (MFTs; see the following section)

Level III ACFT grader-instructors

Level III grader-instructors have completed validation training offered by a Military Training Team or U.S. Army CIMT, and they must be MFTs. You can't become a Level III grader-instructor unless you've already completed the Army's Master Fitness Trainer course and earned the additional skill identifier (ASI) of P5 if you're enlisted or 6P if you're an officer. Level III graders can

>> Serve as a testing OIC or NCOIC to administer a unit ACFT

>> Validate testing locations

>> Validate testing equipment to standard

>> Grade all six ACFT events to standard

>> Administer a 90-day record ACFT

>> Train Level I graders

>> Train Level II graders

Chapter **4**

Breaking Down ACFT Instructions and Scoring

The big, green machine thrives on rules, instructions, and governance, and the ACFT is no different from any other test in the military. Each event has its own specific instructions, and your performance on each event is tied to a point system.

Unlike the point system for the Army Physical Fitness Test (APFT), which was based on age and gender, the ACFT's point system is completely neutral. Whether you're a 60-year old two-star general or an 18-year-old private doesn't matter — you're going to have to earn the score your military occupational specialty (MOS) requires. The highest score you can possibly get is 600 points; the lowest score you can possibly get depends on whether you want to stay in the Army. (You can score zero points, but if you want to avoid involuntary separation, aim for at least the minimum in your physical demand category.) Every MOS falls into one of three physical demand categories, which I cover later in this chapter.

Following the Rules: The Official ACFT Instructions

Before you jump on a pull-up bar and try to shrimp-curl your way to a perfect 600, you need to know how the Army wants you to perform each exercise on the ACFT. So where do you get that knowledge? Right here is a great start, but you can also get it from the Center for Army Lessons Learned (CALL) and your leadership.

REMEMBER

It's your job to read the official ACFT instructions — and understand them — before you show up on test day. The test administrators in your unit make them available to you, but just in case, I cover them all here. You need to know them long before you take the test anyway. On the day you take your ACFT, the OIC or NCOIC reads only a handful of instructions, and *none* of them are about the events. In fact, the person reading is required to say, "It is your responsibility to complete proper preparation and know the event standards prior to taking the ACFT. What are your questions about the event standards?" (And that happens before you even start the Preparation Drill.)

The following sections include all the Army's official instructions for each event, plus performance tips and things to watch out for — as well as what your graders watch out for.

Lifting with your legs: 3 Repetition Maximum Deadlift instructions

The 3 Repetition Maximum Deadlift (MDL) event requires you to stand inside a hex bar loaded with your choice of weight (but never less than 140 pounds). Check out the scores you need to make the grade in Table 4-3. These are the official instructions for the MDL:

> You must step inside the hex bar with feet shoulder-width apart and locate the midpoint of the hex bar handles. On the command "Get set," you will bend at the knees and hips, reach down, and grasp the center of the handles using a closed grip. Arms will be fully extended, back flat, head in line with the spinal column, and heels in contact with the ground. All repetitions will begin from this position. On the command "Go," you will stand up and lift the bar by straightening the hips and knees. After completing the movement up, you will lower the bar to the floor under control while maintaining a flat back. You must not rest on the ground. A successful attempt is three repetitions to standard. If you fail to perform a successful attempt, you will be allowed one re-attempt at the same weight or a lower weight of your choosing. If you complete three correct repetitions on your first attempt, you will be given the option to attempt a higher weight of your choosing to increase your score. The amount of weight successfully attempted will be your raw score.

Trying MDL tips and techniques

The hex bar itself weighs 60 pounds, so practicing lifting with various weights before you take the ACFT is essential.

REMEMBER

If you're not used to lifting with a hex bar, expect to lift 5 to 10 percent less than you normally would — this bar requires you to balance differently than you would with a straight bar. (With practice, you'll be able to lift more.)

To safely and properly execute a deadlift with the hex bar, plant your feet about shoulder-width apart. Sit into a squat and grip the bar. Distribute your weight evenly through your feet and keep your back straight. Keep your shoulders back and down, and stand up by using the muscles in your legs. You use the muscles in your back and forearms, too, as you balance the bar. Stand up in a smooth motion, and ensure your hands are parallel with your thighs when you're standing all the way up. (If you remember your drill and ceremony, think about matching your hand to the seam of your trousers). Figure 4-1 shows various stages of the MDL with proper form.

TIP

Here are some tricks for nailing the MDL:

>> Center your body inside the hex bar.

>> Keep your chin tucked — don't look straight ahead. Keep your spine neutral, from the top of your head all the way down to your tailbone. (You can't keep your core engaged if your neck is tilted back.) You can injure yourself if you're looking ahead, too, so work very hard to keep your spine neutral.

>> When you're standing up and holding the hex bar, reset your body by coming to a complete stop before lowering the bar again. Check your spine alignment.

Watching for trouble spots on the MDL

A grader can call out a safety violation during any of your deadlifts. You must do three in a row, but if your grader calls out a safety violation, that rep doesn't count. For example, if you do one spectacular deadlift and then commit a safety violation (like rounding your shoulders), that rep doesn't count — and you have to start your three repetitions all over again.

The most common safety violations include the following:

>> Having your feet too close together or too far apart

>> Failing to grab the bar's handles in the middle

FIGURE 4-1:
Proper form for
the MDL.

» Failing to keep your back straight

» Failing to lift with your legs

» Allowing your knees to collapse inward

» Slamming down the weights

» Rounding your shoulders

If your grader observes you trying to lift a weight that's too heavy, he or she can tell you to stop and lower your weight. This determination is a judgment call on the grader's part. If the grader believes that continuing is likely to cause you injury, he or she has the final say.

Exercising explosive power: Standing Power Throw instructions

For the Standing Power Throw (e), you stand with your heels in front of the *throw line* (also called the *fault line*), which is behind you. Throw the ball over your head and behind you, using explosive power to launch that bad boy as far down the lane as you can. Your feet can come off the ground as you throw, but when you land, your feet have to be in front of the throw line. See how far you'll have to throw the ball to get the score you want in Table 4-3.

These are the Army's official instructions for the SPT:

> You will face away from the throw line and grasp a 10-pound medicine ball with both hands. Stand with the heels at — but not on or over — the start line. To avoid having the ball slip, grasp firmly and as far around the sides or beneath the ball as possible. You may make several preparatory movements by bending at the trunk, knees, and hips while lowering the ball toward the ground. Attempt to throw the ball as far as possible. Your feet must be stationary and on the ground prior to the throw. You may jump during the throwing movement to exert more power into the throw, but you must not fall, cross beyond, or touch the throw line with your foot. If you do, the throw will not count. The longer of the two attempts will be the one used for your record score.

When you're training for the SPT, use the exercises in Chapter 8 — but do the Standing Power Throw as often as you can, too. That way, you can get a feel for using the right form on the real deal.

Surveying SPT tips and techniques

Brush off the ball before you throw it; if you're not the first thrower, the ball likely has some grass and dirt on it. If it's wet, dry it off. (Test administrators provide rags or towels you can use for this purpose.)

Doing well on the SPT involves a specific technique. Grasp the ball as far around the outer sides as you can. Get a full swing by sitting into a squat with the ball between your legs, and then lift out of the squat by using leg power. At the same time, raise the ball in one fluid movement until it's over your head. You have to release the ball in just the right spot to get it to travel as far as you want it to go, and for most people, that's almost exactly when the hands pass the back of the head. Ideally, you get it over your head and let it go at a 45-degree angle from the ground.

TIP

Think of your body like a loaded spring when you're in the lower position. Load up into a squat and do a full-body extension (your ankles, knees, and hips all straighten), and let go of the ball when your body is completely extended.

WARNING

Work on your timing. If you let the medicine ball go too early, it gets all its distance up in the air (not straight behind you, where it counts). If you let it go too late, you drive it straight into the ground.

Watching for trouble spots on the SPT

With a little practice, you can nail down the right technique on the SPT. On test day, graders are watching for testers stepping over the fault line and/or throwing at an angle.

WARNING

If your medicine ball goes outside your lane, it doesn't matter how far away it lands; what counts is where it crossed the line. You get two record throws, and the one that goes farthest is the one that your grader writes down as your raw score.

Letting it go: Hand Release Push-up – Arm Extension instructions

The Hand Release Push-up – Arm Extension (HRP) exercise is a lot like a tricep push-up. The catch is that you land on your chest, extend your arms and bring them back in before pushing yourself up again. Find out how many HRPs you need to do to pass in your physical demand category by checking out Table 4-3. These are the official instructions:

> On the command "Get set," you will assume the prone position with hands flat on the ground beneath your shoulders. Your chest and the front of your hips and thighs will be on the ground. Toes will be touching the ground, and feet will be together or up to a boot's width apart as measured by the grader's boot. Your ankles will be flexed. Your head does not have to be on the ground. With the hands placed flat on the ground, your index fingers will be inside the outer edge of your shoulders. Your feet will remain on the ground throughout the event. On the command "Go," you will push the whole body up from the ground as a single unit to fully extend the elbows, moving into the front leaning rest position. You will maintain the same straight body alignment from the top of the head to the ankles.

This straight position will be maintained for the duration of the event. Bending or flexing the knees, hips, trunk, or neck during a repetition will cause that repetition to not count. The front leaning rest is the only authorized rest position. While at rest, if you move out of the front leaning rest position, the event will be terminated.

After you reach the up position, your elbows will bend again to lower your body to the ground. Your chest, hips, and thighs will touch the ground. Your head or face does not have to contact the ground. However, your eyes will be focused on the ground throughout the Hand-Release Push-up test event. After reaching the ground as a single unit, without moving the head, body, or legs, you will immediately move both arms out to the side, straightening the elbows into the T position. You will then immediately return your hands to the starting position to complete one repetition. You cannot pause or rest on the ground. If you place a knee on the ground or lift a hand or foot when in the up position, the event will be terminated. You have two minutes to complete as many correct repetitions as possible.

The best way to practice for the HRP is — you guessed it — to do plenty of HRPs. You can check out strengthening exercises for your core, back, chest and legs in Chapter 8, too, which help you execute even more HRPs properly in the two minutes the Army gives you. Check out proper form for the HRP in Figure 4-2.

Harping on HRP tips and techniques

You have to keep moving during the HRP event. The only exception: You can stop in the front leaning rest position to rest. Remember to bring your hands right back to where they started after you make the T-shape — if your index fingers aren't inside the outer edge of your shoulders, your grader doesn't count your rep.

When you begin practicing HRPs, expect to reach muscle fatigue faster than you would if you were doing ordinary push-ups. In fact, you may do 30 percent fewer HRPs than you can standard push-ups until you strengthen your upper back muscles and get used to the fatigue they experience from making the T to complete a rep.

Here are a few more suggestions for getting the HRP right:

>> Practice with a tennis ball between your feet to make sure you're keeping them close enough together.

>> Spread your fingers wide to distribute weight across your hands when you push yourself up.

>> Your elbows may be most comfortable at about a 45-degree angle from your body when you're doing HRPs.

FIGURE 4-2:
Proper form for
the HRP.

Zack McCrory

>> Zip up your core and engage your chest, thighs, and glutes before you come up to ensure that you move as a single unit. If your grader sees you "peeling" up from the ground (where your upper body comes up before your backside does), your rep doesn't count. Flex everything like you're in a plank before you push yourself up.

>> Your hands don't have to stay in contact with the ground when you make the *T*, but they can. The key is extending your arms so your elbows are straight.

>> Don't waste a lot of effort pulling your upper body off the ground when you make the *T*. Keep your chest on the ground while you extend your arms.

Watching for trouble spots on the HRP

Whether you're practicing or doing the real deal, check yourself during every phase of movement. Your graders are watching for these infractions:

>> Having your index fingers or hands outside your shoulders

>> Failing to keep your body in a generally straight line

>> Resting (aside from in the front leaning rest position)

>> Having your feet more than the grader's boot's width apart

WARNING

When the Army says your feet can't be more than the grader's boot's width apart, it means the width of the *toe* — not the boot length. You're looking at 3 to 4 inches, max.

Showing your combat moves: Sprint-Drag-Carry instructions

The Sprint–Drag–Carry (SDC) comprises five separate events, and each one comes with specific rules for proper execution. See how much time you have to complete the event in Table 4-3. The Army's instructions for the SDC are as follows:

You must assume the prone position with hands on the ground beneath your shoulders and with the top of your head behind the start line, ready to complete five consecutive and continuous 50-meter shuttles. For the first shuttle, on the command "Go," stand up and sprint 25 meters before touching the 25-meter line with your foot and hand, turning at the line and sprinting back to the start. If you fail to touch properly, the scorer will call you back before allowing you to continue. For the second shuttle, grasp each pull-strap handle to pull the sled backwards until the whole sled crosses the 25-meter line. If you fail to cross the line with the sled, the scorer will call you back before allowing you to continue. Turn and drag the sled back to the start line.

For the third shuttle, you will perform the lateral for 25 meters, touching the line with the foot and hand before performing the lateral back to the start line. The lateral will be performed leading with the left foot in one direction and the right foot in the other direction. For the fourth shuttle, grasp the handles of the two 40-pound kettlebells and run 25 meters, touching the line with the foot before returning back to the start line. Place the kettlebells on the ground without dropping them. For the fifth shuttle, sprint 25 meters to the line, touching with the foot and hand, before turning and sprinting back to the start line to complete the event.

In plain English, that means you start the SDC on your stomach, in the prone position (just like the starting position for the HRP), and then you spring into action for the first sprint. When you hit the 25 meter line, you touch it with your foot and hand, turn around, and come right back to the starting point. Then you grab your sled handles and drag the sled to the 25-meter line as you run backward. Wheel it over the line, turn around and drag it all the way back across the start line, drop the handles, and go right into your laterals. Hit the line with your hand and come right back (while still facing the same way). Get over the start line and pick up your two 40-pound kettlebells. Carry them to the 25-meter line and back as quickly as you can, and then do your final sprint (down to the 25-meter line and back).

The SDC events are always in the same order: sprint, sled drag, laterals, kettlebells, and sprint.

REMEMBER

Sorting out SDC tips and techniques

The sled drag may not trip you up, but it's likely to pre-fatigue the muscles you need for the remaining events. The two sprints are where you really give it your all; because they're a relatively short distance, you can make up some time if you lose it in other shuttles. Try these other suggestions as well:

TIP

>> Pull your sled straight back and keep your eyes forward while you're moving backward — don't try to turn to look for the 25-meter or finish line. You're not going to miss the line; you see it as soon as you cross it. This way, you can also use your whole body to pull the sled rather than only the side that's closest to it.

>> Use your legs for the sled drag — don't flex your arms by trying to pull the handles in close to your body. Lean back and let your arms extend so you're not pre-fatiguing your grip and your biceps (remember, the Leg Tuck is still on the horizon). Figure 4-3 gives you a look at what your upper body should look like in the Sled Drag.

FIGURE 4-3:
Proper form for
the Sled Drag.

>> Keep your chest tall while you drag the sled and lean back as you pull. Your core muscles and your lats (technically, your latissimus dorsi) work with your legs to provide you with enough power to get the sled across the line.

>> Get into an athletic stance before you do laterals. You go faster — and stay safer — if you get low and leggy. Don't bounce, because bouncing slows you down and wastes valuable energy.

>> Engage your deltoids and lats (see Figure 4-4) to keep your kettlebells under control while you run with them. If you let your kettlebells swing, you can hurt yourself (or drop them, which costs you time).

Watching for trouble spots on the SDC

If you perform something incorrectly on the SDC, your grader calls you back to the start and has you repeat the shuttle. This do-over counts against your time, so looking out for the same things your grader is looking for is in your best interest:

>> Failing to touch the line (with your hand and foot for sprints and laterals and your foot with kettlebells)

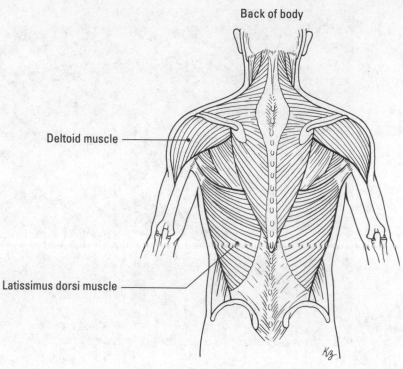

Back of body

Deltoid muscle

Latissimus dorsi muscle

FIGURE 4-4:
Latissimus dorsi
and deltoids.

Kathryn Born

>> Failing to get the entire sled across the line prior to turning around

>> Crossing your feet during laterals

>> Jerking the sled

>> Failing to use the sled's handles

>> Failing to travel facing the same direction during laterals

>> Throwing or carelessly letting go of the kettlebells

>> Running sideways or forward while dragging the sled

Considering core strength: Leg Tuck instructions

The Leg Tuck (LTK) is a quick check on your grip, arm, shoulder, and core strength. It requires you to curl your body up to a pull-up bar, touch your legs (anywhere from your knee to your upper thigh) on your elbows, and lower yourself back down to a hang. Find out how many you need to do in Table 4-3. These are the Army's official instructions for the LTK:

> You will assume a straight-arm hang on the bar with feet off the ground and uncrossed. You must use the alternating grip, with the dominant hand closest to the head. Your body will be perpendicular to the bar. Your elbows will be straight. Your feet cannot contact the ground or the pull-up or climbing bar during the event. On the command "Go," you will flex at the elbows, knees, hips, and waist to raise your knees. Your elbows must flex. They cannot remain fully extended or straight. The right and left knees or thighs must touch the right and left elbows respectively. Your grader must observe both of the knees or the front of the thighs contacting both elbows.

> You will return under control to the straight-arm hang position to complete each repetition. If your elbows remain bent in the straight-arm hang position, that repetition will not count. You do not have to be completely still in the straight-arm hang position, but deliberate, active swinging of the trunk and legs to assist with the upward movement is not permitted. Small, inconsequential or passive movement of the body and twisting of the trunk is permitted. Your grader may assist with controlling these movements if they become excessive. You may rest in the straight-arm hang position. The event will be terminated when you voluntarily stop by dropping from the bar or if you use the ground to rest or push up from to complete a repetition.

Figure 4-5 shows the up position of the Leg Tuck event, where both elbows touch the legs.

Looking for LTK tips and techniques

For some people, the LTK is one of the toughest parts of the ACFT. If you're one of those folks, this event is where you should focus your attention. Getting the technique down is almost as important as strengthening your core muscles.

TIP

The Leg Tuck requires a lot of core strength (front and back). It also requires you to have a good grip, a strong upper body and legs, and a bit of technique. But you can't get around it: To become good at the LTK, you're going to have to practice leg tucks. Because you can't (and shouldn't) do leg tucks every day, check out Chapter 8 for several exercises that help strengthen all the muscles you need to perform well in this event. Keep the following in mind as well:

>> Pull your body up at an angle. You can do that by looking up at the bar or even above your head and leaning back slightly.

FIGURE 4-5:
The up position
of the LTK.

Zack McCrory

>> Involve your hips in the exercise. Tuck them in and curl your body up as you bend your arms.

>> The longer you wait to perform your reps, the more difficult they are. Try not to hang and rest for too long.

>> Don't relax yourself completely between reps; you don't want to go into a complete dead-hang and loosen up all your muscles because then you have to reengage them all to do another leg tuck. Keep your shoulders, core, and lats engaged while you're hanging there.

>> You may find that losing as little as five pounds can make a big difference in your LTK performance. Talk to your primary care provider about losing weight if you're heavier than you want to be. You can also visit the Army Wellness Center on your installation to find out about nutrition options, or jump to Part 4 for information about meeting all your dietary needs.

Watching for trouble spots on the LTK

Graders are trained to watch for

- » Failing to start at and return to a straight-arm hang
- » Failing to touch both elbows to both upper legs
- » Swinging excessively
- » Touching the ground with your feet
- » Using the posts for assistance
- » Moving your hands more than a fist's width apart

Welcoming an old friend: Two-Mile Run instructions

The Army tests your cardiovascular endurance by turning you loose on a two-mile running course and telling you to cross the finish line as quickly as possible (see how fast you have to run to pass in Table 4-3). The official instructions for the Two-Mile Run (2MR) say as much, too. Here they are:

> Prior to starting the ACFT event, you will already know the 2-mile course including the start and finish points, turn around points, or number of laps. On the command "Go," the clock will start and you will begin running at your own pace, completing the 2-mile distance without receiving any physical help. You may walk or pause, but you cannot be picked up, pulled, or pushed in any way. You may pace another soldier or be paced by another soldier. Verbal encouragement is permitted. Leaving the course at any time or at any point during the event will cause the event to be terminated. Your time will be recorded as you cross the finish line at the 2-mile point.

The course can be any flat, improved surface, so your unit may run the ACFT 2MR on a road or a track. If you're on a road, you can expect to see NCOs stationed at waypoints or turn around points.

Marking 2MR tips and techniques

Like any Army run, walking is authorized but highly discouraged. You have to stay on the running course, and you have to complete the run with no physical help from anyone. If your unit isn't already running on Mondays, Wednesdays, and Fridays for PT, or if running is your weak point, you're going to have to mix running into your own fitness routine. You can also check out Chapter 8 for exercises that can help shave a few seconds (or more) off your run time.

Watching for trouble spots on the 2MR

Your grader counts your laps and monitors for no-gos like leaving the designated running course for any reason and receiving physical assistance from anyone.

Even if your grader doesn't tell you to, keeping track of your own laps if you're on a track is a good idea — just like any other time you're running a track with your unit. You don't want to mistakenly think you've completed the event and walk off with one lap to go.

REMEMBER

It seems like you have plenty of time to complete the 2MR, especially if you're comparing it to the APFT standards, but this run is your last of six events, and you've done a full-body workout — so don't take passing it for granted.

Addressing the ACFT's Scoring Scale

The Army scores the ACFT the same for every service member, regardless of gender or age. Whether you're an enlisted soldier, a warrant officer, or a commissioned officer doesn't matter, either. Everyone takes the same ACFT, and everyone has to meet or exceed the standard.

Perusing Physical Demand Categories

Every military occupational specialty falls into one of three Physical Demand Categories: Moderate (Gold), Significant (Gray), or Heavy (Black). The Physical Demand Categories (PDCs) are all outlined in DA PAM 611-21, and they're subject to change over time. Check out Tables 4-1 (enlisted) and 4-2 (commissioned officer) to see which PDC applies to your MOS. All warrant officers, with the exception of MOS 180A, fall into the Moderate (Gold) category.

Jobs that don't require a lot of heavy lifting, such as public affairs, dentistry, and logistics, typically fall under the Moderate (Gold) category. Soldiers in these MOSs have to get 60 points in each event.

Soldiers with jobs that require regular use of physical strength, like military police, combat medics, and aircrew members, usually fall into the Significant (Gray) category. If you're in a Gray MOS, you have to earn at least 65 points in each event.

Infantry and other combat arms jobs always fall into the Heavy (Black) category. Soldiers in these jobs need to score at least 70 points on every event.

TABLE 4-1 **Enlisted Physical Demand Categories**

MOS	Physical Demand Category	MOS	Physical Demand Category
09L	Moderate	35Q	Moderate
09W	Moderate	35S	Moderate
11B	Heavy	35T	Moderate
11C	Heavy	35V	Moderate
12B	Heavy	35X	Moderate
12C	Heavy	35Y	Moderate
12D	Heavy	35Z	Moderate
12G	Significant	36B	Moderate
12K	Moderate	37F	Significant
12M	Heavy	38B	Significant
12N	Moderate	42A	Moderate
12P	Moderate	42R	Moderate
12Q	Moderate	42S	Moderate
12R	Moderate	46Q	Moderate
12T	Moderate	46R	Moderate
12V	Significant	46S	Moderate
12W	Moderate	46Z	Moderate
12X	Moderate	51C	Moderate
12Y	Moderate	56M	Moderate
12Z	Moderate	68A	Moderate
13B	Heavy	68B	Moderate
13F	Heavy	68C	Moderate
13J	Heavy	68D	Moderate
13M	Heavy	68E	Moderate
13R	Heavy	68F	Moderate
13X	Moderate	68G	Moderate
13Z	Moderate	68H	Moderate
14E	Moderate	68J	Moderate

(continued)

TABLE 4-1 *(continued)*

MOS	Physical Demand Category	MOS	Physical Demand Category
14G	Moderate	68K	Moderate
14H	Moderate	68L	Moderate
14P	Significant	68M	Moderate
14S	Significant	68N	Moderate
14T	Moderate	68P	Moderate
14X	Moderate	68Q	Moderate
14Z	Moderate	68R	Moderate
15B	Moderate	68S	Moderate
15C	Moderate	68T	Moderate
15D	Moderate	68U	Moderate
15E	Moderate	68V	Moderate
15F	Moderate	68W	Significant
15G	Moderate	68X	Moderate
15H	Moderate	68Y	Moderate
15J	Significant	68Z	Moderate
15K	Moderate	74D	Moderate
15L	Moderate	79R	Moderate
15M	Moderate	79S	Moderate
15N	Moderate	79T	Moderate
15P	Moderate	79V	Moderate
15Q	Moderate	88H	Heavy
15R	Moderate	88K	Heavy
15S	Significant	88L	Significant
15T	Moderate	88M	Heavy
15U	Moderate	88N	Significant
15W	Moderate	88U	Moderate
15Y	Moderate	88Z	Moderate
15Z	Moderate	89A	Moderate

MOS	Physical Demand Category	MOS	Physical Demand Category
17C	Moderate	89B	Significant
17E	Moderate	89D	Heavy
18B	Heavy	91A	Moderate
18C	Heavy	91B	Moderate
18D	Heavy	91C	Moderate
18E	Heavy	91D	Moderate
18F	Heavy	91E	Moderate
18Z	Moderate	91F	Moderate
19D	Heavy	91G	Moderate
19K	Heavy	91H	Moderate
19Z	Moderate	91J	Moderate
25B	Moderate	91L	Moderate
25C	Moderate	91M	Moderate
25D	Moderate	91P	Moderate
25E	Moderate	91S	Moderate
25L	Significant	91X	Moderate
25M	Moderate	91Z	Moderate
25N	Moderate	92A	Significant
25P	Moderate	92F	Significant
25Q	Moderate	92G	Significant
25R	Significant	92L	Moderate
25S	Moderate	92M	Heavy
25T	Moderate	92R	Significant
25U	Moderate	92S	Significant
25V	Moderate	92W	Significant
25W	Moderate	92Y	Moderate
25X	Moderate	92Z	Moderate
25Z	Moderate	94A	Moderate

(continued)

TABLE 4-1 *(continued)*

MOS	Physical Demand Category	MOS	Physical Demand Category
27D	Moderate	94D	Moderate
29E	Moderate	94E	Moderate
31B	Significant	94F	Moderate
31D	Moderate	94H	Moderate
31E	Moderate	94M	Moderate
31K	Significant	94P	Moderate
35F	Moderate	94R	Moderate
35G	Moderate	94S	Moderate
35L	Moderate	94T	Moderate
35M	Moderate	94W	Moderate
35N	Moderate	94Y	Moderate
35P	Moderate	94Z	Moderate

TABLE 4-2 ## Officer Physical Demand Categories

MOS	Grade Band	PDC	MOS	Grade Band	PDC
11A	O1-O6	Heavy	61G	O1-O6	Moderate
12A	O1-O6	Heavy	61H	O1-O6	Moderate
13A	O1-O2	Heavy	61J	O1-O6	Moderate
13A	O3-O6	Moderate	61K	O1-O6	Moderate
14A	O1-O2	Significant	61L	O1-O6	Moderate
14A	O3-O6	Moderate	61M	O1-O6	Moderate
15A	O1-O2	Moderate	61N	O1-O6	Moderate
15B	O3-O6	Moderate	61P	O1-O6	Moderate
15C	O3-O6	Moderate	61Q	O1-O6	Moderate
15D	O3-O6	Moderate	61R	O1-O6	Moderate
17A	O1-O6	Moderate	61U	O1-O6	Moderate
17B	O1-O6	Moderate	61W	O1-O6	Moderate
18A	O1-O6	Heavy	61Z	O1-O6	Moderate

MOS	Grade Band	PDC	MOS	Grade Band	PDC
19A	O1-O2	Heavy	62A	O1-O6	Moderate
19A	O3-O6	Moderate	62B	O1-O6	Moderate
25A	O1-O2	Significant	63A	O1-O6	Moderate
25A	O1-O6	Moderate	63B	O1-O6	Moderate
25G	O1-O2	Significant	63D	O1-O6	Moderate
25G	O3-O5	Moderate	63E	O1-O6	Moderate
25Z	O6	Moderate	63F	O1-O6	Moderate
26A	O1-O5	Moderate	63H	O1-O6	Moderate
26B	O1-O5	Moderate	63K	O1-O6	Moderate
26Z	O6	Moderate	63M	O1-O6	Moderate
27A	O1-O6	Moderate	63N	O1-O6	Moderate
27B	O1-O6	Moderate	63P	O1-O6	Moderate
30A	O3-O6	Moderate	63R	O1-O6	Moderate
31A	O1-O2	Significant	64A	O1-O3	Moderate
31A	O3-O6	Moderate	64B	O3-O6	Moderate
34A	O3-O6	Moderate	64C	O3-O6	Moderate
35A	O1-O6	Moderate	64D	O3-O6	Moderate
35B	O3-O6	Moderate	64E	O3-O6	Moderate
35D	O1-O6	Moderate	64F	O3-O6	Moderate
35E	O1-O6	Moderate	64Z	O3-O6	Moderate
35F	O1-O6	Moderate	65A	O1-O6	Moderate
35G	O1-O6	Significant	65B	O1-O6	Moderate
36A	O1-O6	Moderate	65C	O1-O6	Moderate
37A	O3-O6	Moderate	65D	O1-O6	Moderate
37X	O1-O6	Moderate	65X	O3-O6	Moderate
38A	O3-O6	Moderate	66B	O1-O6	Moderate
38G	O3-O6	Moderate	66C	O1-O6	Moderate
38X	O1-O6	Moderate	66E	O1-O6	Moderate

(continued)

TABLE 4-2 *(continued)*

MOS	Grade Band	PDC	MOS	Grade Band	PDC
40A	O3-O6	Moderate	66F	O1-O6	Moderate
40C	O3-O6	Moderate	66G	O1-O6	Moderate
42B	O1-O3	Moderate	66H	O1-O6	Moderate
42C	O1-O6	Moderate	66N	O1-O6	Moderate
42H	O4-O6	Moderate	66P	O1-O6	Moderate
46A	O1-O6	Moderate	66R	O1-O6	Moderate
46X	O3-O4	Moderate	66S	O1-O6	Moderate
47	O5-O6	Moderate	66T	O1-O6	Moderate
48	O3-O6	Moderate	66W	O1-O6	Moderate
49	O3-O6	Moderate	67A	O1-O6	Moderate
50A	O3-O6	Moderate	67B	O1-O6	Moderate
51	O3-O6	Moderate	67C	O1-O6	Moderate
52B	O1-O6	Moderate	67D	O1-O6	Moderate
56A	O1-O6	Moderate	67E	O1-O6	Moderate
56D	O1-O6	Moderate	67F	O1-O6	Moderate
56X	O1-O6	Moderate	67G	O1-O6	Moderate
57A	O3-O6	Moderate	67J	O1-O2	Significant
59A	O3-O6	Moderate	67J	O3-O6	Moderate
60A	O1-O6	Moderate	70A	O1-O6	Moderate
60B	O1-O6	Moderate	70B	O1-O6	Moderate
60C	O1-O6	Moderate	70C	O1-O6	Moderate
60D	O1-O6	Moderate	70D	O1-O6	Moderate
60F	O1-O6	Moderate	70E	O1-O6	Moderate
60G	O1-O6	Moderate	70F	O1-O6	Moderate
60H	O1-O6	Moderate	70H	O1-O6	Moderate
60J	O1-O6	Moderate	70K	O1-O6	Moderate
60K	O1-O6	Moderate	71A	O1-O6	Moderate

MOS	Grade Band	PDC	MOS	Grade Band	PDC
60L	O1-O6	Moderate	71B	O1-O6	Moderate
60M	O1-O6	Moderate	71E	O1-O6	Moderate
60N	O1-O6	Moderate	71F	O1-O6	Moderate
60P	O1-O6	Moderate	72A	O1-O6	Moderate
60Q	O1-O6	Moderate	72B	O1-O6	Moderate
60R	O1-O6	Moderate	72C	O1-O6	Moderate
60S	O1-O6	Moderate	72D	O1-O6	Moderate
60T	O1-O6	Moderate	73A	O1-O6	Moderate
60U	O1-O6	Moderate	74A	O1-O6	Moderate
60V	O1-O6	Moderate	88A	O1-O2	Heavy
60W	O1-O6	Moderate	88A	O3	Moderate
61A	O1-O6	Moderate	89E	O1-O3	Heavy
61B	O1-O6	Moderate	89E	O4-O6	Moderate
61C	O1-O6	Moderate	90A	O3-O6	Moderate
61D	O1-O6	Moderate	91A	O1-O3	Moderate
61E	O1-O6	Moderate	92A	O1-O2	Heavy
61F	O1-O6	Moderate	92A	O3	Moderate

Many officers' requirements differ based on pay grade. For example, second and first lieutenants in the Quartermaster field fall into the Heavy (Black) physical demand category, while their captain counterparts fall into the Moderate (Gray) category. That's because the jobs these officers perform typically depend on their pay grades, with higher-ranking officers generally being less responsible for heavy lifting than their juniors are.

So what about O7s and above? General officers are all categorized as Moderate (Gold), regardless of MOS. If that's not a great reason to work toward promotion, I don't know what is.

When an MOS's duties or tasks change, PDCs can change with them.

REMEMBER

Weighing your score on the scale

When you complete an ACFT event, you get a raw score. That raw score translates into points. Your grader writes both scores on your scorecard. (I discuss the scorecard in the following section.) Table 4-3 shows the number of points you receive for each raw score. The table stops at 60 points, because a score below 60 is an ACFT failure. If you fail one event, you fail the whole test. The ACFT has no extended scale, so the highest score you can achieve on the test is 600. The lowest score you can get and still pass is 360.

TABLE 4-3   ACFT Scoring Scale

Points	MDL	SPT	HRP	SDC	LTK	2MR
100	340	12.5	60	1:33	20	13:30
99		12.4	59	1:36		13:39
98		12.2	58	1:39	19	13:48
97	330	12.1	57	1:41		13:57
96		11.9	56	1:43	18	14:06
95		11.8	55	1:45		14:15
94	320	11.6	54	1:46	17	14:24
93		11.5	53	1:47		14:33
92	310	11.3	52	1:48	16	14:42
91		11.2	51	1:49		14:51
90	300	11.0	50	1:50	15	15:00
89		10.9	49	1:51		15:09
88	290	10.7	48	1:52	14	15:18
87		10.6	47	1:53		15:27
86	280	10.4	46	1:54	13	15:36
85		10.3	45	1:55		15:45
84	270	10.1	44	1:56	12	15:54
83		10.0	43	1:57		16:03
82	260	9.8	42	1:58	11	16:12
81		9.7	41	1:59		16:21

Points	MDL	SPT	HRP	SDC	LTK	2MR
80	250	9.5	40	2:00	10	16:30
79		9.4	39	2:01		16:39
78	240	9.2	38	2:02	9	16:48
77		9.1	37	2:03		16:57
76	230	8.9	36	2:04	8	17:06
75		8.8	35	2:05		17:15
74	220	8.6	34	2:06	7	17:24
73		8.5	33	2:07		17:33
72	210	8.3	32	2:08	6	17:42
71		8.2	31	2:09		17:51
70 (Heavy)	**200**	**8.0**	**30**	**2:10**	**5**	**18:00**
69		7.8	28	2:14		18:12
68	190	7.5	26	2:18	4	18:24
67		7.1	24	2:22		18:36
66		6.8	22	2:26		18:48
65 (Significant)	**180**	**6.5**	**20**	**2:30**	**3**	**19:00**
64	170	6.2	18	2:35		19:24
63	160	5.8	16	2:40		19:48
62	150	5.4	14	2:45	2	20:12
61		4.9	12	2:50		20:36
60 (Moderate)	**140**	**4.5**	**10**	**3:00**	**1**	**21:00**

Tallying up your score on the new ACFT scorecard

You fill in the identifying information on your scorecard before you begin the ACFT, like your name, your unit and location, the date, your pay grade, and your MOS. You also include your age and gender, but they don't affect the scores you need to pass. Figure 4-6 has a sample scorecard.

ARMY COMBAT FITNESS SCORECARD

For use of this form, see *ACFT IOC, OCT 2019.*

NAME: LAST, FIRST, MI:

GENDER: MALE/FEMALE

UNIT/LOCATION:

TEST ONE					TEST ONE			
DATE	GRADE	MOS	AGE		DATE	GRADE	MOS	AGE

HEIGHT (inches)	BODY COMPOSITION				HEIGHT (inches)	BODY COMPOSITION		
	WEIGHT: ___ LBS		BODY FAT: ___ x			WEIGHT: ___ LBS		BODY FAT: ___ x
	GO	NO GO	GO	NO GO		GO	NO GO	GO	NO GO

3 REPETITION MAXIMUM DEADLIFT: weight lifted - circle heaviest (lbs)

1ST ATTEMPT	2ND ATTEMPT	POINTS	GRADER INITIALS

STANDING POWER THROW: distance thrown - circle longest (meters: centimeters)

1ST THROW	2ND THROW	POINTS	GRADER INITIALS

HAND RELEASE PUSH-UP: number of correctly performed repetitions

REPETITIONS	POINTS	GRADER INITIALS

SPRINT-DRAG-CARRY: overall event time (minutes: seconds)

TIME	POINTS	GRADER INITIALS

LEG TUCK: number of correctly performed repetitions

REPETITIONS	POINTS	GRADER INITIALS

TWO-MILE RUN: overall event time (minutes: seconds)

TIME	POINTS	GRADER INITIALS

5K ROW/1K SWIM/15K BIKE (circle one): overall time to reach required distance

TIME	PASS/FAIL	GRADER INITIALS

Soldier Signature: _____   TOTAL POINTS

OIC/NCOIC Last, First, MI   OIC/NCOIC Signature/Rank

FIGURE 4-6:
The Army Combat
Fitness Test
scorecard.

© *John Wiley & Sons, Inc.*

Army Regulation 600-9 requires your height and weight to be measured every 6 months (at minimum) and also encourages commanders to allow at least seven days between a physical fitness test and a weigh-in so that soldiers don't try to drop weight and negatively impact their performance on the test. If you need to be taped — that is, if the Army needs to measure your body composition — your body fat percentage is written on your scorecard and marked "Go" or "No Go." Get a closer look at the Army's height and weight requirements, as well as the Army Weight Control Program, in Chapter 20.

Your grader fills in your raw scores and your scaled scores. Your *raw scores* are those that reflect your time, distance, or weight lifted on the PT field. Your *scaled scores* are the raw scores translated into points (like you see in Table 4-3 in the preceding section). For example, if you threw your 10-pound medicine ball 9.5 meters, that's your raw score. Your 9.5-meter raw score translates into 80 points earned toward your overall score.

REMEMBER

You sign your scorecard before you leave the PT field. When you sign it, you're saying that you agree with your scores.

Accounting for the ACFT MOD

If you qualify to take the ACFT MOD — that is, if you're on a permanent profile and you have clearance from your primary care provider — you have to score at least 60 points in both the MDL and the SDC. You also have to complete one of four aerobic events: the Two-Mile Run, the 5,000-Meter Row, the 12,000-Meter Bike, or the 1,000-Meter Swim. You must complete your alternate aerobic event within 25 minutes. (The 2MR rules are exactly the same as they are on the standard ACFT, but you must complete the course in 21 minutes.)

REMEMBER

The requirements for the ACFT MOD are subject to change.

Sailing through the 5,000-Meter Row

If you're rowing your way through the ACFT, you get some time to warm up. Then, your event supervisor reads you these instructions:

> The 5,000-Meter Row event measures your level of aerobic fitness. On the command "Go," the clock will start and you will begin rowing at your own pace. You may pause and rest during the test. However, you may not get off the rower. You must complete the 5,000-meter distance. You will be scored on your time. To pass, you must complete 5,000 meters in 25 minutes. What are your questions about this event?

TIP

Do a complete stroke each time you row. The rowing machine measures your distance, so don't stop yourself shy — extend your arms all the way forward (until you're almost touching the machine) and lean all the way back so that your body is almost parallel to the ground. Pull the handles to your chest, not your bellybutton.

Braking for the 15,000-Meter Bike

The 12,000-Meter Bike event is another way the Army can measure your cardio-vascular fitness. Your event supervisor reads you these instructions after giving you a short time to warm up:

> The 12,000-Meter Bike event measures your level of aerobic fitness. On the command "Go," the clock will start and you will begin pedaling at your own pace. You may pause and rest during the test. However, you may not get off the bike. You must complete the 12,000-meter distance in 25 minutes or less. You will be scored on your time. What are your questions about this event?

TIP

Take some time to adjust the bike to your body before your event starts. You don't want to stop during the test to tweak it because that cuts into your time.

Soaking up the 1,000-Meter Swim

The 1,000-Meter Swim is the third option available on the ACFT MOD. You get a few minutes in the pool to acclimate and warm up before your event supervisor reads these instructions:

> The 1,000-Meter Swim measures your level of aerobic fitness. You will begin in the water; no diving is allowed. At the start, your body must be in contact with the wall of the pool. On the command "Go," the clock will start. You should then begin swimming at your own pace, using any stroke or combination of strokes you wish. You must swim [appropriate number based on lap length] laps to complete this distance. You must touch the wall of the pool at each end of the pool as you turn. Any type of turn is authorized. You must complete the 1,000-meter distance in 25 minutes. You will be scored on time. Walking on the bottom to recuperate is authorized. Swimming goggles, swim caps, and civilian swimming attire are permitted, but no other equipment is authorized. What are your questions about this event?

TIP

Pace yourself and work with your best strokes (the ones that allow you to cover the most distance with the least effort on your part). Your grader tells you how many laps you need to do to reach 1,000 meters and keeps track of how many you've done, but keeping track yourself is a good idea.

Taking Another Shot: Army Policy on ACFT Failures

You aren't supposed to take the ACFT if you're sick or injured, or if you're on a temporary profile that limits what you can do. If you start the test, you're acknowledging that you're physically able to perform to the best of your ability and that you understand the test standards. However, if you fail to reach the minimum passing score on any event, you fail the whole ACFT.

ACFT failure can have serious consequences — both in the short and long term. When you fail a record PT test, your unit puts a flag in your file that suspends all favorable actions. That flag, which is authorized in AR 600-8-2, prevents you from going to school (including leader development schools and schools where you pick up additional skill identifiers, like Air Assault, Airborne, Pathfinder, or

Tech Escort). You can't get promoted, either, and you can't reclass into another MOS. (If you're in the Guard or Reserves, a flag can even prevent you from changing units — so if you move but can't pass your ACFT, you're going to be doing some serious traveling.) You can't reenlist while you're flagged, either.

AR 350-1 says that your commander can allow you to retake the ACFT after a failure as soon as you (and your commander) feel that you're ready. However, the Army considers you a "repetitive failure" when you fail a record test, you're given adequate time and assistance to condition (not more than 90 days), and you fail the test again. That's when your command can bar you from reenlistment completely or even process you for separation under AR 600-8-24 (for officers) or AR 635-200 (for enlisted soldiers).

REMEMBER

You can't take an ACFT if you're on a temporary profile. You have to come off profile and recondition first. If you're on a permanent profile, you may be eligible to take the ACFT MOD, which requires you to complete at least the MDL and SDC, plus one aerobic event. Flip to the earlier section "Accounting for the ACFT MOD" for more details.

2

Training for the ACFT on Your Own Time

Chapter **5**

Putting the (Mandatory) "Fun" in Functional Fitness

The Army needs combat-ready soldiers who are less prone to injury and who can perform on the battlefield, which means functional fitness is in and old PT plans are out. To pass the ACFT with flying colors, you probably need to do PT on your own time, not just with your unit Monday through Friday. Sure, the Army requires you to knock out some components of its Holistic Health and Fitness program from 0630 to 0730, but you need to create your own functional fitness routines that include full-body muscle-based movement training.

Mastering the Science of Movement Training

If you walked into a gym right now, you'd most likely see rows of machines dedicated to training just one muscle at a time. Those are great for bodybuilders but not necessarily for the average soldier. Because most MOSs have at least minimal physical demands (that's where the physical demand categories I cover in Chapter 4 come in), and because those demands require real-world movement, many of the machines at the gym are great supplements to your training. However, you definitely need movement training, too.

Distinguishing muscle training from movement training

Improving athleticism, which is what the Army is really testing with the ACFT, requires a combination of muscular and movement-based training. Movement training is unlike muscle training. It harnesses your natural human kinetics — the way you move — and makes your movements stronger, more stable, and safer.

In standard muscle training, you have to isolate a muscle (or a group of muscles) to focus all your work there. Your intent is to put force in just one region of your body, like your chest, while the rest of your body is stabilized and still, and your goal is to see just how much force you can send into that region and still execute a movement, such as a chest press. You don't want to "cheat" by using momentum because that means other muscles are pitching in to help you execute the movement. That's fine if that's the type of training you're doing.

But when you need motor skills you can use outside the gym, and if you need to be efficient with your movement (like you do on the ACFT and on the battlefield), you need your muscles to work together to accomplish a result. Whether you're putting together a GP Medium or carrying one of your squad members to safety, your movement training kicks in. Movement training is about improving motor tasks that take you outside the linear plane. Movement training integrates your whole body.

And with the ACFT, the Army is testing your ability to pull off complex movements — not just your ability to use your pecs and a few smaller muscles to push yourself off the ground. That means you have to cross-train, use three-dimensional movements and your planar movements, and use weight training to complement everything you're doing if you want to perform well on the ACFT.

These 3D movements come with a wide range of other benefits, too, such as improved

>> Aerobic capacity

>> Coordination

>> Joint health

>> Resiliency in multidirectional movements outside the gym

>> Tensile strength in your connective tissues

TECHNICAL STUFF

The more momentum you can harness while controlling your form, the more efficiently you work. Your brain automatically wants to execute all your body's movements in ways that are easiest to accomplish — but not necessarily in ways that prevent injury (think about the last time you did bicep curls and threw your back into them, or picked up a box from the floor without bending your legs).

Playing with planar movement

With physical training, you can do your work in one or more of the three planes of motion: the sagittal plane, the frontal plane, and the transverse plane.

If you're working in the *sagittal plane*, you're moving two-dimensionally — up and down or back and forth. In the *frontal plane*, you're making side-to-side movements. Finally, in the *transverse plane*, you're using twisting or rotating movements. Work in any of these planes can be *unloaded*, which means you have only your body weight, or *loaded*, which means you're using an external mass while moving. An external mass can be anything from a barbell loaded with weight to your Improved Outer Tactical Vest, or IOTV.

Most exercises in the three planes of motion fall into one or more of four main categories:

>> **Unloaded linear movements:** Linear movements are in the sagittal plane or the frontal plane. You're running, cycling, or performing some types of strength training. Linear exercises move only horizontally or vertically.

>> **Unloaded 3D movements:** Movements that cross over the borders between the sagittal, frontal, and transverse planes are 3D movements. Things like sports (tennis, football, baseball, and a number of others), dancing, and many types of martial arts use unloaded 3D movements.

>> **Loaded linear movements:** Loaded movements keep you in the sagittal or frontal plane and involve external weight. Running while carrying a litter, squatting with a bar on your back, and doing everyday bicep curls are loaded linear movements. The external weight can range from resistance bands and barbells to the flywheel of an adjustable stationary cycle or full battle rattle.

>> **Loaded 3D movements:** Working through different planes with an external weight means you're doing loaded 3D movements. These movements, like agility drills, modified exercises (such as shoulder extensions with a trunk rotation), and lateral lunges with a plate reach involving rotation.

TIP

Strictly training in loaded linear movements can easily result in overuse injuries. Working in 3D allows other muscles, connective tissues, and joints to pitch in to complete a task, which "shares the load."

Sectioning off the 4Q model

The *4Q model* allows you to group exercises together by type: unloaded linear, unloaded 3D, loaded linear, and loaded 3D. (Check out the preceding section for more on these types of movements.) Figure 5-1 shows the 4Q model, as well as some of the exercises that belong in each quadrant.

LOADED

Loaded Linear Training	**Loaded 3D Movement Training**
• Bicep curls	• Lap pull-down with rotation
• Bench presses	• Multidirectional lunges holding weights or wearing a weighted vest
• Dead lifts	
• Shoulder presses	• Shoveling snow
• Weighted calf raises	
• Weighted lunges	

LINEAR _____ **3D**

Unloaded Linear Training	**Unloaded 3D Movement Training**
• Sit-ups	• Tai Chi and other martial arts
• Pushups	• Agility drills
• Planks	• Dancing
• Squats	
• Swimming	
• Iron Mikes	
• Pull-ups	

UNLOADED

FIGURE 5-1:
The 4Q model.

© *John Wiley & Sons, Inc.*

REMEMBER

Training in all four quadrants is essential for optimal results. If your goal is overall strength and endurance, you can't leave one (or more) out.

Unloaded training

Unloaded training — commonly called *body weight training* — refers to exercises like push-ups and pull-ups. Despite what you've heard, body weight training isn't inherently easier than loaded training is. The Leg Tuck on the ACFT is a perfect illustration of that; it's all body weight, but for many people, it's one of the most difficult exercises to perform.

LOADED MULTI-PLANAR (3D) TRAINING FOR THE ACFT

Loaded multi-planar training is relatively new — at least in the gym. Classic strength training isolates muscles with the purpose of strengthening only those muscles, as evidenced by people hitting the gym for "chest day" or "cardio day." (Everyone knows what happens when "leg day" isn't part of a weekly routine.) But loaded multi-planar movement falls into the upper-right quadrant in the 4Q model (see the nearby "Sectioning off the 4Q model" section), and training there is absolutely essential for passing the ACFT. The bottom line is that functioning in and out of the Army requires the human body to move mass while in motion, and most of the time, you have to move that mass in a way that asymmetrically loads your body or puts it in a weird position. If you're only training to carry something by using both biceps evenly at the same time, without any help from your back or legs, you're not going to perform as efficiently or as safely as you would if you practiced loaded movement training that integrated your whole body.

Loaded training

Loaded training requires you to add external mass to movement. Any mass counts, whether it's a 1-kilogram plate alone or a bar loaded with 400 pounds. How much mass you need to move to make gains and improve your fitness level depends on your current level of physical fitness. Your body will adapt to larger loads over time, provided that you use something that challenges you and forces a change in your muscles. When your body adapts to a certain amount of weight, it's no longer going to force your muscles to adapt, so if you want to become stronger, you have to increase the mass of the loads you're working with.

REMEMBER

Loaded movements are movements that involve an external mass that's not part of your body. Running is an unloaded linear movement, while running while wearing your IOTV is a loaded linear movement. Throwing your rucksack over a wall is a loaded 3D movement, and climbing up the wall after it (if you're not wearing your kit) is an unloaded linear movement. (If you're wearing your kit, it becomes a loaded linear movement.) Going over the top of the wall to come down on the other side is a 3D movement; it's unloaded or loaded depending on whether you're wearing your kit.

ACFT events in the 4Q model

Table 5-1 shows whether each of the ACFT events falls into the loaded linear or unloaded linear quadrant of the 4Q model. The test is mostly about linear movement, but training to perform well on the test requires you to work in all four quadrants. Each event gives the Army a good look at how you perform 3D movements, such as surmounting an obstacle or extracting a casualty from a vehicle, which are hard to grade. Some of the events require a combination of muscular strength and endurance plus cardiovascular endurance, such as the drag and carry shuttles of the Sprint-Drag-Carry. Flip to Chapter 1 to read more about each individual event and how it correlates to battlefield tasks; Chapter 6 has info on Army fitness components like endurance.

TABLE 5-1 **ACFT Events in 4Q Quadrants**

Loaded Linear Movement	Unloaded Linear Movement
3 Repetition Maximum Deadlift (MDL)	Hand Release Push-Up – Arm Extension (HRP)
Standing Power Throw (SPT)	Sprint-Drag-Carry (SDC)
Sprint-Drag-Carry (SDC)	Leg Tuck (LTK)
	Two-Mile Run (2MR)

Note that the Sprint-Drag-Carry falls under two quadrants: loaded linear movement and unloaded linear movement. That's because this single event comprises four individual activities. The sprints and laterals are unloaded linear movements, while the drag and carry are loaded linear movements.

Finding Functional Fitness Basics

Functional fitness really just means training that prepares your body for real-life movements — and in the Army, your real-life moves are in action in garrison and downrange. Functional fitness requires strength and stability in every part of your body, including your muscles, connective tissues, and joints. It also requires you to have enough cardiovascular endurance for sustained work, the kind you need to carry a litter for 1,500 meters or push through a 12-mile ruck with a 35-pound load in three hours.

All your muscles work together to keep you moving throughout the day, which is why functional fitness is so important — and exactly why the Army tests it. The following sections introduce the muscle groups and some individual muscles involved in functional fitness (some muscles fall into more than one group); you can see the body's major muscles in Figures 5-2 and 5-3. Flip to Chapter 6 to get an inside look at the Army's reasoning for implementing Physical Readiness Training and the ACFT, as well as the functions you need each muscle group to perform.

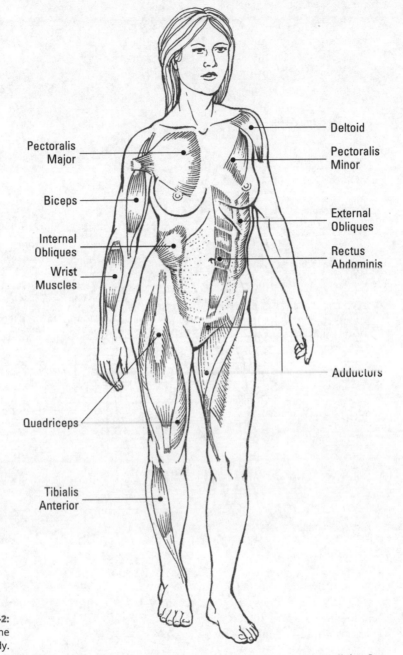

Pectoralis
Major

Biceps

Internal
Obliques

Wrist
Muscles

Quadriceps

Tibialis
Anterior

Deltoid

Pectoralis
Minor

External
Obliques

Rectus
Abdominis

Adductors

FIGURE 5-2:
Muscles of the
front of the body.

Kathryn Born

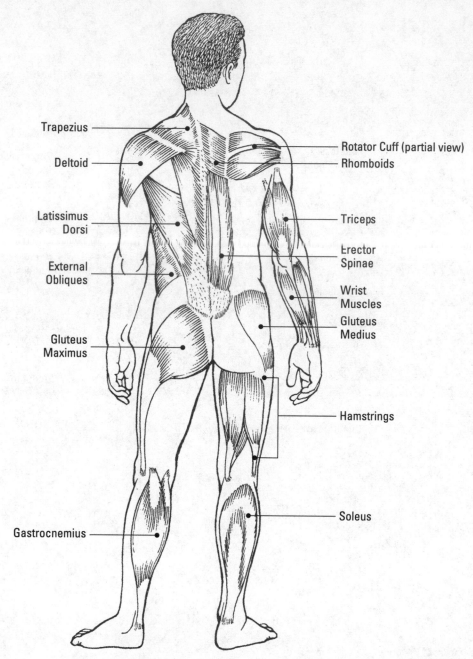

Trapezius

Deltoid

Latissimus
Dorsi

External
Obliques

Gluteus
Maximus

Gastrocnemius

Rotator Cuff (partial view)

Rhomboids

Triceps

Erector
Spinae

Wrist
Muscles

Gluteus
Medius

Hamstrings

Soleus

FIGURE 5-3:
Muscles of the
back of the body.

Kathryn Born

Core strength

You hear a lot about core strength, especially in functional fitness. Your *core* is really your trunk, and it provides your body with all kinds of stability during different tasks. You have an *anterior core* in the front and a *posterior core*, which is in the back. Every day, you flex, extend, and rotate your trunk by using a series of muscles that help you with virtually every physical activity you do.

Your anterior core, which you can see most of in Figure 5-2, includes the following

>> Rectus abdominis

>> External obliques

>> Internal obliques

>> Transversus abdominis (beneath your internal obliques)

>> Adductors

Your posterior core muscles show up on your back (and many also make an appearance in Figure 5-3). They include:

>> Trapezius

>> Rhomboids

>> Latissimus dorsi

>> Erector spinae (a group of muscles and tendons that go from your tailbone to the base of your skull)

>> Multifidus (the muscle that runs straight up and down each side of your spine)

>> Quadratus lumborum, deep in your back, which starts at your lowest rib and ends at the top of your pelvis

>> Gluteal complex, which includes gluteus maximus, gluteus minimus, and gluteus medius

Table 5-2 explains the actions, appearance, and core muscles you use to perform everyday movements. It also shows which ones you use in ACFT events.

Leg strength

Leg strength gets you from Point A to Point B, propels you forward on your Two-Mile Run, and helps you lift heavy objects. You extend your leg (put it behind you), flex it (put it in front of you), abduct it (move it out to the side), and adduct it (move it in) multiple times a day, and on test day, you have a chance to show off all the muscles and connective tissues that make those things happen. Figures 5-2 and 5-3 illustrate the basic anatomy of a leg.

TABLE 5-2   ## Core Muscles in Action

Action/Event	Movement Appearance	Primary Muscles Used
Flexion	Bending forward or curling up	Rectus abdominus
Extension	Standing up straight from a bent-over position, bending backward	Erector spinae
Rotation	Twisting to the left or right in a 3D movement	Internal and external obliques
Lateral flexion	Bending to the side	Internal and external obliques, rectus abdominus, erector spinae
Compression	Sucking in your stomach	Transversus abdominis
Spinal stability	Keeps your spine stable during movement	Multifidus
3 Repetition Maximum Deadlift (MDL)	Bending forward, erecting the spine, moving upward with weight, moving downward with weight	Internal obliques, transversus abdominus, adductors, trapezius, latissimus dorsi, erector spinae, multifidus, quadratus lumbar
Standing Power Throw (STP)	Bending forward, moving upward with weight, bending backward, throwing overhead	Rectus abdominus, external obliques, internal obliques, transversus abdominis, adductors, trapezius, latissimus dorsi, erector spinae, multifidus, quadratus lumbar, gluteal complex
Hand Release Push-Up – Arm Extension (HRP)	Pushing upward, lowering to the ground, extending arms from a prone position	Rectus abdominis, transversus abdominis, adductors, trapezius, latissimus dorsi, erector spinae, multifidus, quadratus lumbar, gluteal complex
Sprint-Drag-Carry (SDC)	Picking up a load, spinal stability, carrying a load while running, bending to the side	Trapezius, gluteal complex, internal obliques, transversus abdominis, rectus abdominis, multifidus, erector spinae
Leg Tuck (LTK)	Curling upward, maintaining trunk stability	Rectus abdominis, external obliques, internal obliques, transversus abdominis, adductors, latissimus dorsi, erector spinae, multifidus, trapezius, quadratus lumbar
Two-Mile Run (2MR)	Continuous forward motion with legs	Adductors, gluteal complex

TECHNICAL STUFF

Your hip flexors are groups of muscles in the pocket area of your pants, and they include the psoas major, psoas minor, iliacus, iliopsoas, and sartorius. Your primary hip extensors include the gluteus maximus, adductor magnus, and hamstrings.

Table 5-3 shows you which leg muscles you use to perform everyday activities and the ACFT events.

TABLE 5-3   ## Leg Muscles in Action

Action/Event	Movement Appearance	Primary Muscles Used
Hip flexion	Lifting your thigh upward in front of you	Hip flexors
Hip extension	Moving your thigh behind you	Hip extensors
Hip abduction	Lifting your leg out to the side, squatting	Gluteus medius and minimus (located below the medius and behind the maximus)
Hip adduction	Returning your leg from abduction	Adductor magnus
External hip rotation	Rotating your leg out from the midline of your body	Piriformis
Knee flexion	Bending your knee	Hamstrings
Knee extension	Straightening your knee	Quadriceps
Ankle plantarflexion	Standing on tiptoes, pointing your toes	Gastrocnemius and soleus
Ankle dorsiflexion	Lifting toes from the floor (toward shin), flexing foot	Tibialis anterior
3 Repetition Maximum Deadlift (MDL)	Lifting to a standing position, squatting to a seated position	Hip flexors, quadriceps, gluteal complex, hip extensors, gastrocnemius
Standing Power Throw (SPT)	Squatting and extending	Hip flexors, quadriceps, tibialis anterior, gluteal complex, hip extensors, gastrocnemius
Hand Release Push-Up – Arm Extension (HRP)	Holding the body in a straight line	Hip flexors, quadriceps, tibialis anterior, gluteal complex, hip extensors, gastrocnemius
Sprint-Drag-Carry (SDC)	Sprinting, moving a load backward using your legs, performing laterals, running under load	Hip flexors, quadriceps, tibialis anterior, gluteal complex, adductor magnus, piriformis, hamstrings, quadriceps, hip flexors, hip extensors, gastrocnemius
Leg Tuck (LTK)	Curling up	Hip flexors, quadriceps, tibialis anterior
Two-Mile Run (2MR)	Running	Hip flexors, quadriceps, tibialis anterior, gluteal complex, hamstrings, quadriceps, hip flexors, hip extensors, gastrocnemius

Back strength

Your back has a tremendous number of muscles and connective tissues, and they're layered. *Deep muscles* are beneath other muscles, while *superficial muscles* are those you can see beneath your skin when you use them. Your back helps keep your spine stable to protect your spinal cord; without that protection, you'd be in serious trouble. Figure 5-3 shows the major deep and superficial back muscles so you can see what works (and what hurts) while you're moving.

Table 5-4 lists the main ways your back muscles move during a normal day, as well as which ones get a piece of the action on the ACFT.

TABLE 5-4   ## Back Muscles and Movement

Movement/Event	Movement Appearance	Primary Muscles Used
Shoulder elevation	Shrugging your shoulders	Upper trapezius, levator scapulae (deep beneath your trapezius, running from your neck to your shoulder blade)
Shoulder depression	Pushing your shoulders down	Lower trapezius
Retraction	Pushing your shoulder blades together	Rhomboids, middle trapezius
Protraction	Rounding your shoulders forward	Serratus anterior (deep muscles attached to your first through ninth ribs)
Upward rotation	Putting your arms overhead	Upper and middle trapezius
Downward rotation	Putting your arms at your sides from an up position	Rhomboids
Spinal rotation	Twisting in the trunk	Erector spinae and latissimus dorsi
3 Repetition Maximum Deadlift (MDL)	Picking up, holding, stabilizing, and putting down a hex bar	Rhomboids, infraspinatus (part of your rotator cuff), teres minor and major (also in the rotator cuff), latissimus dorsi, levator scapulae, erector spinae, serratus posterior inferior (four muscles attached to your lower ribs), external and internal obliques
Standing Power Throw (SPT)	Rounding your shoulders forward, coming upright, and throwing the medicine ball behind your head	Trapezius, splenius cervicis (a neck muscle that covers deeper back muscles), levator scapulae, rhomboids, infraspinatus, teres minor and major, latissimus dorsi, serratus posterior inferior, external and internal obliques

Movement/Event	Movement Appearance	Primary Muscles Used
Hand Release Push-Up – Arm Extension (HRP)	Pushing your body upright in a single unit, lowering your body to the ground, reaching your arms out in a *T* position	Trapezius, splenius cervicis, levator scapulae, deltoids, rhomboids, teres minor and major, latissimus dorsi, serratus posterior inferior, erector spinae, external and internal obliques
Sprint-Drag-Carry (SDC)	Carrying weight while in motion	Trapezius, splenius cervicis, levator scapulae, rhomboids
Leg Tuck (LTK)	Holding your body weight on the bar, flexing your body to curl toward the bar, lowering your body under control	Trapezius, splenius cervicis, deltoids, infraspinatus, teres minor and major, rhomboids, erector spinae, serratus posterior inferior, latissimus dorsi, external and internal obliques

You do use your back muscles in the 2MR, but only to keep your spine erect. They're the same muscles you use when you walk or sit, such as your erector spinae.

Chest strength

You use your chest muscles every day, whether you're pulling open or closing a door, doing push-ups during morning PT, or shoving someone in combatives. The chest has two major muscles — *pectoralis minor* and *pectoralis major* — so this group is a lot simpler than many of the others you use on the ACFT. Get a look at these two essential muscles in Figure 5-2.

The pectoralis minor and pectoralis major work together to help you rotate your arms, extend them to the side or in front of you, lower them to a natural position, and perform pushing motions. They also help you breathe by pulling on your rib-cage so your lungs can expand (which pretty much cinches their involvement in all the ACFT events).

Bicep, tricep, forearm, and shoulder strength

Your arms play a major role in nearly everything you do. They even help you balance so you can stay upright on two feet. Your major arm muscles are your biceps on the front of your arm, your triceps on the back, and your brachioradialis on the lower half of your arm. The primary shoulder muscle you use is your deltoid (you have one on each side), but you have some supporting shoulder muscles, too, as Figures 5-2 and 5-3 illustrate.

Check out how your arms and shoulders help you muscle your way through each day — and through the ACFT — in Table 5-5. (*Note:* Some arm and shoulder movements rely on chest and back muscles as well, such as the latissimus dorsi and pectoralis major.)

TABLE 5-5   ## Arm and Shoulder Muscles

Movement/Event	Movement Appearance	Primary Muscles Used
Elbow flexion	Bending your elbow	Biceps brachii
Elbow extension	Straightening your elbow	Triceps brachii
Wrist flexion	Bending your palm toward your forearm	Wrist flexors
Wrist extension	Bending the back of your hand toward your forearm	Wrist extensors
Shoulder abduction	Lifting your arms out to your sides	Deltoids
Shoulder adduction	Lowering your arms to your sides	Pectoralis major and latissimus dorsi
Shoulder flexion	Lifting your arms in front of you	Deltoids with the pectoralis major
Shoulder extension	Lowering your arms from shoulder flexion and lifting your arms behind your body	Teres major with the latissimus dorsi
Horizontal abduction	Moving your arms to the side from a position of extension in front of you so you form a *T* shape	Deltoids with latissimus dorsi
Horizontal adduction	Moving your arms to the front from a *T* shape so they're directly in front of you	Deltoids and pectoralis major
Grip	Grasping an object	Wrist flexors, extensors, forearms flexors, brachioradialis
3 Repetition Maximum Deadlift (MDL)	Grasping the hex bar and holding it steady	Wrist flexors, extensors, forearms flexors, brachioradialis
Standing Power Throw (SPT)	Grasping a medicine ball and raising your arms in front of you with a load	Deltoids, wrist flexors, extensors, forearms flexors, brachioradialis
Hand Release Push-Up – Arm Extension (HRP)	Pushing your body up from the ground and extending your arms to a *T* position	Deltoids, teres minor and major with help from the trapezius, triceps, wrist flexors, extensors, forearms flexors, brachioradialis

Movement/Event	Movement Appearance	Primary Muscles Used
Sprint-Drag-Carry (SDC)	Carrying 40-pound kettlebells and dragging a 90-pound sled	Biceps, triceps, wrist flexors, extensors, forearms flexors, brachioradialis
Leg Tuck (LTK)	Raising your body toward the bar, maintaining a grip on the bar, and lowering yourself from the bar	Deltoids, biceps, triceps, wrist flexors, extensors, forearms flexors, brachioradialis

The 2MR doesn't really require you to put forth any effort with your arms (unless you trip over nothing, like I often do, and have to push yourself back up from the ground). Your arms move naturally without your focusing on exerting them.

Chapter **6**

Stacking Up the Army's Physical Fitness Components

Having a buff bod — or even passing the ACFT — doesn't matter much if your body is actually broken down and injured. Functional fitness is all about healthy mobility so you can exercise and perform day-to-day tasks safely, minimizing your risk for injury and making doing your job in (or out of) the Army easier. I introduce some of the basics of functional fitness in Chapter 5; in this chapter, I get into its influence on Army physical training and the ACFT.

REMEMBER

Stretching your muscles is an integral part of recovery, which your body needs to perform its best. Professional athletes, PT stars, and everyday exercisers all know the value of stretching to give the body some much-needed TLC. Stretching keeps your muscles flexible, healthy, and strong; failure to stretch makes your muscles shorten and become increasingly tense, which makes you prone to injury. Check out Chapter 9 to read more about recovery and take a deep dive into stretching that helps protect your body and keep it running like a well-oiled machine.

Tracing the Origins of PRT and the ACFT

The Army takes functional fitness so seriously that it began the Physical Readiness Training (PRT) program in 2005. The main premise of the PRT program is to develop an agile, versatile, and lethal force that can operate in complex environments. During the beginning of Operation Enduring Freedom, and even into Operation Iraqi Freedom, the Army began facing serious challenges with recruits who weren't "fit to fight." Recruits would get to Basic Combat Training and suffer immediate injuries. But PRT's rollout drastically reduced the number of injuries during Initial Entry Training.

Each part of PRT, which has now been migrated into the Holistic Health and Fitness System, or H2F, features techniques designed to improve a soldier's overall level of conditioning and prevent future injuries. Musculoskeletal conditions account for more than half of the Army's post-service disability ratings, resulting in compensation of about $125 million each year, so leaders anticipate that h2F and the ACFT will lower that figure, too.

REMEMBER

Restructuring the existing PT program, which primarily consisted of running Monday, Wednesday, and Friday with muscle failure exercises on Tuesdays and Thursdays, wasn't an overnight job; the Department of the Army pulled from decades of research on physical fitness to come up with new PT programs and the test.

First, the Army conducted the Baseline Soldier Physical Readiness Requirements and Physical Demands Study. The study identified ten major components of physical fitness and how they correlated with success on the battlefield:

>> Muscular strength

>> Muscular endurance

>> Power

>> Speed

>> Agility

>> Aerobic endurance

>> Balance

>> Flexibility

>> Coordination

>> Reaction time

Using those components (which you can read more about in the following section), the Army zeroed in on the most effective test to assess its soldiers. Military fitness experts from the United Kingdom, Canada, Australia, France, the Netherlands, and many other countries threw in their two cents as well. The Army also consulted with the U.S. Military Academy, the Army Physical Fitness School, and a whole host of other agencies to put together the six events you see on the ACFT.

Counting on the Army's Ten Fitness Components

The ten fitness components, or *performance basics,* that the Army wants to test are good indicators of how well a soldier will perform on the battlefield, but they also help predict how well a soldier can avoid injury. The overarching idea behind these performance basics is to transform the Army fitness culture and shift focus from training for a PT test (such as by doing push-ups, sit-ups, and a two-mile run) to training for real-world scenarios. Soldiers have to be fit enough to lift and move heavy loads from the ground, jump across and over obstacles, carry ammunition from one place to another, and conduct dismounted movements safely.

Every MOS in the Army falls into one of three Physical Demand Categories (PDCs, which I cover in Chapter 4), and the PDCs correlate pretty well with the day-to-day demands each job requires. For example, infantry soldiers fall into the "Heavy" category, while a Military Working Dog Handler falls into the "Significant" category and a Human Resources Specialist usually faces "Moderate" physical demands on the job. You can find exercises that help you meet each of the Army's performance basics in Chapter 8, and stretches that help you recover in Chapter 9.

Muscular strength

You don't have to be able to bench-press 300 pounds to pass the ACFT or squeak by in your Army job, but you do have to be able to perform mission-essential tasks that align with your PDC. *Muscular strength* relates to your ability to lift and move mass, and it's measured by how much force you can exert and how much weight you can lift over a short period of time.

Workouts that develop muscular strength and power include exercises like weightlifting and body weight training (you can read more about power later in the chapter). Loaded 3D movements, which I explain in Chapter 5, fall into that category as well. You build muscle by lifting heavier weights in fewer repetitions.

The ACFT tests muscular strength through the 3 Repetition Maximum Deadlift, the Standing Power Throw, the Sprint-Drag-Carry, and the Leg Tuck.

Muscular endurance

Muscular endurance is similar to muscular strength (see the preceding section), but it's more specific — it refers to how long you can exert force over time.

Workouts that develop muscular endurance include things like long-distance running, cycling, or swimming, as well as circuit training and repeated body weight exercises. You develop muscular endurance by lifting lighter weights for more repetitions.

The ACFT tests muscular endurance through the Hand Release Push-Up – Arm Extension, the Standing Power Throw, and the Leg Tuck.

Power

Power represents your body's ability to exert a maximal force in as short a time as possible. That means accelerating, jumping, and throwing mass — so really, power refers to speed. Power ties into muscular strength, which I discuss earlier in the chapter.

REMEMBER

Muscular strength is the amount of force you can apply to an object; power shows how quickly you can do it.

You can increase your power by participating in some sports (like boxing or martial arts), running against resistance, or doing *plyometric* training, such as aerobic exercises that require you to push your muscles to their maximum potential in a short period of time.

The ACFT tests your power in the Standing Power Throw event.

Speed

In physical fitness terms, *speed* is your ability to move quickly, whether you're running, doing laterals, or moving your limbs. To be an *actual* high-speed soldier, you need good muscle strength and power (and the low-drag part requires you to meet the requirements in AR 600-9).

You can increase your speed by doing interval workouts and exercises that require you to use explosive power, like plyometrics.

The ACFT tests your speed during the Sprint-Drag-Carry and the Two-Mile Run.

Agility

Moving like a professional athlete is the hallmark of *agility*, which is your ability to move and change direction or position quickly and effectively while still under control. Agility ties into your balance, coordination, and speed.

You don't have to float like a butterfly and sting like a bee, but if you float more like a lead balloon and sting more like a mosquito, you need to work on your agility through exercises like high knees and butt-kickers, box jumping, and side-to-side lateral drills. (And for the record, I know mosquitoes don't sting.)

The ACFT tests your agility on the Sprint-Drag-Carry event.

Aerobic endurance

Aerobic endurance refers to your ability to sustain medium- to high-intensity exercise for an extended period of time. These endurance exercises, like jogging, swimming, and cycling, increase your heart rate and your oxygen consumption.

The best way to increase your aerobic endurance is to do cardio. If you're not able to run two miles without stopping right now, start small and work your way up to it. Increase your distance gradually with a goal of doing 30 minutes of cardio training five days a week, which is what the American Heart Association recommends for all adults.

The ACFT tests your aerobic endurance with the Two-Mile Run event.

Balance

Your *balance* is your body's ability to stay upright and maintain control over your movement. Essentially, it's maintaining equilibrium and not falling over when it counts. Balance exercises, like back leg raises and calf raises, can help you improve your ability to maintain equilibrium, and tai chi helps, too. So can most other activities that keep you on your feet and moving.

Balance comes in two types: static and dynamic. *Static balance* is being able to maintain your equilibrium when you're stationary (like when you're standing on one foot trying to do a quad stretch at PT), and *dynamic balance* is maintaining your equilibrium while you're moving, like you'd do if you were walking on a balance beam.

The ACFT tests your balance during the 3 Repetition Maximum Deadlift and Standing Power Throw.

Flexibility

Flexibility equals the range of motion in a joint (or a group of joints). It also refers to your ability to move those joints through a complete range of motion. Being flexible improves your athletic performance, which is a big bonus for the ACFT, and it helps decrease your risk of injury, which is a big bonus on its own.

Stretching your muscles before and after workouts — and in between workouts — can do a lot to improve your flexibility and range of motion. Check out recovery stretches you can use anytime, anywhere, in Chapter 9.

The ACFT tests your flexibility on the 3 Repetition Maximum Deadlift and the Standing Power Throw.

Coordination

Coordination is your ability to move two or more body parts smoothly and efficiently under control. It's the difference between throwing your ruck on the back of a five-ton and climbing up behind it and getting tangled up in the straps as it falls on your face.

People on the Army's eSports team have plenty of hand-eye coordination, but to develop the kind of coordination you need for the ACFT, you can do standing balance exercises while tossing a ball, reaction squats, and D&C, which requires hand-foot coordination.

The ACFT tests your coordination during the 3 Repetition Maximum Deadlift, the Standing Power Throw, the Hand Release Push-Up – Arm Extension, and the Sprint-Drag-Carry.

Reaction time

Reaction time is your ability to respond quickly to a stimulus. The Army definitely values quick reaction time on the battlefield and in garrison, and there's always room for improvement.

Quickness drills can improve your ability to accelerate and decelerate. Try partner drills where you spend 30 seconds switching among a slow jog, a run, and a sprint when your battle buddy blows a whistle at random, playing catch, or doing plyometric drills on your own.

The ACFT tests your reaction time during the Sprint-Drag-Carry.

Getting Heart Smart for Aerobic Exercise

The American Heart Association recommends that the average American get at least 150 minutes of moderate-intensity aerobic activity or 75 minutes of vigorous aerobic activity each week; a brisk walk counts as moderate intensity, and running is vigorous. But you need more than the minimum if you're planning to do well on the ACFT. Success on the Army's newest PT test is all about conditioning your body well before the big day.

Cardiovascular endurance is your ability to exercise without getting wiped out right away. It involves your lungs' bringing in oxygen and supplying it to your heart, which spreads the love to all the tissues in your body. The more efficiently your body manages this process, the lower your breathing rate is — you don't need to suck in oxygen frantically to get enough to survive during physically challenging activities. Even better, though, is that a well-conditioned cardiovascular system helps you experience less fatigue (because your body doesn't have to work as hard just to get oxygen around), keeps you more relaxed, and helps you respond better to challenges.

Calculating your resting heart rate

Your *resting heart rate* is the number of times your heart beats per minute when you're at rest. You should check your resting heart rate first thing in the morning, before you get out of bed and certainly before you have your first cup of coffee. (If you're a warrant officer on the coffee continuum, ask your PCM if you *have* a resting heart rate.) If you have a wearable fitness tracker, check your app; you may well already have your resting heart rate recorded. Otherwise, here's how to check your heart rate — resting or otherwise — on your own:

1. **Find the artery in your wrist.**

   It's on the inside, on the same side as your thumb.

2. **Use the tips of your first two fingers (not your thumb, which has a pulse of its own) and press lightly over the artery.**

3. **Count your pulse for 30 seconds and multiply the final number by two to get your heart's beats per minute.**

Keep track of your resting heart rate for several days, and then calculate the average.

For most people, a resting heart rate between 60 and 100 beats per minute (bpm) is normal. Athletes and more-active people have lower resting heart rates (sometimes as low as 40 bpm) than less-active people do. Medications, stress, anxiety, and even hormones can affect your resting heart rate, though, so everyone's is a little bit different. The bottom line is that the lower your resting heart rate is (medications and stress aside), the more efficient your heart is at shuttling oxygen around your body. Higher resting heart rates are often linked with lower physical fitness levels as well as higher body weight and blood pressure.

Finding your target heart rate for aerobic exercise

You can improve your cardiovascular fitness with regular aerobic exercise, provided that you perform it within in a target range of 50 to 85 percent of your maximum heart rate, or MHR. Check out average maximum heart rates in Table 6-1. Your heart muscle grows stronger and more efficient, pumping more blood with each beat. Your blood vessels become more elastic, which can reduce your blood pressure, and your capillaries (the tiny delivery drivers that supply oxygen to your tissues) create more branches. You even increase your body's mitochondrial density, which means you feel more energetic.

TABLE 6-1   **Average Target and Maximum Heart Rate Zones**

Age (in years)	Target Heart Rate Zone (50 to 85%)	Average Maximum Heart Rate (100%)
20	100–170 bpm	200 bpm
30	95–162 bpm	190 bpm
35	93–157 bpm	185 bpm
40	90–153 bpm	180 bpm
45	88–149 bpm	175 bpm
50	85–145 bpm	170 bpm
55	83–140 bpm	165 bpm
60	80–136 bpm	160 bpm
65	78–132 bpm	155 bpm
70	75–128 bpm	150 bpm

If you're a 25-year-old soldier, exercising so that your heart rate is between 100 and 170 beats per minute for a sustained period of time (at least 30 minutes) can help improve your aerobic endurance. (The American Heart Association puts 20- to 30-year-olds in the same target heart rate zones, which is why you don't see a separate age bracket for 25-year-olds in Table 6-1.)

TIP

You can get a better ballpark range for your max heart rate if you subtract your age from 220, and then calculate your ideal percentage from there. For example, if you're 37, your max target heart rate is 220 – 37 = 183. Half (50 percent) of that is 91.5, and 85 percent is 155.5. That's where you want your heart rate to be if you're going for an improvement in cardiovascular endurance.

WARNING

Before you start any exercise program, even those listed in this book to help you perform well on the ACFT, make sure you have a green light from your primary care manager (what the Army calls your PCM). If you're taking certain medications, your heart rate may naturally be higher or lower than those of your peers who are in similar physical condition. You should make sure you're good to go before you try something new.

If your heart rate is too high, you're straining, and that can be dangerous for your health (especially if you're pretty new to working out). In fact, studies have found that those who continuously exceed their target and maximum heart rates have poor rates of recovery when they finish exercising — and they may also be at increased risk for cardiac events such as arrhythmias (that means the heart beats too fast, too slow, or with an irregular pattern), chest pains, and discomfort.

On the other hand, if your heart rate is too low, you're not improving your cardiovascular endurance. It's not always fun, but you're going to have to get your heart pounding (and keep it that way for several minutes) if you want to get a boost in the cardio fitness department.

WHAT IS RUNNER'S HIGH, AND SHOULD YOU AIM FOR IT?

You've probably heard of — or maybe even experienced — *runner's high*. This euphoric post-exercise feeling may be hard-wired into our brains thanks to our ancestors, who had to chase down dinner — or run to avoid *being* dinner. When you engage in moderate to heavy exercise over a sustained period of time, specialized neurons in your brain will likely create endorphins, which are natural painkillers. And every cell in your body is capable of producing endocannabinoids under stress, too, which contribute to feelings of calmness. Your body produces these natural chemicals and spreads them through your nervous system in response to physical discomfort, so short, casual runs aren't likely to produce enough discomfort to trigger that rush. Neither are grueling, gut-busting runs that are way off the healthy end of the spectrum when it comes to your physiology and physical fitness level. You have to find a happy medium — working within 70 to 85 percent of your target heart rate for a sustained period of time — and stay hydrated, get enough sleep, and avoid chronic stress if you want to get that feeling after cardio exercise.

Fitting FITT Principles into Your Workout

When you know your resting heart rate, you can develop a cardio regimen that works for your body by using FITT principles. (Head to the earlier section "Calculating your resting heart rate" for details on getting that measurement.) FITT stands for frequency, intensity, type, and time. Keep in mind that if you're running with your unit on Mondays, Wednesdays, and Fridays, that time counts toward your cardio tally.

Frequency

The American College of Sports Medicine and a whole host of other heart-smart organizations recommend that healthy adults dive into moderate aerobic exercise at least 30 minutes a day, five days a week. The American Heart Association says 75 minutes of vigorous cardio should be on your weekly calendar, too. Try to avoid more than two days of rest between cardio workouts; if you wait too long, your body can "detrain," which really means it'll go off the rails and force you to start from scratch.

Intensity

Your cardiovascular endurance improves when you elevate your heart rate between 60 and 80 percent of your max heart rate, which you can read about in the earlier section "Finding your target heart rate for aerobic exercise." You can use these formulas to find your upper and lower range so you know what to target:

$$\left(\left(MHR - RHR\right) \times 0.60\right) + RHR = \text{lower limit of range}$$

$$\left(\left(MHR - RHR\right) \times 0.85\right) + RHR = \text{upper limit of range}$$

MHR represents your max heart rate, and RHR represents your resting heart rate, which I cover in the earlier section "Calculating your resting heart rate."

So what do you do with these numbers? Try to hit and sustain your lower limit during longer workouts (those exceeding 30 minutes) and your upper limit during shorter workouts. Even better, do some interval training that features alternating bursts of moderate-intensity and high-intensity exercise. You can measure a workout's intensity by using the Borg Rate of Perceived Exertion scale (no, not *those* Borg). It's a 15-point scale based on heart rate (add a zero to the right of the rating to find your own most likely heart rate). Check out Table 6-2 for a look at the Borg RPE scale (which starts with the number 6, according to the Swedish psychologist who created it) and Table 6-3 for the Modified Borg RPE Scale. Both are based on averages.

TABLE 6-2 ## The Borg RPE Scale

Exertion Level	Borg Rating	Heart Rate	Examples
None	6	60 bpm	Watching TV or reading a book
Very, very light	7–8	70–80 bpm	Tying your shoes
Very light	9–10	90–100 bpm	Housework that takes a little effort, like sweeping or folding laundry
Fairly light	11–12	110–120 bpm	Walking at a leisurely pace, which requires some effort but not enough to increase your breathing
Somewhat hard	13–14	130–140 bpm	Brisk walking that requires moderate effort; activities that speed up your heart rate but don't make you feel breathless
Hard	15–16	150–160 bpm	Cycling, swimming, running, and other activities that take vigorous effort; things that make your heart pound and increase your breathing
Very hard	17–18	170–180 bpm	The highest level of activity you can sustain, such as running your fastest on a PT test
Very, very hard	19–20	190–200 bpm	A burst of activity that you can't maintain for long, such as sprinting to the finish line on a PT test when you have fewer than 10 seconds left to pass

TABLE 6-3 ## The Modified Borg RPE Scale

Exertion Level	Modified Borg Rating	Heart Rate	Examples
Very light	1	50–60 percent of your maximum	Barely any exertion, but more than watching TV or reading
Light	2–3	60–70 percent of your maximum	Activity that's easy to maintain; you can carry on a conversation while performing light activities
Moderate	4–6	70–80 percent of your maximum	Activity that requires you to breathe heavily, but during which you can still hold a short conversation; noticeably challenging
Vigorous	7–8	80–90 percent of your maximum	Activity that makes you short of breath, and that's fairly uncomfortable
Very hard	9	90–100 percent of your maximum	Activity with an intensity that's difficult to maintain; difficult to speak more than a few words
Max effort	10	90–100 percent of your maximum	Activity with an intensity that's impossible to maintain; completely out of breath and unable to talk

Which scale you use is up to you, but looking at (and keeping track of) how you feel when you're performing different activities can help you develop a plan.

REMEMBER

Although the Borg scale is highly subjective — you're rating your own workout, and you may call something more or less intense than I or anyone else would — it's still a fairly effective measure for your personal fitness goals. Athletes and their trainers frequently use it to judge their own levels of exertion.

Type

What type of cardiovascular exercise you choose doesn't matter, as long as you stay in your training zone. Pick things you enjoy and that you can fit into your daily routine, and aim for variety in endurance exercises so you don't get bored. Variety helps you avoid overuse injuries, too. Consider joining a group fitness class or working out with a friend. Check out the aerobic exercises in Chapter 8 to get some ideas.

TIP

Strength training can also help you meet your cardiovascular goals, provided that you eliminate the time you rest between exercises and you keep your heart rate elevated in the right zone.

Time

The duration of your workouts matters. Try to stay in your target range for at least 30 minutes a day (or 20 minutes if you're doing interval training). If you're having a tough time doing 30 minutes at once, break it up throughout the day — 10 minutes here and there are still helpful. Try to keep your heart rate up for a little longer each day.

Powering Your Way through Life with Anaerobic Exercise

Anaerobic exercise and your ability to perform it well are important to the Army because they support battlefield functions. Need to carry ammo from one truck to another under fire? Have to fight off a combatant in close quarters? You rely on your anaerobic power to do so.

Anaerobic exercise is different from aerobic exercise because anaerobic exercise doesn't use a continuous supply of oxygen to sustain an activity. This type of exercise forces your body to demand more energy than your aerobic system can produce. In fact, *anaerobic* means "without oxygen." The energy you use during anaerobic exercise comes from glucose stored in your muscles.

Glucose is available for quick, short bursts of movement, so that's what your body relies on when your aerobic system is maxed out. The process is called *glycolysis*, and it occurs inside your cells. Glycolysis also produces lactic acid, which builds up and creates the burn you feel when you're intensely using your muscles. Lactic acid is also why you feel so wiped out after an energy burst, but the more anaerobic exercise you do, the more effectively your body can deal with it and eliminate it, which means you don't get as tired after using the glucose in your muscles. Your *lactic threshold* is the maximal effort or intensity you can maintain with little or no increase in lactate in your blood. The higher your lactic threshold is, the longer you can perform an exercise or movement without being stopped by "the burn."

Anaerobic exercise, like lifting weights, jumping rope, doing plyometrics, sprinting, and doing high-intensity interval (HIIT) training, is hard — but the potential benefits are huge. This type of exercise can

>> Increase your bone strength and bone density

>> Help you maintain a steady weight

>> Increase your power

>> Boost your metabolism

>> Increase your lactic threshold

>> Reduce your risk of disease

>> Improve your mood

>> Protect your joints

>> Increase your energy levels

IN THIS CHAPTER

» Discovering all three corners of the Army's Performance Triad

» Knowing where to find H2F regulations

» Understanding how PRT coordinates with the ACFT

» Homing in on H2F drills and ACFT-targeted exercises

» Squeezing the Army's PT plan into your schedule

Chapter **7**

Examining P3, PRT, H2F, and the ACFT

The Army has dramatically shifted gears over the past few decades. It's now looking at the "whole soldier" concept, which says that every service member should be well-balanced. The Army wants soldiers who thrive while working in any capacity, from earning college credits to staying physically fit. Health and wellness is an essential component of the "whole soldier" concept, and it falls under the Army's Holistic Health and Fitness program, or H2F. That means that H2F also includes the Army's Performance Triad (P3), Physical Readiness Training (PRT), and the ACFT.

Cornering the Army's Performance Triad

H2F operates on three basic tenets — sleep, activity, and nutrition — that make up the Army's Performance Triad. P3 is the Army's answer to soldiers' sustaining personal strength, endurance, and mental agility, which leads to unit readiness.

Under P3, optimizing soldier performance is the foundation on which the Army can build a fitter, more lethal force. P3 applies to every soldier, so I cover each piece of the triad in the following sections.

Sleep

I'm not going to pretend that your unit lets you get enough sleep, especially if you're deployed or on a high OPTEMPO. But sleep is the first corner of the Performance Triad, and Big Army recognizes that getting enough rest is critical to mission success. A lack of sleep slows your reaction time, your ability to detect and engage enemies, and your ability to move in a coordinated way. In fact, lack of sleep is often responsible for accidents, poor morale, and impaired judgment — and that's just the tip of the iceberg. The bottom line is that you can't perform as well as you need to on the ACFT (or in your job), keep your weight under control, and let your muscles recover properly without adequate rest.

I'm not saying you should tell your first line leader that you won't make it to PT formation because you're tired, though — I'm saying that if you're trying to become healthier, regardless of whether you're prepping for the ACFT, you may need to start hitting the rack a little earlier than you normally do.

Activity

Physical fitness (stop me if you've heard this one) is the cornerstone of combat readiness. You know it, I know it, and the Army certainly knows it. Practicing the principles of safe and effective training lets you maintain your physical readiness, which really means that you're staying healthy. If you want to keep your job in the military, you have to stay fit — and that's part of the reason that the Army developed PRT and implemented the ACFT. You can look at it this way: They're trying to ensure you're a lean, green, fighting machine, and they're giving you the tools to get started. PRT won't make you the toughest soldier in the barracks, but it'll help you pass the ACFT. (Notice that I said "help," though. You shouldn't rely on morning PT sessions using PRT to help you pass the test. Everyone needs to put in the work on his or her own time to perform well on the test.)

In P3, the Army even says, "Despite obtaining some activity through structured unit physical readiness training, many soldiers are sedentary over the course of the day." That means although soldiers are typically more active than their civilian counterparts are, PRT isn't quite enough to keep you healthy and ready to deploy.

Nutrition

When Napoleon Bonaparte said, "An Army marches on its stomach," he meant that troops needed food to stay fit to fight. That's still true today — soldiers can only function effectively if they're getting the right fuel. That's what the P3 nutrition component is all about. You have to eat the right foods, drink enough water, and police up your consumption of things that drag your body down.

Following good nutrition principles helps you improve your focus and concentration, manage your weight, and perform physical activities well. (Don't worry, though. None of your favorites are vacating the PX's food court, so you'll still have access to tacos, subs, and the winner of the Great Chicken Sandwich War of 2019). You can read more about finding the right fighting fuel for your body in Chapters 20 through 23.

Reading Up on PRT Documentation

H2F contains a complete set of exercises designed by the Army to keep you fit to fight. If you're proficient in each of them, the Army feels you should be able to meet the ACFT's minimum standards. You can find all the PRT exercises in ATP 7-22.02, *Holistic Health and Fitness Drills and Exercises*, which you can get from the Army Publishing Directorate. You can also check with your platoon sergeant, your operations NCO, or headquarters platoon — most leaders should have a hard copy.

Army Regulation 350-1, *Army Training and Leader Development*, was revised in 2017 and points to FM 7-22 as "the primary reference for developing soldier physical readiness." AR 350-1 also says that PRT develops all the components the Army needs its soldiers to have when it comes to physical capacity and movement.

The same regulation says that all soldiers must be physically fit in all five components of the "physical capacity domain." Those components are

>> Cardiorespiratory endurance

>> Muscular strength

>> Muscular endurance

>> Flexibility

>> Body composition

PRT addresses the first four components, and the Army believes that if you're conducting PRT as prescribed (and following the Army's H2F program), you'll meet the body compositions outlined in AR 600-9, *The Army Body Composition Program.* You can find more about AR 600-9 and the H2F program in Chapter 20, where you also get a peek at the Army standards on the minimum and maximum weight for your height.

Matching PRT Drills and ACFT Events

You probably do PRT every day when you report for accountability and PT formation. The Preparation Drill and Recovery Drill are both standard Monday through Friday, even if the exercises you do between those two drills aren't exactly described in FM 7-22. But no matter what workouts you do with your unit, PRT falls into 11 main parts; I discuss these drills in more detail in the later section "Taking a Closer Look at PRT and Its Drills":

>> Preparation Drill (PD)

>> 4 for the Core (4C)

>> Conditioning Drills 1, 2, and 3 (CD1, CD2, CD3)

>> Climbing Drills 1 and 2

>> Hip Stability Drill (HSD)

>> Push-Up and Sit-Up Drill

>> Shoulder Stability Drill (SSD)

>> Running, Endurance, and Mobility Activities

>> Military Movement Drills 1 and 2 (MMD1, MMD2)

>> The Strength Training Circuit (STC)

>> Guerilla Drill

>> Recovery Drill

The Army has zeroed in on specific PRT exercises that it believes help you perform your best on the ACFT. Table 7-1 provides a quick reference for the military's top three for each event.

TABLE 7-1　　**Top PRT Exercises for the ACFT**

MDL	SPT	HRP	SDC	LTK	2MR
1. Sumo squat	1. Power jump	1. Supine chest press	1. Straight-leg deadlift	1. Bent leg raise	1. Sprint intervals
2. Alternate staggered squat jump	2. Overhead push-press	2. 8-count push-up	2. Bent over row	2. Leg tuck and twist	2. Release run
3. Forward lunge	3. Tuck jump	3. Incline bench	3. 300-meter shuttle run	3. Alternating grip pull-up	3. Hill repeats

Table 7-2 outlines the PRT drills most likely to help you with the entire ACFT, along with lists of standard equipment and alternate equipment you can use if Army-issued equipment isn't available.

TABLE 7-2　　**Top PRT Drills and Equipment for the ACFT**

	MDL	SPT	HRP	SDC	LTK	2MR
PRT drill	Strength Training Circuit	Conditioning Drill 3	4 for the Core	Guerilla Drill	Climbing Drill	60:120s
Standard equipment	60-pound hex bar and plates	10-pound medicine ball	Kettlebells	Two 40-pound kettlebells and 90-pound sled	Climbing bar	Two-mile running route
Alternate equipment	Ammo cans, duffle bags, rucksack, five-gallon water cans, tow bars, PVC pipe, wooden handles	10-pound sandbag, slam ball, kettlebell	Ammo cans, tow bar, IOTV	40-pound duffle bag, 40-pound rucksack, 90-pound sked/stretcher, 90-pound litter, 90-pound log, tires	Pull-up bar, suspension trainer, stretch cords	Treadmil

You can download a Physical Readiness Training Quick Reference Card (nomenclature GTA 07-08-003) from rdl.train.army.mil without CAC access. The reference card doesn't include details on how to perform each exercise, but ATP 7-22.02 does. However, anyone who's been to Basic Leader Course (BLC) should know the proper way to execute all PRT exercises. You can also talk to your unit's Master Fitness Trainer (or another unit's MFT if you don't have one) about proper form and execution of any PRT exercise. Proper form is essential so you can avoid injury.

REMEMBER

Army-issued ACFT equipment is as good for practicing on as it is for taking the test, and plenty of on-post fitness centers and outdoor fitness areas have hex bars, pull-up bars, and other gear you can use — in addition to several two-mile running courses — to get yourself ready for the ACFT between test days. Your unit should be conducting the Army's prescribed PRT Monday through Friday. You can do PRT on your own, too, in addition to a good mix of exercises in Chapter 8 and stretches in Chapter 9.

Despite PRT's years-long shaky start, it's designed to train you up for the ACFT. PRT exercises are an excellent beginning — or supplement — to your ACFT prep. Explore your PRT options in the following sections so you can mix them into your off-time training.

Maximizing PRT for the 3 Repetition Maximum Deadlift

The best exercises to help you max your MDL score are the sumo squat from the Strength Training Circuit Drill, the alternate staggered squat jump from Conditioning Drill 3, and the forward lunge from the Preparation Drill.

The sumo squat

If you're not familiar with Army-style sumo squats, start training with an empty straight bar or a PVC pipe so you can get your squat technique down to a science. (Need help? Ask a Master Fitness Trainer in your unit.) After you get your squat form down, give yourself a two-to-four-week base phase during which you work with a load of only 40 to 50 percent of your body weight *or* 25 to 50 percent of your *one-repetition maximum* (1RM, the most you can lift safely just one time).

Equipment: kettlebell, straight bar weighting 45 pounds, weight plates, and collars

Movement execution:

1. **Stand in a straddle stance with your feet out wider than your shoulders and your toes pointed outward.**

Make sure your feet are wider than shoulder-width apart and that your knees are in line with your toes.

2. **Hold a single kettlebell or straight bar with both hands; your grip should face inward so your palms are facing your body.**

   Technically, that's called a *pronated* grip; its cousin is the *supinated* grip, in which your palms are facing out from your body.

3. **Squat while keeping your head in line with your spine, leaning only slightly forward.**

   Don't let your heels lift up from the floor. Keep a neutral spine and avoid rounding your shoulders or letting your knees collapse inward.

4. **Move down until your thighs are parallel to the ground and then return to the starting position.**

Complete two to three sets of 12 to 15 reps using 50 to 65 percent of your 1RM.

See Figure 7-1 to check out the sumo squat in action.

FIGURE 7-1:
The sumo squat.

Zack McCrory

Alternate staggered squat jump

The alternate staggered squat jump from CD3 helps you develop balance and works on your explosive power.

Equipment: a level surface

Movement execution:

1. **Squat in a staggered stance (put one foot slightly forward and one foot slightly back) and touch the ground between your legs.**

   Keep your trunk mostly straight with a slight bend forward at the hips. Keep your chest up and your back straight.

2. **Jump into the air as explosively as you can, switching your legs in midair so that you land with your opposite leg in the front.**

   Land as softly as you can on the balls of your feet and lower your heels after you make contact with the ground.

3. **Continue jumping, switching legs each time.**

Complete one set of 5 to 10 repetitions.

Figure 7-2 shows the start and execution of the alternate staggered squat jump.

Forward lunge

The forward lunge is a short-stride lunging movement. If you're a beginner, start with 5 reps, no weight, and a limited range of movement, and increase to 10 reps over a two-to-four-week base phase.

Equipment: a level space

Movement execution:

1. **Start with a staggered stance and step forward.**

2. **Let your forward knee bend until your thigh is parallel to the ground and then return to the starting position.**

   Keep your forward heel flat on the ground and raise your rear heel. Try not to extend your knee past the ball of your foot; if you find that you're doing so, shift your weight backward, into your hips. Your movements should remain smooth — don't jerk your trunk backward to stand up.

3. **Repeat the process with your other leg, alternating until you've completed the right number of reps for your workout.**

FIGURE 7-2:
The alternate staggered squat jump, step by step.

Zack McCrory

You can add weights when you're sure you have proper form. Figure 7-3 illustrates an example of using weights during the forward lunge. Start with 5-pound weights in each hand, gradually working your way up to 20 pounds. Use your waist to bend slightly forward, bringing your weights to each side of your forward leg.

Complete one to three sets of 5 to 10 reps each.

FIGURE 7-3: The forward lunge with weights.

Zack McCrory

Stepping up PRT for the Standing Power Throw

If you're trying to improve your distance and explosive power on the SPT, the Army recommends you do the power jump from CD1, the overhead push-press from the STC, and the tuck jump from CD3.

Power jump

The power jump in Conditioning Drill 1 can help develop your leg strength and explosive power. If you're just starting out, do 5 reps with a limited range of movement, at least until you get your form down. Then, start increasing your reps until you reach 10 over a two-to-four-week range. Figure 7-4 shows the proper execution of the power jump.

Equipment: a level surface

FIGURE 7-4:
The power jump.

Zack McCrory

Movement execution:

1. **Stand with your legs about shoulder-width apart and your hands on your hips.**

2. **Squat with your heels flat to the ground as you bend forward (but keep your back straight) until your straightened arms reach the ground.**

Try to touch the ground with your palms.

3. **Jump straight up, raising your arms overhead with your palms facing inward.**

Make sure your spine stays neutral and your feet remain shoulder-width apart. Extend your arms fully overhead.

4. **Control your landing and repeat.**

Land softly on the balls of your feet before lowering your heels.

Complete one set of 5 to 10 repetitions.

Overhead push-press

The overhead push-press from PRT's Strength Training Circuit can help develop strength in your arms, shoulders, and grip. Figure 7-5 shows this exercise in action.

FIGURE 7-5:
The overhead
push-press.

Zack McCrory

Equipment: If you're new to the overhead push-press, start with light kettlebells, barbells, an empty straight bar, a piece of PVC pipe, or a wooden handle; then graduate to heavier weights.

Movement execution:

1. **Start with your feet about shoulder-width apart, holding one kettlebell or barbell in each hand in front of your collarbones.**

   You can also use a straight bar in place of the kettlebells. Maintain a neutral grip with your palms facing each other.

2. **Slightly flex your hips and knees, but keep your feet flat on the floor.**

   Look straight ahead or slightly upward while keeping a neutral spine.

3. **Forcefully extend your hip, knee, and ankle joints while you extend your elbows to raise your weight(s) overhead.**

   Press the weight(s) up in a controlled, continuous motion. When you straighten your elbows, don't lock them.

4. **Return to your starting position while flexing your hips and knees.**

   Control the descent so you don't hurt yourself. Try to absorb some of the movement in your lower body to reduce the impact on your shoulders.

Complete one to three sets of 5 to 10 repetitions.

Tuck jump

The tuck jump can help you develop better balance and coordination while improving your legs' explosive power. It's an explosive movement that pushes you up in the air, and with practice, you'll jump higher and more powerfully. Check out the tuck jump in Figure 7-6.

Equipment: a level surface

Movement execution:

1. **Sit into a half squat and swing your arms backward.**

2. **Jump up, driving your arms forward at the same time.**

3. **Draw your knees into your chest while wrapping your hands around them.**

   Keep your eyes forward and avoid rounding your back.

FIGURE 7-6:
The tuck jump.

Zack McCrory

4. **Land in a half squat position.**

   Land softly on the balls of your feet before you lower your heels. Move slowly
   between jumps as you repeat the process to meet the target number of reps.

   Complete one set of 5 to 10 repetitions.

Practicing PRT for the Hand Release Push-Up – Arm Extension

The Hand Release Push-Up – Arm Extension tests your muscular endurance, and
it requires you to use your whole body. The Army's top three exercises to improve
your performance on the HRP include the supine chest press from STC, the
8-count T push-up from CD2, and the incline bench (the chest press from
FM 7-22).

Supine chest press

The supine chest press from the Strength Training Circuit strengthens your chest, shoulders, and triceps. Talking to your unit's MFT is a good idea if you're not sure about form — doing this exercise the wrong way can easily result in injury. Figure 7-7 shows the supine chest press in the starting and fully extended positions.

Equipment: kettlebells and a level space

Zuck McCrory

FIGURE 7-7: The supine chest press.

Movement execution:

1. **Lie on the ground with your knees bent at 90 degrees and your feet 8 to 12 inches apart and flat on the ground.**

   Keep your head on the ground throughout the exercise.

2. **Hold the kettlebells over your shoulders, close to your chest, with your palms facing up and toward the midline of your trunk.**

   Rest the backs of your upper arms (your triceps) on the ground. Your forearms should be perpendicular to the ground.

3. **Extend your elbows to raise the kettlebells until your upper arms are straight but not locked.**

   Keep the kettlebells parallel to each other.

4. **Lower the kettlebells back to your starting position, keeping your movements under control.**

Complete one set of 5 to 10 repetitions.

8-count T push-up

CD2's 8-count T push-up develops strength and endurance in your arms, upper back, and legs, and it requires core strength, too. This exercise is one of the slowest in PRT — the cadence is slow for all eight counts (shown in Figure 7-8).

Equipment: a level surface

Movement execution:

Start at the position of attention and then begin your 8-count T push-up by using these steps:

1. **Assume the squat position.**

2. **Kick your legs back to the front leaning rest position.**

3. **Bend your elbows and lower your body to the ground, moving as one unit.**

4. **Release your hands from the ground and straighten your arms out in a *T*, just like the HRP.**

5. **Bring your hands back under your shoulders.**

6. **Push yourself up into the front leaning rest position.**

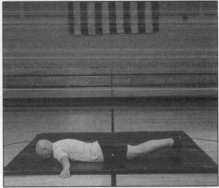

FIGURE 7-8:
The 8-count T
push-up.

Zack McCrory

7. **Quickly jump to the squat position.**

   The Army calls this move a *reverse thrust.*

8. **Return to the position of attention before you repeat Step 1.**

Complete one set of 5 to 10 repetitions.

TIP

Keep your hands directly below your shoulders and open your fingers to spread out your weight distribution. Keep your heels together when you're doing the push-up (it's great practice for the HRP, in which your feet can't be more than a grader's boot's width apart).

WARNING

Zip up your core so your trunk doesn't sag. Letting your trunk sag strains your back. If you can't keep your body in a generally straight line while performing a push-up, it's time to stop and try again later (or even on another day).

Incline bench

The incline bench is a press exercise that strengthens your chest, shoulder, and arm muscles. If you're a beginner, practice with an empty straight bar, PVC pipe, or even a broom handle until you nail down the proper form. Then work for two to four weeks pressing 40 to 50 percent of your body weight. For example, if you weigh 150 pounds, you'll press between 67.5 pounds and 75 pounds. Alternatively, you can press 25 to 50 percent of your 1RM; that means if you can press as much as 200 pounds one time, you can train with 50 pounds to 100 pounds.

TIP

Maintain a fairly constant weight during the first two to four weeks, and when the exercise becomes easier, increase the number of reps you do. Don't increase the weight until you're out of your base phase.

Check out the incline bench exercise in Figure 7-9, which shows the starting "up" position and the "down" position.

Equipment: a straight bar, weight plates, incline bench, collars, and a spotter

Movement execution:

1. **Adjust the bench seat so you can form a 90-degree angle between your upper and lower arms when your shoulders are directly below the handgrips.**

2. **Lie on the bench with your hips, shoulders, and head touching the bench while you maintain a neutral spine.**

   Keep your feet on the ground and a natural arch in your lower back throughout the exercise.

3. **Grasp the bar with a closed grip and your hands about shoulder-width apart.**

   You can go wider if it's more comfortable.

FIGURE 7-9:
The incline bench.

Zack McCrory

4. Lower the bar in a controlled manner until your upper arms are parallel to the ground.

5. Immediately return the bar to the up position by fully extending your arms (but don't lock your elbows).

Don't bounce the bar off your chest, either.

Complete three sets of 8 to 10 repetitions at 60 to 70 percent of your 1RM.

Surveying PRT for the Sprint-Drag-Carry

The Sprint–Drag–Carry requires you to be flexible, agile, and strong, so the Army recommends three PRT exercises that help you develop the skills you need: the straight–leg deadlift from the STC, the bent over row from the STC, and the 300-meter shuttle run from PRT's Running, Endurance, and Mobility Activities.

Straight-leg deadlift

The Army's answer to developing strength, endurance, and mobility in your trunk and lower body and improving your grip strength is the straight–leg deadlift.

If you're new to deadlifts, practice with an empty bar or broom handle until you find the right form. Work for two to four weeks lifting 40 to 50 percent of your body weight. If you weigh 150 pounds, that translates to 67.5 to 75 pounds. You can train with 25 to 50 percent of your 1RM, too, so again, if you can lift 100 pounds, you train with a weight that ranges between 25 pounds and 50 pounds. Perfect your straight–leg deadlift by checking out the moves in Figure 7-10.

FIGURE 7-10:
The straight-leg deadlift.

Zack McCrory

TIP

If you're a beginner, keep the same weight on your bar for two to four weeks, and when the exercise becomes easier, add reps rather than weight.

Equipment: a straight bar, plates, collars, or alternate equipment

Movement execution:

1. **Pick up the bar and stand with your legs planted firmly on the ground about shoulder-width apart.**

2. **Keep a secure, pronated grip (with your palms facing behind you) just outside your thighs and try to push your shoulder blades together.**

   WARNING

   Keep your knees soft throughout the entire exercise; don't lock them.

3. **Flex at your hips to lower the bar toward the floor. Keep your spine straight and your shoulders back.**

   WARNING

   Keep your spine neutral. Avoid looking straight ahead or up while you're lowering or raising the bar. I tell participants in my strength training classes, "Take your head and neck with you!" Don't round your spine or allow your knees to fold inward.

4. **Return to the upright position under control.**

Complete three sets of 8 to 10 reps using 60 to 70 percent of your 1RM.

Bent over row

The bent over row develops strength, endurance, and mobility in your upper back, your trunk, and even your legs. It also helps with your grip strength. The Army typically uses kettlebells for this exercise, but FM 7-22 allows for a straight bar (which I personally prefer).

New to the bent over row? It's not as intimidating as it sounds. Start training with an empty bar until you can feel which muscles are supposed to be working — and until you get your form down to a T. You can really hurt yourself without proper form, so talk to an MFT if you're not sure about where to go with the row.

Beginners should do the bent over row for two to four weeks with a load of just 10 to 25 percent of body weight (between 15 and 37.5 pounds if you weigh 150) or 25 to 50 percent of 1RM. It sounds light now, but just wait. Don't increase your weight during your base phase. Increase your reps instead. Get a good look at form (using kettlebells) in Figure 7-11.

FIGURE 7-11:
The bent over
row.

Zack McCrory

Equipment: kettlebells or a straight bar, plates, and collars

Movement execution:

1. **Pick up the weight from the ground and move into the forward leaning rest position.**

   The forward leaning rest position starts with feet shoulder-width apart and knees and hips flexed so your back is at about a 45-degree angle from the ground (give or take a few degrees). In the forward leaning rest position with kettlebells, hold the handles with your palms toward your thighs. If you're using a bar, the bar is hanging around your knees, your palms are facing your thighs, and your hands are just outside your thighs in a natural position.

   Some weightlifting pros bend over farther than 45 degrees, and that's okay. However, for the Army's bent over row, you're at or around a 45-degree angle.

   TIP

2. **Squeeze your shoulder blades together and pull the weight up toward the area between your bellybutton and your chest.**

   Use your upper back to pull the kettlebells or bar up. Send your elbows straight back — don't chicken-wing them out. Absorb every phase of the movement in your flexed legs.

3. **Return to the starting position before you repeat.**

Complete three sets of 8 to 10 repetitions using 60 to 70 percent of your 1RM.

TIP

The flexion always comes from your hips in the bent over row — not from rounding your lower back. Take your head and neck with you, too; maintain a neutral spine and don't look straight forward (unless you're stealing a quick glance in the mirror to check your form).

300-meter shuttle run

The 300-meter shuttle run is designed to max out your ability to sprint, sprint, and sprint some more with a few directional changes mixed in. It improves your anaerobic endurance, speed, and agility.

Equipment: a level surface marked off at 25-meter intervals

Movement execution:

1. Stagger your stance behind the start line.

2. Sprint like a Specialist when the First Sergeant asks for weekend volunteers.

3. Touch the ground and turn around at the 25-meter mark and sprint back to the start line.

   Slow down and plant your feet before you touch the ground and change direction. If you come in too hot, you can't bend your trunk and squat when you reach for the ground.

4. Repeat Steps 1 through 3 until you've gone back and forth a total of 12 times.

Complete one full set.

TIP

Alternate touches between your left and right hand to mix things up.

Looking at PRT for the Leg Tuck

The LTK is a key component of the ACFT, and the people who created the test put it at the end to create a good chance you're already wiped out by the time you get to it. The Army recommends conditioning yourself with three exercises long before test day: the bent-leg raise from 4 for the Core, the leg tuck and twist from Conditioning Drill 1, and the alternating grip pull-up from Climbing Drill 1.

Bent-leg raise

The bent-leg raise is essential core work that develops strength, endurance, and mobility in your whole trunk. If you're new to core work, you're coming off a pregnancy profile, or you've been injured in the past, start with 20-second repetitions and keep a limited range of movement. Increase your intervals over the first two to four weeks you're practicing the bent-leg raise. Check out the proper crunch and extension in Figure 7-12.

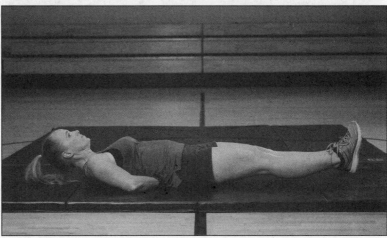

FIGURE 7-12: The bent-leg raise.

Zack McCrory

Equipment: a level surface

Movement execution:

1. **Lay on your back with your knees flexed like you're about to do a sit-up and put your hands between the small of your back and the ground with your elbows flexed out.**

   From the top, it looks like your hands are on your hips, but they're under your body.

2. **Raise your head 2 to 3 inches off the ground while also raising your feet off the ground until your hips and knees both flex to 90 degrees.**

   TIP

   If you wear a bun, don't rest on it. In fact, if you're practicing, let your hair down — that way, you can use your neck muscles to raise and lower your head in a full range of motion.

3. **Contract your abs, focusing on how much pressure you're generating on your hands, which are still on the ground beneath your lower back.**

4. **Maintain the same amount of pressure in your hands and straighten your legs slowly; hold that position for 30 to 60 seconds while keeping your feet together.**

   TIP

   You can extend your legs at a higher angle or bend your knees to take a little heat off your abs and hip flexors. If you're ready for more heat, straighten your legs more and lower your feet farther to the ground. As you become stronger, you'll be able to get straight legs closer to the ground. See if you can challenge yourself to keep your feet six inches from the ground during this exercise.

Complete three reps, each with a 30- to 60-second hold.

Leg tuck and twist

The leg tuck and twist is designed to improve your balance while developing core strength and mobility. It's from CD1, so if you're like most soldiers, you've done this exercise dozens — if not hundreds — of times. If you're not familiar with it, though, start with just five reps and control your range of movement. Increase the number of reps you do over a two-to-four-week period. For a quick peek at proper form, scope out Figure 7-13.

FIGURE 7-13:
The leg tuck and
twist.

Zack McCrory

Equipment: a level surface

Movement execution:

1. **Sit on the ground with your legs straight out in front of you.**
2. **Lean back to a 45-degree angle, keeping your legs on the ground.**

   Use your arms to prop yourself into position so that the space between your arms and your back looks like an upside-down *V*.
3. **Raise your straight legs 8 to 12 inches from the ground.**

   You're now in the starting position for the leg tuck and twist.
4. **Draw your knees toward your right shoulder while rotating on your right buttock and then return to the starting position in Step 3.**
5. **Repeat Step 4, using your left shoulder and buttock.**
6. **Continue alternating sides until you reach the desired number of reps.**

Complete two sets of 5 to 10 repetitions.

TIP

Keep your legs, knees, and feet together throughout the exercise. Don't move your head and trunk. Protect your back by keeping your movements smooth and controlled — no jerking allowed.

Alternating grip pull-up

The Army designed the alternating grip pull-up to help develop the muscles you need to pull your body up with — you guessed it — an alternating grip. If you haven't done these exercises before, or if you're not sure about your upper-body strength, you should start training with a spotter, a step bench, or an assistive stretch cord. Work for two to four weeks with assistance, increasing the number of reps you knock out as you become stronger. Have a look at proper form in Figure 7-14.

Equipment: a climbing bar, pull-up bar, or suspension trainer

Movement execution:

1. **Hang on the bar, using an alternating grip and keeping your arms straight.**

   The LTK event on the ACFT requires you to keep your dominant hand closest to your body.

REMEMBER

FIGURE 7-14:
The alternating
grip pull-up.

2. Pull your body upward, moving your head out of the way so you don't ring your bell on the bar.

Your body doesn't have to go straight up and down. It's natural for your body to reach a slight angle in the flexed position. Keep your feet together (and uncrossed) while you're pulling yourself up.

3. Return to the starting position in a controlled manner and pull yourself up again.

You can pair up with a partner and help each other reach the fully flexed position after you're fatigued.

TIP

Complete one set of 5 to 10 repetitions.

You can also do this exercise with a lat pull-down machine if you have one available. Start at 50 percent of your body weight; if you weigh 180 pounds, that's 90 pounds.

TIP

Tackling PRT for the Two-Mile Run

The Two-Mile Run event on the ACFT is the Army's best way to test your cardio-vascular endurance, so it's definitely something you should train for if you want to pass the test. PRT has a few fancy tricks you can do to improve your run time: sprint intervals (you know them as 30:60s and 60:120s), release runs, and hill repeats. Of course, you should be running a few times a week for at least a couple of miles — if not with your unit, then on your own.

REMEMBER

The Two-Mile Run is the last event on the ACFT, so by the time you reach the event, you may be pretty fatigued. Fortunately, the allowable run times are pretty forgiving. You can check out the scoring table in Chapter 4 to see how quickly you need to reach the finish line.

Sprint intervals (30:60s and 60:120s)

Sprint intervals, formally known as Fartlek training, are a great way to work on acceleration and deceleration while improving your resistance to fatigue. You go through cycles of moderate and intense effort to increase both your aerobic and anaerobic endurance. (Chapter 6 has more on aerobic and anaerobic exercise.)

Equipment: a level surface such as a field, track, or running route

Movement execution:

1. **Sprint at full speed for 30 seconds.**
2. **Jog for 60 seconds.**

TIP

Replace the 30-second sprint with a 60-second sprint and the 60-second jog with a 120 second jog after a few weeks of training.

Complete 4 to 10 reps of 30:60s per week, increasing to 5 reps of 60:120s and, after several weeks, 10 reps of 60:120s.

Release run

Running at your own pace is good for your heart, your lungs, and your muscles. If you're new to running, or if it's been a while because you were on profile, start at a moderately sustainable pace for 5 to 10 minutes at a time. Gradually increase your time pounding the pavement to 10 to 15 minutes in a single stretch during the first two to four weeks.

Equipment: a level surface such as a field, track, or running route

Movement execution:

1. **Run at a comfortably difficult pace — not so fast that you're sprinting, but faster than the Airborne Shuffle.**

2. **Over time, increase the time you spend running until you reach 25 minutes.**

Complete 25 minutes of running at a comfortably difficult pace.

TIP

Don't run every day. On the days you do run, don't forget to warm up first. Your goal is to run at the same pace for the entire period, so starting small and working your way up to a longer duration is okay.

Hill repeats

Whether you ran up Tank Hill at Fort Jackson, Misery Hill at Knox, or Car Wash Hill at Leonard Wood, you probably did more hill repeats than you could count during Basic Combat Training and Advanced Individual Training. You may even run up Kolekole Pass at Schofield Barracks or Custer Hill at Fort Riley now — and that's great news for your 2MR score. Uphill and downhill repeats are both great exercises.

Equipment: a steep hill with a running surface at least 40 yards long, or a long, gently sloping hill at least 60 yards long

Uphill movement execution:

1. **Warm up by jogging on a level surface for 10 to 20 minutes.**

2. **Sprint 40 to 60 meters uphill.**

3. **Walk downhill, reaching the bottom within 60 to 90 seconds.**

4. **Repeat Steps 2 and 3 six to ten times.**

Downhill movement execution:

1. **Warm up by jogging on a level surface for 10 to 20 minutes.**

2. **Sprint down the hill in 15 to 20 seconds.**

3. **Walk up the hill in 60 to 90 seconds.**

4. **Repeat Steps 2 and 3 six to ten times.**

Complete one each of uphill and downhill repeat runs once a week, each consisting of six to ten repetitions.

Taking a Closer Look at PRT and Its Drills

Army PRT is the Army's plan for keeping soldiers fit to fight, but it can be complicated. Not all soldiers are at the same level of fitness at any given moment; some are on profile, some have just recovered after being on profile, and some are newer to fitness than others are. Usually, looking at PRT under the Army Force Generation, or ARFORGEN, model is helpful. ARFORGEN is the Army's process for meeting combatant commanders' requirements. It's an Army-wide process that synchronizes how units train (and stay trained). That means keeping more units fully trained and fully ready than ever before. The ARFORGEN model allows the Pentagon to tap into the Army's total strength, including both active and reserve units.

ARFORGEN features a three-stage cycle: Reset, Train/Ready, and Available. PRT follows that three-stage cycle so that more units, and more individual soldiers, are ready to deploy at any given time. (Two additional phases, the Initial Conditioning phase and the Toughening phase, deal with new soldiers in BCT and AIT.) Here's how the three-stage portion works:

>> **Reset phase:** Soldiers returning from deployment are in the reset phase. They're supposed to have downtime and reconnect with their families and friends before a return to their regular training schedule.

>> **Train/Ready phase:** During the Train/Ready phase, soldiers and their units begin to train more extensively, and they're eligible for deployment. The Train/Ready phase is also the time when units can prepare for a specific overseas mission.

>> **Available phase:** The Available phase signifies that soldiers and units are ready for deployment.

The ARFORGEN model isn't just about physical training, but every category of PRT belongs within in the ARFORGEN model. All soldiers in the three main phases are required to be able to execute the exercises in all PRT drills. You can read more about the drills in the following sections and some individual exercises earlier in the chapter.

Preparation Drill

The Preparation Drill is your warm-up, and it comprises ten exercises that are always performed in the same order and at the same cadence. Table 7-3 outlines these calisthenic exercises.

TABLE 7-3

Preparation Drill

Exercise	Reps	Cadence
Bend and reach	5–10	Slow
Rear lunge	5–10	Slow
High jumper	5–10	Moderate
Rower	5–10	Slow
Squat bender	5–10	Slow
Windmill	5–10	Slow
Forward lunge	5–10	Slow
Prone row	5–10	Slow
Bent-leg body twist	5–10	Slow
Push-up	5–10	Moderate

The Preparation Drill is designed as a full-body warmup, which means it covers everything from your head to your toes. Check out Table 7-4 to see the focus areas for each exercise in the PD so you can use what you need when you're training on your own time.

TABLE 7-4

Focus Areas for the Preparation Drill

	Hips	Thighs	Lower Legs	Chest	Back	Core	Shoulders	Arms
Bend and reach	x	x			x	x	x	
Rear lunge	x	x	x		x	x		
High jumper	x	x	x		x	x	x	
Rower	x	x	x		x	x	x	x
Squat bender	x	x	x	x	x	x	x	x

	Hips	Thighs	Lower Legs	Chest	Back	Core	Shoulders	Arms
Windmill	x	x	x	x	x	x	x	x
Forward lunge	x	x	x		x	x		
Prone row	x			x	x	x	x	x
Bent-leg body twist	x	x			x	x		
Push-up	x	x	x	x	x	x	x	x

4 for the Core

The 4 for the Core drill, or 4C, was designed to maximize your strength in your abdomen, lower back, and pelvic area. Having a strong core is essential for stability. Your limbs need to rely on your core to generate powerful movements. Although 4 for the Core didn't make it into the H2F program, your unit is still likely to perform these exercises. This group contained four total exercises, and they all focused on strengthening your front and back core:

>> Bent-leg raise

>> Side bridge

>> Back bridge

>> Quadraplex

The goal in 4C is to hold each exercise position for 60 seconds. You can do these exercises anywhere you find a level surface.

You can read about the bent-leg raise, which can help you perform better on the LTK event, in the earlier section "Bent-leg raise." Figure 7-15 shows the side bridge, back bridge, and quadraplex.

Conditioning Drills 1, 2, and 3

The Army included five conditioning drills in CD1 and CD2, and ten conditioning drills in CD3. CD1 is the least complex of all the conditioning drills, and CD3 is the most complex; CD2 falls somewhere in the middle. Many Army units don't routinely do CD3 because commanders have to balance the needs of the many with the needs of the few — and in a typical PT formation, you're working with new soldiers and those who are already conditioned. That makes CD2 the happy medium, and it's where you find exercises like the turn and lunge, supine bicycle, half jacks, swimmer, and the 8-count push-up (see the earlier section "8-count T push-up"). CD3 has a heavy focus on the lower body, and the exercises are more complicated (like the tuck jump, which I discuss in the earlier section "Tuck jump" as a way to improve your Standing Power Throw performance on the ACFT). It also includes the single-leg deadlift, half-squat laterals, and frog jumps.

FIGURE 7-15: Side bridge, back bridge, and quadraplex.

Zack McCrory

Climbing Drills 1 and 2

Climbing Drill 1 is designed to improve soldiers' upper-body and core strength, which translates into the ability to negotiate obstacles on the battlefield. It includes the straight-arm pull, heel hook, pull-ups, leg tucks, and the alternating grip pull-up (see the earlier section "Alternating grip pull-up"). Climbing Drill 2 features the same exercises (save the straight-arm pull), but with higher reps and more sets — and it includes the flexed-arm hang.

The Guerilla Drill

The Guerilla Drill includes only three exercises: the shoulder roll, the lunge walk, and the soldier carry. Each is designed to improve agility, cardiorespiratory endurance, muscular endurance, and muscular strength.

The Hip Stability Drill

The Hip Stability Drill trains your hips and quads by using 3D movements like those I explain in Chapter 5. The PRT Hip Stability Drill includes the lateral leg raise, medial leg raise, bent-leg lateral raise, single-leg tuck, and single-leg over, which are all great complements to the training exercises in Chapter 8.

The Push-Up and Sit-Up Drill

Push-ups and sit-ups develop upper body strength, muscular endurance, and mobility, and they were absolutely essential for the APFT, predecessor to the ACFT. They're still part of a good physical training regimen, but the ACFT doesn't grade you on straight push-ups or sit-ups.

The Shoulder Stability Drill

The Shoulder Stability Drill is designed to develop shoulder strength and promote stability, and it includes only five exercises, commonly called "I," "T," "Y," "L," and "W" raises. In each exercise, you lie in the prone position (on your stomach) with your head slightly elevated and in line with your spine. Your feet and toes are together to the rear, and your arms form the shape of each letter.

Running, Endurance and Mobility Activities: Military Movement Drills 1 and 2

The Army's Running, Endurance and Mobility Activities include Military Movement Drills 1 and 2. MMD1 and MMD2 cover verticals, laterals (just like the ones you're tested on during the ACFT), shuttle sprints, the power Skip, crossovers, and crouch Runs.

PRT's Running, Endurance and Mobility Activities also feature sprints, hill repeats, 30:60s, release runs, and unit formation runs. (Flip to the earlier section "Tackling PRT for the Two-Mile Run" for details on the first four of those exercises.) Even ruck marching is part of this category, which is all about improving soldiers' cardiovascular endurance and developing motor efficiency.

The Strength Training Circuit

Strength training is important for any good PT plan, and the Army has a specific circuit design that runs soldiers through all the exercises necessary to train for individual physical demands — and, more importantly, for combat. Figure 7-16 shows the Army's ideal Strength Training Circuit, or STC, and the order in which you should perform the exercises (many of which I discuss earlier in the chapter).

Here's the order of exercises in the STC:

1. Do the sumo squat and then run verticals (high-knee) to Station 2.
2. Do the straight-leg deadlift and then run laterals (left) to Station 3.
3. Do the forward lunge and then run laterals (right) to Station 4.
4. Do the step-up and then run to Station 5.
5. Do the pull-up or straight-arm pull and then run to Station 6.
6. Do the supine chest press and then run laterals (left) to Station 7.
7. Do the bent over row and then run laterals (right) to Station 8.
8. Do the overhead push-press and then run verticals to Station 9.
9. Do the supine body twist and then run backward to Station 10.
10. Do the leg tuck and then run backward to Station 1.

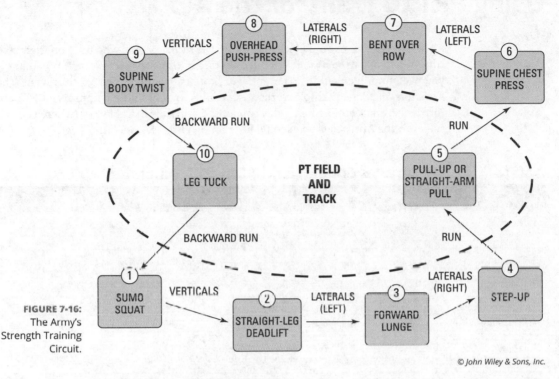

STRENGTH TRAINING CIRCUIT

FIGURE 7-16:
The Army's
Strength Training
Circuit.

© John Wiley & Sons, Inc.

Recovery Drill

Most people do the Recovery Drill after PT Monday through Friday, but the stretches it covers are great to use any time — in the gym, at home, or anywhere you can squeeze them in. The eight stretches are the overhead arm pull, the rear lunge, the extend and flex, the thigh stretch, the single-leg over, the groin stretch, the calf stretch, and the hamstring stretch. Each focuses on a different area of the body except the extend and flex, which focuses on everything. In PRT, you're supposed to hold each of these stretches for 20 to 30 seconds on each side and call it a day, but if you're using them on your own time, you can hold for that long and repeat as necessary.

TIP

Recovery is essential, and it's just as important as eating right and getting enough sleep. Flip to Chapter 9 for more about recovery and stretching so you can give your body everything it needs to reach optimal — or even just improved — performance.

Using PRT to Train for the ACFT

Although you can use only PRT to train for the ACFT, people who train on their own time *in addition to doing unit PT* generally fare a lot better on test day. If you know you need improvement in any event, you should absolutely train for that event. The Army has published sample workout schedules to help soldiers improve ACFT performance, and I outline its 14-day condensed schedule in Table 7-5 (where you can see even the Army says you should be training with PRT on Saturdays).

TABLE 7-5 **The Army's Condensed 14-Day PRT Schedule**

Day	PRT Strength Training	PRT Endurance Training
1. Monday	Bent-leg raise, quadraplex, sumo squat, forward lunge	
2. Tuesday		HSD, MMDs, six to ten hill repeats
3. Wednesday	Bent-leg raise, quadraplex, incline bench, overhead push-press, bent over row	
4. Thursday		MMDs, release run
5. Friday	I, T, Y, L, and W raises, alternating grip pull-up, power jump, leg tuck and twist	
6. Saturday		HSD, MMDs, five to ten 30:60s
7. Sunday	Rest day	Rest day
8. Monday	I, T, Y, L, and W Raises, 8-count push-ups, tuck jump, alternate staggered squat jump	
9. Tuesday		MMDs, one to three 300-meter shuttle runs
10. Wednesday	Bent-leg raise, quadraplex, power jump, leg tuck and twist	
11. Thursday		HSD, MMDs, release run
12. Friday	I, T, Y, L, and W Raises, alternating grip pull-up, overhead push-press, bent over row	
13. Saturday		MMDs, five 60:120s
14. Sunday	Rest day	Rest day

REMEMBER

When you're conducting PRT, doing the Preparation Drill and Recovery Drill each time is a good idea. They help warm up and cool down your body so that you can exercise and recover safely. You can read more about those drills (and many of the exercises in Table 7-5) earlier in the chapter.

Chapter **8**

Training to Standard on the ACFT

L
ike any other test, you have to practice the subject matter to do well on the ACFT. That includes doing the test events yourself — especially the events you know you need to work on. If your leg tuck skills are a little shaky, you need to dangle from a pull-up bar and push yourself to do regulation-style leg tucks. Though training on the exercises you perform on the ACFT helps you get the score you need, dozens of other exercises (too many to include in just one book) can boost your muscular strength, cardiovascular and cardiorespiratory endurance, and anaerobic power, too. Using other exercises to improve your ACFT performance is a great way to keep training, improve your fitness level, and avoid burnout. I explain some of these moves here and in Chapter 9, where I cover stretching and recovery, and the Army uses some of them in its PRT program.

REMEMBER

Whipping yourself into great shape for the ACFT (or for any other reason) involves a lot more than just working out. You also need to stretch, recover, and choose the right fuels for your body. I cover all those things in Chapters 9 and 23, respectively.

Doing the exercises in this chapter properly is really important — you can hurt yourself if you're not using good form. Read the instructions and advice for each move carefully to make sure your form is on-point.

Getting the Basics Down Before You Exercise

When you perform nearly any exercise, keeping a *neutral spine* is important to avoid injury. That means letting your back stay in its most natural position, which is about halfway between a flat back and arched back. Your spine has four major sections (cervical, thoracic, lumber, and pelvic), and when you exercise, they should all be in their natural positions. That starts with the way your pelvis is tilted. If you tip your pelvis forward and stick your rear end out (an anterior pelvic tilt), your lumbar spine curves too much to safely exercise; if you tip your pelvis back and tuck in your backside (a posterior pelvic tilt), your lumbar spine extends and puts you at risk for injury. Your spine is in a neutral position when you stand up straight with your shoulders back and away from your ears, don't tuck in or push out your backside, and let your hips sit naturally (a neutral pelvic tilt). Figure 8-1 shows the sections of your spine and these three postures. (Turn this book sideways, and you can imagine what these spinal positions look like on a bench or the floor, too.)

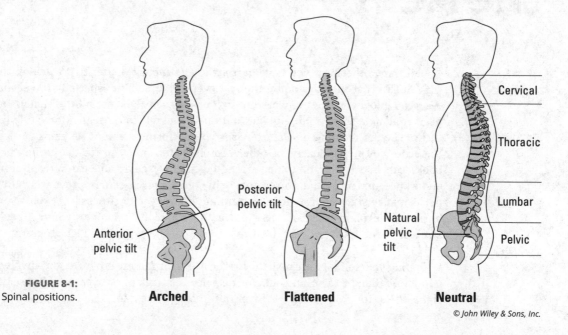

Anterior pelvic tilt

Posterior pelvic tilt

Natural pelvic tilt

Cervical

Thoracic

Lumbar

Pelvic

Arched **Flattened** **Neutral**

FIGURE 8-1: Spinal positions.

© John Wiley & Sons, Inc.

You also need to know about the athletic stance, a standing position that lets you maximize your strength, power, and speed in any direction. The *athletic stance* (or *athletic position*, if you prefer) is

» Feet shoulder-width (or slightly wider) apart

» Neutral spine

» Shoulders down (away from your ears)

» Knees slightly bent

» Weight evenly distributed over both feet, from your heels to your toes

You modify the position by changing the angles of your ankles, knees, or torso, depending on the direction you need to move or exert strength.

Throughout the exercises, I also tell you to *engage your core*, which means that all four sections of your abdominal muscles need to work together with the muscles connected to your spine. Engaging your core keeps you stable and protects your back (and it even lends you a little strength to perform exercises).

TECHNICAL STUFF

The four sections of your abdominal muscles are your transversus abdominis (the deepest muscles in your abdomen, which are the biggest actors in keeping your trunk stable), rectus abdominis (the ones that make up a "six-pack"), external obliques (the muscles on your sides that pull you to one side when you twist), and your internal obliques (the muscles on your sides that push you to the side you're twisting toward).

Other common terms you encounter include the following:

» **Repetitions (reps):** This term refers to the number of times you perform one complete exercise from start to finish.

» **Sets:** A *set* is a group of reps. For example, if a workout says you should do three sets of 10 reps, you perform the exercise a total of 30 times.

» **One-repetition maximum (1RM):** Your *1RM* is the maximum amount of weight you can lift one time for an exercise.

So how much weight should you lift in each of these exercises? Everybody — and every *body* — is different, so figure out your 1RM (and write it down) for every exercise you do so you can create a plan. The best way to determine your exact 1RM is to lift as much as you can one time, successfully. Your 1RM is different from one exercise to the next, which is why I suggest writing it down.

REMEMBER

The number of reps I prescribe for each exercise varies based on your goals, and you should absolutely customize them to your needs. As a general rule, you probably want to work with 70 to 85 percent of your 1RM and perform three sets of exercises at moderate speeds, giving yourself 30 to 60 seconds to rest in between. Check out Table 8-1 for a look at the rep ranges for different goals.

TABLE 8-1 **Rep Ranges and Goals**

Goal	Percent of 1RM	Number of Reps
Endurance	60–70 percent	13–20
Strength	70–85 percent	7–12
Power	85–100 percent	1–6

WARNING

If an exercise hurts, stop doing it immediately. These exercises are supposed to make you uncomfortable (what's that saying about killing you or making you stronger?), but it's a good kind of uncomfortable — the kind that means your muscles are working hard. If you feel pain, *don't* push through it. (There's another saying about that — something to do with playing stupid games.) Discomfort because you're working hard is a lot different from pain, which you'll likely experience if you're using bad form or you're doing more than your body can handle. The last thing you need is to get stuck on profile with an ACFT on the horizon, or worse, sustain a serious injury because you were training for a physical fitness test.

Back and Legs: Maxing the 3 Repetition Maximum Deadlift Score

The 3 Repetition Maximum Deadlift, or MDL, is the first event you run into on test day. You get a 10-minute warm-up for the event; during that time, you have a chance to add or remove weight from the hex bar you're going to use. Long before you take the ACFT, though, you can start a workout routine that includes the exercises in this section. They're all designed to strengthen the muscles in your back and legs, which helps you meet your goals on the test.

REMEMBER

Don't work out the same muscle groups on back-to-back days if you're working out until you reach muscle failure. As you probably already know from conducting PT on Tuesdays and Thursdays, *muscle failure* is where you work a muscle (or muscle group) until you just can't perform any longer. You can alternate cardio and strength training, which will probably yield you the best results (both performance-wise and looks-wise). You don't get stronger *during* your workout; you get stronger *between* your workouts, which is why recovery days are so important.

TIP

If you still have some gas in the tank at the end of a workout, add more weight the next time (as long as you can do so safely without injuring yourself).

Sumo squats

Sumo squats are part of the Strength Training Circuit in PRT, and to do them, you need a kettlebell and a flat surface. But you can only lift so much weight with a kettlebell, which means your goal here is the number of reps you can knock out, not increasing the amount of weight you're lifting. In a sumo squat, your feet and knees are facing outward, rather than forward like they would with a traditional squat, and you're in a wide stance. The sumo squat engages your glutes, quads, inner thighs, hamstrings, and core muscles, and because your goal is reps (not weight), you're training for muscular endurance. You're not going to get Schwarzenegger-style quads from these exercises, but you are going to improve your endurance so you don't have to low-crawl across the finish line on the Two-Mile Run.

Figure 8-2 shows the weighted sumo squat, Army-style.

FIGURE 8-2:
The weighted
sumo squat.

Zack McCrory

Here's how to properly execute a sumo squat.

1. **Stand with your feet more than shoulder-width apart in an athletic stance.**

2. **Point your toes out at 45-degree angles.**

3. Lower your body into a squat.

Bend at the hips and knees while you sit back. Keep your chest up and knees out, and keep your spine neutral. Lower your body until your thighs are parallel to the ground.

4. Stand back up so you're at the starting position.

TIP

You don't have to use a kettlebell, especially if you're new to exercise. Instead, you can raise your arms in front of you with each squat so that your hands are parallel to your shoulders. When the unweighted squat stops sending you into muscle failure, add a kettlebell. You know you're going far enough down when the kettlebell almost touches the ground.

You can turn the sumo squat into two other exercises for a little more variety: the sumo jump squat and the kettlebell swing (I cover the latter in the later section "Kettlebell swings"). You can turn a sumo squat into a jump squat when you're not using a kettlebell. Simply drive your body back up explosively from a squat (like you do in the Standing Power Throw event) and reach above your head. Land softly and squat again.

EXAMPLE

You can work sumo squats into your routine by aiming for three or four sets of 8 to 15 reps.

Staggered squats

Staggered squats are just like regular squats, where your feet are shoulder-width apart, but your feet are staggered. It's not quite a lunge, which requires your back leg to stay perpendicular to the ground; it's a halfway point between a lunge and a squat, like a crouch. Figure 8-3 shows a staggered squat, which you can do with a weight bar across your back or dumbbells in your hands for more of a challenge (just keep that neutral spine so I don't have to go all old-school drill sergeant on you).

EXAMPLE

Incorporate staggered squats into your strength training workouts by doing three sets of 12 to 15 reps at a time. If you're doing bodyweight-only training, you can increase the number of sets you do; if you're using weights, increase your weight but do the same number of reps.

Lunges

Standard lunges are a great way to keep it simple while strengthening your quads and glutes. If you're new to working out, or if you're just getting back into the game, do lunges without weight until they become easier. Then you can add dumbbells or a bar. Figure 8-4 shows a bodyweight-only lunge with proper form.

FIGURE 8-3:
The bodyweight-only staggered squat.

FIGURE 8-4:
The bodyweight-only lunge.

EXAMPLE

Start adding lunges to your workout routine with bodyweight only. Do one set of 8 to 12 reps on each side. Add weights as necessary to keep challenging yourself.

Conventional deadlifts

Deadlifts strengthen everything you need for the MDL and then some. They hit your

>> Quadriceps

>> Glutes

>> Adductor magnus (inner thigh)

>> Hamstrings

>> Erectors

>> Lats

>> Traps

>> Rhomboids

>> Abs

>> Obliques

When you perform deadlifts safely, you challenge — and strengthen — all the muscles across your posterior chain (that's everything on the back of your body from your neck to your heels). You boost your grip strength and improve your core stability.

But all of that means you have to start light and perfect your form before you start lifting heavier. Even a minor form issue can cause serious injury.

Here's how to do it right:

1. **Put your feet flat on the floor and bend at the knees.**

Keep your spine neutral by looking at a spot on the floor 6 to 10 feet in front of you. Tighten your core so your spine stays stable throughout the exercise.

2. **Grab the bar from the floor with your hands shoulder-width apart.**

   Always squeeze the bar as tightly as you can before you lift it. Make sure your shoulders are back and down.

3. **Stand up powerfully, using your legs and glutes to push yourself into a standing position.**

   Your shoulders should be slightly in front of your hands until the bar passes the middle of your thigh. At that point, you can put your back into the exercise by pulling your shoulder blades back. Keep your core engaged to protect your back as you lift with your legs.

4. **Control your movement downward and place the bar back on the floor.**

Figure 8-5 shows proper form for a standard deadlift.

FIGURE 8-5: The deadlift.

Zack McCrory

WARNING

Don't hunch forward over the bar — keep your back straight and your spine neutral. Hunching takes away your ability to engage your core the right way and opens you up to the possibility of a back injury.

TIP

Switch things up with your deadlifts by changing your grip. Use an overhand grip with both hands or, for a change, do one overhand grip and one underhand grip. Alternate between sets so you get an even workout. (A reverse grip lets you lift heavier.)

If you're not very experienced, squeeze deadlifts into your workout routine by doing four sets of six reps with the same weight on the bar each time. If you're pretty familiar with them, do three sets of five reps with the same weight on your bar, and if you're advanced, do five sets of five reps, starting small and ramping up to your heaviest weight for the last set.

Bent over rows

Bent over rows are spectacular for working out your upper back. In fact, they blast your lats, posterior shoulders, rhomboids, scapular stabilizers, forearms and biceps or triceps (depending on your grip), spinal erectors, hamstrings, and glutes. You can do bent over rows with a bar or dumbbells, and plenty of variations help you keep your workouts fun and fresh. Here's how to do a standard bent over row, which you can see in Figure 8-6:

1. **Grasp the bar, loaded with your weight of choice, with an overhand grip and stand up using your legs (leave your back out of it for now).**

2. **Standing in an athletic posture, roll your shoulders back and down to set your spine and core up for success.**

   The bar should be resting in your hands in front of your thighs. If you can feel the bar pulling your shoulders forward, extending your muscles when you try to flex in an athletic posture, put it down and take off some weight.

3. **Bend your knees slightly and tip at the hip so you're leaning forward at an angle between 60 and 80 degrees.**

   Keep a neutral spine and engage your core, which helps you balance. You can be more upright, especially if you're having balance issues, but don't let yourself go higher than 45 degrees.

4. **Let the bar hang with your arms straight.**

   If you're standing close to 90 degrees, your bar should hang below your knees. If your posture is more upright, the bar hangs above your knees. Don't hunch your back, and keep your shoulders back and down.

5. **Double-check your core and make sure it's engaged.**

6. **Squeeze your shoulder blades together to row the weight up so it touches the bottom of your sternum or the area just below your breasts, or in toward a spot between your bellybutton and sternum.**

   Try to tuck your elbows in toward your body — don't let them flap out like wings. Think of it this way: You're not pulling the bar up; you're pulling your elbows behind you. This process is a deliberate and steady movement. You don't have to do it at sloth speed, but if you look like you're leaning over a jackhammer, you're doing it wrong.

FIGURE 8-6:
Bent over row.

Zack McCrory

WARNING

Don't let your shoulders create momentum. Focus on keeping them back and down throughout the whole exercise. If you need your shoulders to create momentum, your weight is too heavy and your form will suffer (and that almost inevitably leads to injury).

7. **Stop the movement and pause for a moment when you can't get your shoulder blades any closer to each other.**

WARNING

If you can't pause for a moment at the top of each rep, your weight's too heavy. Shave some off your bar and see where that takes you.

8. **Lower the bar back to the starting position and repeat Steps 1 through 7.**

EXAMPLE

Put bent over rows into your workout regimen by doing four sets of 8 to 10 reps. If you're not fatigued or close to muscle failure, add more weight next time.

You can vary the bent over row in a few ways. To mix things up, think about using the following:

>> An underhand grip

>> Dumbbells rather than a barbell while standing

>> Dumbbells while facedown on a 45-degree inclined bench

TIP

You can do a Pendlay row by tipping to a 90-degree angle and lifting the barbell from the ground, although this move can be tough on your body. You can also do a Yates row, where your torso is at a 30- to 45-degree angle to the floor; this one requires you to row the bar toward your lower abs while squeezing your lats, and it activates your mid- to lower traps.

Grip work

A lot of the training you do for the ACFT improves your grip simply because you're using it. You can do extra grip work by trying a few of these exercises:

>> Clenching a tennis ball or stress ball repeatedly

>> Grip clenches, which require you to use a spring-loaded grip trainer

>> Towel wrings, where you soak a towel and wring it out in both directions

>> Dead hangs for as long as you can

>> Farmer's carries, which require you to hold a dumbbell while walking

>> Plate pinches, where you grab a 10-pound bumper plate by its edges using only your fingers

>> Static holds, where you grasp and hold any weight in a fixed position for 30 to 60 seconds

Explosive Power: Training for the Standing Power Throw

You have to use all your quick, explosive power to knock the Standing Power Throw, or SPT, out of the park. Training with a 10-pound medicine ball on a lane is ideal (and you should definitely do it whenever you can), but you can do plenty of other exercises to max out your score on this ACFT event.

Power jumps

The power jump, which is part of Conditioning Drill 1 in PRT, is a great way to kick off your explosive power training. It helps you practice balance and coordination while developing explosive strength in your legs by using the anaerobic power I explain in Chapter 6. You can check out the power jump in Figure 8-7 to see how these rules of the road apply:

1. **Get into an athletic stance.**

   Stabilize your trunk by engaging your core, and keep it that way throughout the whole exercise.

2. **Squat with your feet flat (with equal pressure across your soles) until your hands touch the ground.**

3. **Jump forcefully into the air while raising your arms overhead, like you're blocking a spike at a volleyball net.**

4. **Control your landing so both feet hit the ground at the same time, from the balls of your feet to your heels.**

Spring for these jumps a couple of times a week in your fitness routine. Try two or three sets of two to six reps each, letting yourself rest for a minute in between.

FIGURE 8-7:
Power jump.

Zack McCrory

Overhead push presses

The overhead push press — sometimes called a dumbbell push press — works you from top to bottom. It uses your calves, quads, core, deltoids, and triceps, which are all muscles you use on the ACFT. This explosive movement challenges your stability and gives you an edge on the SPT because you're using many of the same muscles. Figure 8-8 depicts an overhead push press with a barbell (although you can do it with dumbbells, too), so read these instructions and check it out:

1. **Stand in an athletic stance with a loaded bar resting on the front of your shoulders.**

   Keep your elbows facing forward and your weight evenly distributed through your feet. Wrap your thumbs around the bar and keep your grip pretty narrow, sticking to around shoulder-width.

2. **Drop into a shallow squat with your weight centered under the bar.**

   Bend your knees only slightly. You don't need to go into a full squat; you need only to fold enough to spring up with explosive power.

3. **Press up with your whole body, through your feet and legs, to drive the bar over your head.**

   At the end of this movement, your arms should be straight above your head, holding the bar. Keep looking forward through the entire exercise, and keep the bar path straight the whole time. Don't let the bar go too far in front of you *or* too far behind you. It should go straight up and down.

FIGURE 8-8:
Overhead push
press.

Zack McCrory

WARNING

Don't arch your back at any point. If you catch yourself arching (you may notice it when the bar is at its highest point), think about splitting your stance on the next rep.

4. **Lower the bar down to your chest.**

EXAMPLE

Push these (or their variations) into your workout regimen one or two times a week. Do them in sets of eight each, and when you become comfortable with the weight you're using, inch it up a little.

You can vary your workout by trying these, too:

» Shoulder presses, which are the same movement without adding explosive power and momentum from the legs

» Military presses, which are just like shoulder presses — except you don't rest the bar on your chest

» Arnold (as in Schwarzenegger) presses, which require you to hold dumbbells with an underhand grip just above your shoulders (palms facing you) and extend your arms overhead with a rotation so your palms are facing out

HANG CLEANS AND POWER CLEANS

Hang cleans and power cleans are a great way to develop more explosive power. If you're new to cleaning (at least in a weightlifting sense), start with the hang clean. You hold the bar with a shoulder-width grip in front of your thighs and do a quarter squat. Drive through your heels and explode upward, using the momentum to propel the bar upward to chest height, running it straight up your body. Flip your elbows so they're facing forward and catch the bar from a squat position. If you drive up with enough power, the bar flies up so all you have to do is catch it. Lower the bar back to its spot in front of your thighs under control and do it again. After you get that exercise down, you can try power cleans. They're similar, but your bar starts on the ground, and you deadlift it and then clean it. You should be able to stand a few inches from a mirror or wall and execute the whole exercise without hitting it with the plates. (The threat of breaking the mirror can keep you in check.) Start with the bar only until you can nail down your form.

Tuck jumps

Tuck jumps are part of a lot of high-intensity interval training workouts because they engage the lower body and help boost power — and that's exactly what you need for the SPT (and other ACFT events). As you can see in Figure 8-9, you don't need any equipment to do tuck jumps, so you can really do them whenever you feel like it. Here's how:

1. **Stand with your feet a little less than shoulder-width apart.**

2. **Drop into a quarter squat with a neutral spine.**

3. **Explode into the air with power from your legs.**

   Swing your arms for momentum if you want to.

4. **Pull your knees toward your chest while you're in the air.**

   Don't lean forward into your knees while you're in the air. Bring your knees to your chest.

WARNING

5. **Control your landing.**

FIGURE 8-9: Tuck jump.

Zack McCrory

EXAMPLE

Aim for three sets of three reps each, one or two times per week.

You can swap out the tuck jump for the Army's alternate staggered squat jump from CD3 to mix things up and get similar benefits. Check it out in Chapter 7.

Romanian deadlifts

Romanian deadlifts (shown in Figure 8-10) work your posterior chain, which you need for explosive power on the SPT. You hit your erector spinae, glutes, hamstrings, and adductors, so these super-effective exercises help strengthen your core and your lower body in one shot. They're a lot like conventional deadlifts, but you keep your legs fairly straight throughout so you're not relying as heavily on your quads and glutes. Here's how:

1. **Start with the bar in your hands (as opposed to the floor, like you do with a standard deadlift).**

Keep your knees soft, your feet shoulder-width apart, and your spine neutral. Look at a spot on the floor 10 feet in front of you.

2. **Slowly lower your bar by tipping at the hip and bending your knees slightly.**

Keep tipping until you feel a stretch in your hamstrings or you've gone just below your knees.

3. **Push your hips forward (without tilting your pelvis) to straighten back up to a standing position.**

FIGURE 8-10: Romanian deadlift.

Zack McCrory

Maintain the same position in your lower back throughout the exercise. In a Romanian deadlift, you don't lower the bar to the ground — you're working your hamstrings, not your lower back.

EXAMPLE

Raise the bar on your workouts by doing three sets of four to six reps once or twice a week. Aim for 80 to 85 percent of your 1RM.

Kettlebell swings

Kettlebell swings activate a tremendous number of muscles, including your hips, glutes, hamstrings, lats, abs, shoulders, and pecs — and they help you work on your grip strength, too. As far as athletic movements go, this one gets you a lot of bang for your buck. Here's how to perform the kettlebell swing, which you can see in Figure 8-11:

1. **Perform a sumo squat with a kettlebell, and stop when your thighs are parallel to the ground.**

    Refer to the earlier section "Sumo squats" for details on that exercise.

2. **Swing the kettlebell back, between your legs.**

3. **Thrust your hips forward and stand up while swinging the kettlebell to shoulder height.**

4. **Swing the kettlebell back down under control.**

FIGURE 8-11:
Kettlebell swing.

Zack McCrory

Squeeze in three to five sets of 10 reps each a couple of times per week. You can work your way up to 10 sets over time.

Medicine ball power jumps

The medicine ball power jump is really similar to the SPT, and it works out a lot of the same muscles. You're going to exercise your shoulders, triceps, pecs, calves, back, and core when you do it properly. Check it out in Figure 8-12:

1. **Stand over the ball with your feet shoulder-width apart and the ball between your feet.**

2. **Squat down to pick it up.**

3. **Pull the ball up to your chest as you explode upward.**

4. **When your heels leave the ground, continue moving the ball upward.**

5. **As you come down to a soft landing, lower the ball and touch the ground with it.**

Aim for two or three sets of 10 reps a couple of times a week.

FIGURE 8-12: Medicine ball power jump.

Zack McCrory

Standing front shoulder raises with bands

If you have exercise bands, the standing front shoulder raise is your jam — and if you don't, you can sub in dumbbells. This exercise works out the fronts of your shoulders (your anterior deltoids, to be specific), which spring into action for a split second during the SPT. Check it out in Figure 8-13 with bands after reading these instructions:

1. Stand on your band with your feet hip-width apart.

2. Grasp one handle in each hand and stand up straight, maintaining a neutral spine and a zipped-up core.

3. Straighten your arms so your palms are facing the tops of your thighs.

4. Raise your arms straight out in front of you until your hands are at eye level and 6 inches apart.

5. Lower your arms under control.

EXAMPLE

Do three sets of five reps to start. Work your way up to three sets of eight reps over time.

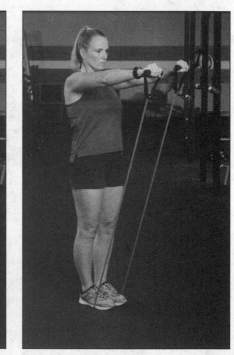

FIGURE 8-13:
Standing front shoulder raise with bands.

Zack McCrory

Practice Makes Perfect: Doing More Hand Release Arm–Extension Push-Ups

The best way to get better at push-ups is, well, to do push-ups. (The 8-count T-push-up from Conditioning Drill 2 in PRT is a great start; head to Chapter 7 for that exercise.) But a handful of other exercises can help you maximize your Hand Release Push-Up – Arm Extension score by working the same muscles you use on test day (and then some). These support exercises also work out your body's backup dancers — the muscles that contribute to your performance on the HRP event.

Supine chest presses

The supine chest press in PRT's Strength Training Circuit works your chest, shoulders, and triceps. You need a pair of kettlebells and a flat surface (you can be on the ground or on a bench). Then, follow these steps, which you can see in Figure 8-14:

1. **Hold the handles of your kettlebells and tuck your elbows in at your sides.**

   If you're on the ground, bend your knees at 90 degrees and keep your feet 8 to 12 inches apart. If you're on a bench, put your feet flat on the ground.

2. **Extend your elbows to raise the kettlebells until your arms are straight and perpendicular to the ground.**

   Make sure your arms are directly over your shoulders at the top position. Don't lock your elbows.

TIP

3. **Lower your arms to the starting position.**

EXAMPLE

Do three sets of eight reps once or twice a week.

Zack McCrory

FIGURE 8-14:
Supine chest
press.

Incline bench presses

The incline bench press (shown in Figure 8-15) primarily works your pecs, anterior delts, and triceps — all of which you need to kick into high gear for the HRP event. You can do bench presses on a flat bench, too, which works out your traps and back a little more. For an incline bench press, raise your bench to a 45-degree angle (give or take) and follow these instructions:

1. Slide down into the bench's seat and engage your core.

2. Grasp the barbell with a grip slightly wider than shoulder-width, squeezing as tightly as you can.

3. Hold the bar directly over your shoulders with your arms straight; this is the starting position.

FIGURE 8-15:
Incline bench
press.

Zach McCrory

4. **Lower the bar under control to the upper part of your chest.**

   Pull your elbows in during downward movement. If you let them flare out to the sides, you're putting stress on your shoulders, which can lead to pain and injury — and worse, you're not in the right position to produce as much strength as possible. They should be at about a 45-degree angle from your body when you're at the bottom of a rep. Your elbows should also be parallel with your back. Don't let them extend below the bench.

   Don't lower the bar to the bottom of your chest or your stomach, and while you're at it, avoid bouncing the bar off your chest.

WARNING

5. **Press your feet into the ground and press the bar up powerfully, back to the starting position.**

Do three sets of eight reps two or three times a week.

You can vary the incline bench press by using dumbbells, which helps build shoulder stability. You can also do incline hex presses, which require you to hold two dumbbells together and press them straight up from your chest.

Chest flys

Chest flys don't let you use a massive amount of weight, but they put plenty of power into your pecs. These strengthening exercises also add a dash of stress to your shoulders, triceps, and biceps. Check out the chest fly in Figure 8-16 and then follow these instructions to crank out a few of your own:

1. **Lie with your head and shoulders supported by an inclined or flat bench, keeping your feet flat on the floor.**

2. **Hold a dumbbell or plate in each hand, directly above your chest with your palms facing each other.**

   If you're using plates, put your thumbs in the center holes.

3. **Lower the weights in an arc out to your sides, but don't let your arms dip below the surface of the bench.**

   You want to keep tension in your pecs the whole time.

   Keep your weights on an imaginary line over the center of your chest from start to finish. That line may be lower than you think it is, but when you hit it, you feel it in your pecs.

4. **Squeeze your pecs to bring the weights back above your chest.**

   Keep a slight bend in your elbows so you can keep the load on your pecs.

Don't arch your lower back or press it hard into the bench. Keep a neutral spine.

Do two to four sets of 8 to 12 reps each a couple of times a week. If you can knock out a few sets of a dozen each without coming close to muscle failure, you need a heavier barbell or plate.

Mess with range and speed a little bit to make your flys more dynamic. For example, raise the dumbbells only halfway or two-thirds of the way up before coming back down, or practice doing flys with the beat of your favorite slow jam. When you change the range *and* speed, there's a good chance that the weight fairy will show up and add a few phantom pounds to what you're lifting.

You can also do flys on a stability ball, which brings extra muscles to the party (especially in your core) to keep you stable.

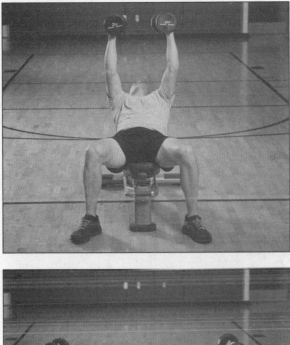

FIGURE 8-16:
Chest fly.

Zack McCrory

Renegade row push-ups

Renegade row push-ups, which you can see in Figure 8-17, create a perfect storm for your upper body and core — it's like getting two exercises for the price of one. This exercise also helps you maintain a straight line when you're performing HRPs because it emphasizes core stability. You need a flat surface and a pair of dumbbells (light to start; you can go heavier after you get the form down) to follow these instructions:

1. **Get into a push-up position with a dumbbell in each hand.**

2. **Perform a push-up and stay at the top.**

FIGURE 8-17:
Renegade row
push-ups.

Zack McCrory

3. **Shift your weight to your right side and row the dumbbell in your left hand to your side.**

Spread your feet a little wider than shoulder-width if you find that you're rotating too much on the row. When you get better at keeping your hips still and preventing your spine from rotating, you can bring your feet closer.

4. **Shift your weight to your left side and row the dumbbell in your right hand to your side to complete the first rep.**

Row slowly, and focus on pushing the other dumbbell and your toes into the ground to help you stay stable.

Try to pull off three or four sets of five to seven reps each with 60 seconds of rest in between.

Medicine Ball push-ups

Core stability is the name of the game on practically every ACFT event, and medicine ball push-ups can get you there. They also help you experiment with how low you have to go for the HRP (and give you a good feel for what it's like to push yourself back up). You can do them with one or both hands on the ball at a time, but I recommend starting with one. Check out what they look like in Figure 8-10 before you roll with these steps:

1. **Rest your right hand on a medicine ball and your left hand on the ground, and assume the push-up's starting position.**

2. **Lower your chest to about an inch above the floor.**

3. **Push yourself back up and move your left hand to the ball to perform another push-up.**

Do three or four sets of 10 to 15 reps each, and if you're experienced in the gym, do them following any other pressing exercise. You can increase the challenge by performing medicine ball push-ups explosively (so your hand comes off the ball) or by putting both hands on the ball at once.

FIGURE 8-18:
Medicine ball
push-ups.

Zack McCrory

Training for the Sprint-Drag-Carry to Boost Your Battlefield Skills

Perhaps the most well-rounded event on the ACFT, the Sprint-Drag-Carry (SDC) is a high-intensity series of exercises that demands peak performance from your upper and lower body. You should practice the event itself whenever you get the chance and also tackle tough workouts that contribute to muscle development, endurance, and anaerobic capacity.

TIP

The bent over row I cover earlier in the chapter can help you on the SDC *and* other events, so if you have to pick only a handful of exercises to put into your workout routine, this row should be one of them.

Shuttle runs

Kids in PE class hate shuttle runs, but they're definitely necessary to improve acceleration, speed, and anaerobic fitness. (It's me. I'm kids in PE class.) The good news is that they're really simple to set up and do. After you're warmed up, follow these steps:

1. Set up markers or cones 25 meters apart (that's how far apart they are on the SDC).

2. Sprint from one marker to the other and back, touching the ground at each.

EXAMPLE

Do six reps as fast as you can so you've sprinted a total of 300 meters.

Straight-leg deadlifts

Straight-leg deadlifts (sometimes called stiff-leg deadlifts) target hip flexion and extension, two valuable skills on the SDC. They also develop the muscles you need for powerful, explosive movements, speed changes, and directional changes. To perform this kind of deadlift properly, you need to master the hip hinge, which you can see in Figure 8-19. Here's how to do it:

1. **With your feet shoulder-width apart, pick up a barbell in an overhand grip.**

   Your hands should be a little wider apart than your feet are.

2. **Tip at the hip, keeping your spine neutral, and lower the bar to a point below your knees (but not to the floor).**

   Squeeze your glutes at the top of the movement and keep all ten toes on the ground. Keep your legs reasonably straight; you need only a little flexion in your knees to do this exercise properly.

   Don't round your back over the bar, and don't lock your legs.

WARNING

FIGURE 8-19: Straight-leg deadlifts.

Zack McCrory

3. **Pause at the bottom and then reverse the movement to return to the starting position.**

Aim for two or three sets of 8 to 12 reps each.

Zercher carries

Zercher carries mimic real-world scenarios, like carrying moving boxes or picking up your kids. These exercises help improve trunk stability while sculpting your forearms, biceps, anterior deltoids, and pecs, and you can completely customize them to reach your goals. You can use a bar, a log, that big tire your platoon sergeant keeps behind the storage shed, or even a bag of dog food. Follow these instructions and have a peek at Figure 8-20.

1. **Squat down slightly to pick up a load (don't start from the ground unless you have to).**

2. **Balance the load in the crooks of your elbows and cradle it in your elbow crease.**

Hold the load tightly. Use your arm strength to keep it stable.

FIGURE 8-20:
Zercher carry.

Zack McCrory

3. **Engage your core and stand up all the way.**

4. **Start walking (any distance is fine), and then stop and turn around at your pre-designated turn around point (like the end of your hallway).**

EXAMPLE

Start with a measured distance — say, 25 meters — and a relatively light weight. Walk back and forth across the distance to complete one rep, and do a total of six reps to complete a full set.

Planks

Planks are a lot like the front leaning rest position. In fact, they *are* the front leaning rest position. Some variations work out different muscles, but a standard plank gets your erector spinae, abs, transverse abdominis, back, and shoulders. See what a solid plank looks like in Figure 8-21 and follow these instructions to do your own:

1. **Place your hands slightly wider than shoulder-width apart, like you would if you were doing a hand release push-up.**

2. **Press your toes into the floor with your feet nearly touching.**

   If you're a beginner, you can start wide and work your way in over time.

3. **Raise your body with a neutral spine so you're in the front leaning rest position, and look at a spot on the floor about a foot in front of your face.**

   If you're new to planking, or if it's been a while, limit your time on the floor to avoid injury. Start with 15-second stretches at a time and work your way up to 30 seconds. When you're more experienced, hold three 60-second planks.

FIGURE 8-21:
Plank.

© John Wiley & Sons, Inc.

WARNING

Don't let your lower back collapse, and don't move into a hip pike — you need to keep your body straight. Try to pull your bellybutton into your spine. If you find yourself sagging in the middle or flexing your hips, decrease the time you're trying to hold your plank.

EXAMPLE

Try to fit planks into your schedule every day. You can do them while you're watching TV, on a conference call with your first sergeant, or waiting for your soldiers to come back with 6 feet of flight line or an exhaust sample.

You can switch up your plank routine by trying the following:

>> Forearm planks, where your forearms are on the floor and your elbows are right below your shoulders.

>> Side planks, which engage your obliques. Lie on your side with your legs stacked, then prop your body on your hand or elbow.

>> Single-leg planks, where you lift one leg toward the ceiling and hold it there without rotating your hips. Switch legs every 15 to 30 seconds.

>> Medicine ball planks, which require you to put your hands on a medicine ball. These planks increase the demand on your core because you have to keep your body stable with only a round ball keeping you from falling.

Glute-hamstring raises

If you haven't figured it out based on this exercise's name, glute-hamstring raises work your glutes and hamstrings. They improve your muscular endurance throughout your whole posterior chain — basically, everything on the back side of your body. Glute-hamstring raises (GHRs) can improve sprinting speed and jumping capability, and they can help prevent hamstring injuries in the future. You can see what this exercise looks like in Figure 8-22 before you jump on a GHR bench at your post's fitness center:

1. Place your knees either directly on or slightly behind the pad and your feet firmly on the platform with the backs of your calves pressed lightly against the upper ankle hook.

2. Keep your back straight, cross your arms in front of your chest, and fold your body over the pad under control.

3. Contract your hamstrings to raise your torso until you're parallel to the floor, pressing your toes into the foot plate.

FIGURE 8-22:
Glute-hamstring
raise.

Zack McCrory

WARNING

Don't hyperextend your body in the up position. Just keep your spine neutral and your core engaged. If you feel it in your lower back, your form is probably off.

Do three sets of 6 to 10 reps each. If you're struggling, cut back — form is infinitely more important than a huge number of reps.

EXAMPLE

You can change things up by stopping halfway through or at the bottom of the motion and holding that position for three to five seconds. Need more of a challenge? Hold a plate across your chest, or put on your body armor or a weighted vest.

Grip, Hips, Shoulders, and Elbows: Training for the Leg Tuck

Your favorite and mine — the Leg Tuck (LTK) — is how the Army assesses your strength in four key areas: your grip, arms, shoulders, and trunk. They're all the same moving parts you use to get over an obstacle or climb a rope. You'll get better at the LTK with practice, but you can do plenty of other exercises to improve your performance, too.

Bent-leg raises

Bent-leg raises were part of 4 for the Core in PRT, and they target your abs, hip flexors, and other parts of your core. All you need is body weight and a flat surface. Here's how to do what you see in Figure 8-23:

1. **Lie faceup on the floor with your palms facing down.**

2. **Get into the starting position by bending your hips and knees 90 degrees so it looks like you're sitting in a chair.**

    Keep your spine neutral — don't press it into the ground.

3. **Hold your upper body still and extend your legs until they're straight, hovering your feet 6 inches above the floor.**

4. **Bring your body back to the starting position to complete one rep.**

Try to do three sets of 10 reps each, keeping your pace steady for every rep.

TIP

EXAMPLE

The leg tuck and twist

This exercise develops strength and mobility while enhancing your balance as part of Conditioning Drill 1 in Army PRT. You don't need any equipment to do it just like it's depicted in Figure 8-24:

1. **Sit with your spine and trunk straight while leaning backward 45 degrees.**

2. **Point your legs directly in front of you and raise them 8 to 12 inches off the ground to get into the starting position.**

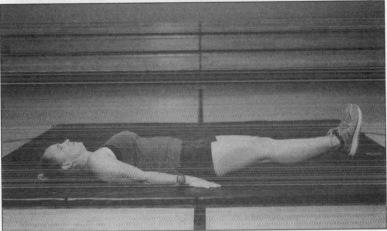

FIGURE 8-23:
Bent-leg raise.

Zack McCrory

3. **Tighten your core and rotate on your right buttock while drawing your knees toward your right shoulder.**

WARNING

Don't jerk your legs. Keep your movements slow and steady.

4. **Return to the starting position and rotate on your left buttock, drawing your knees to your left shoulder before returning to the starting position again to complete one rep.**

EXAMPLE

Shoot for three sets of 10 reps each.

FIGURE 8-24:
Leg tuck and
twist.

Zack McCrory

Mixed-grip pull-ups

The mixed-grip pull-up is another two-in-one exercise that gets you bonus results. This simple exercise works your back, biceps, delts, forearms, and traps, which you need for the LTK. Check out what it looks like in Figure 8-25 and do a few yourself like this:

1. **Grasp a pull-up bar with an alternating grip (one palm facing you and the other facing away from you).**

   Straighten your arms completely at the bottom, but don't lock out your elbows or let them overextend.

FIGURE 8-35:
Mixed-grip
pull-up.

2. **Zip up your core and pull yourself up until your chest is even with the bar; then pause.**

Act like you're pulling the bar down — it's a head game. And bring your back muscles to the party when you're halfway up. Don't rely only on your arms!

3. **Lower yourself under control to complete one rep.**

TIP

WARNING

Never let the tension leave your back, even when you're in the lower position. A dead hang can put too much strain on your bicep tendons and rotator cuffs.

EXAMPLE

Pull-ups are a hard exercise to gauge, because outside the gym, few people can actually do them. Start with assisted pull-ups twice a week if you're struggling to knock out one — have a battle buddy hold your knees and lend a hand when necessary — and try to work your way up to 8 to 10 unassisted pull-ups over time. Then, you can start doing them in sets. The key: Keep pulling that bar down toward the ground until you reach muscle failure and have to drop from the bar.

Rope climbs

Rope climbs are all about upper body strength, although you should use your feet as brakes (and your legs as backup muscles if you need them). You can use several techniques for rope climbing, but they all involve pulling yourself up hand-over-hand. The one that's most likely to help you prep for the LTK on the ACFT goes like this:

1. **Grab the rope high with your dominant hand higher than your non-dominant hand.**

2. **Let the rope fall on the outside of one of your legs.**

3. **Scoop up a length of rope with the foot opposite it, pressing the foot closest to the rope down so it looks like you're standing on a step.**

   The rope at your feet should look like a sideways *S*. The foot that's closest to the rope is standing in it, while the other foot is holding up the bottom portion of the *S*. (Figure 8-26 shows the proper foot position.)

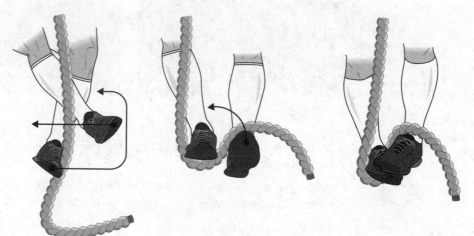

FIGURE 8-26: Foot position for the rope climb.

©John Wiley & Sons, Inc.

4. **Pull up your feet by bending your hips, keeping the rope between your feet.**

5. **Push yourself up using your leg muscles so you return to a standing position.**

6. **Keep repeating until you reach the top, and then release a little tension in your hands and feet to slide back down the rope under control.**

EXAMPLE

Try to climb the rope two or three times a week. Get as high as you can each time. When you've mastered the technique using your feet, take a little leg work out of it and rely more on your upper body to pull yourself up.

Isometric hangs

Remember when you were a kid and did the "bent-arm hang" in gym class? That's a type of isometric exercise (and the one I'm about to describe). *Isometric training* is work that exerts tension without lengthening or shortening the muscle, so when you're holding a heavy bag of groceries, doing a plank, or pausing at the top of a pull-up, you're doing isometrics. The bent-arm hang is one of the best isometric exercises you can do to prep for the LTK, so get a look at the starting position in Figure 8-27 and follow these instructions:

1. **Using an over- or underhand grip, grasp a pull-up bar or rings with your hands shoulder-width apart.**

TIP

   The underhand grip may be a little easier if you're a beginner.

2. **Raise your body (alone or assisted) so that your elbows are slightly flexed.**

3. **Hold the position for 30 to 60 seconds and then lower yourself under control.**

TIP

Engage all your upper body muscles and don't let any of that tension go until you let go of the bar.

FIGURE 8-27:
Starting position of an isometric hang with underhand or overhand grip.

Zack McCrory

EXAMPLE

Try to work these into your routine twice a week, doing two or three sets of three hangs each.

Side pillar holds

A static side pillar hold in Figure 8-28 is a side plank, and it's a great variation of the standard plank I discuss in the earlier section "Planks." This full-body exercise strengthens your whole core, plus your hips, pecs, and shoulders, with a big-time focus on your obliques. Here's how you do it safely and effectively:

1. **Lie on your side with your feet stacked and one elbow directly below your shoulder so that your forearm points out in the direction you're facing.**

2. **Contract your core and raise your hips until your body is in a straight line from head to toe.**

   Balance on the side of your foot, not the sole.

3. **Hold the position without letting your hips drop, and when you're done on that side, switch to the other.**

   If your hips sag, you risk injury, so sagging means you need to tighten your core for one last effort or switch sides.

EXAMPLE

Do three or four side pillar holds at a time. Hold them for as long as you can. You can do these exercises every day (except on rest and recovery days, which I cover in Chapter 18).

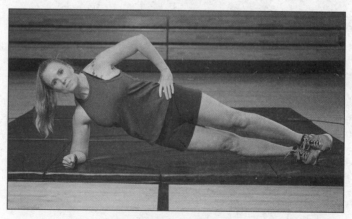

FIGURE 8-28: Side pillar hold.

Zack McCrory

The contralateral dead bug

Contralateral dead bugs aren't as gross as they sound. Runners use this exercise to target trunk muscles, such as the erector spinae, obliques, rectus abdominis, and transverse abdominis, because they help maintain good form while running — and they're all going to help you on the LTK, too. The contralateral dead bug in Figure 8-29 goes like this:

1. **Lie flat on your back with a natural curve in your spine.**

2. **Extend your arms straight up above your shoulders and your legs straight up above your hips; this is the starting position.**

   Perform this movement (and all the movements in the exercise) slowly and deliberately.

FIGURE 8-29: Contralateral dead bug.

Zack McCrory

3. Slowly lower your right leg to the ground while simultaneously lowering your left arm so it goes above your head.

Your arm and leg should nearly touch the ground. Hover at the bottom for five seconds.

WARNING

Don't arch your back. Arching can defeat the purpose of the exercise and cause injury. Stay on the safe side and keep a neutral spine at every point (which means you need to engage your core right out of the gate).

4. Raise your right leg and left arm to the starting position under control.

5. Slowly lower your left leg and right arm, mirroring the position you held in Step 3.

EXAMPLE

This exercise seems easy when you first start, but after you've completed three sets of 5 to 10 reps on each side, you may think differently. If you're ready for a bigger challenge, lower both arms and both legs at the same time.

Is, Ys, and Ts

Shoulder stability does more than help you on the ACFT. It helps prevent injuries, too. One of the simplest ways to become more stable in the shoulders and develop those small muscles is to do Is, Ys, and Ts. Choose a pair of dumbbells with a manageable shoulder weight, find a stability ball, and check out Figure 8-30. (You can do these moves on the floor if you don't have a stability ball.) Then, keep your thumbs pointed toward the ceiling and do the following:

1. Lie on your stomach over the stability ball.

2. Holding the dumbbells, extend your arms in front of you so your body looks like the letter *I*.

Lift your arms by squeezing your shoulder blades together in your back. Keep your shoulders down, away from your ears, throughout each movement.

3. Lower your arms to the ground.

4. Raise your arms at a 45-degree angle from your shoulders, forming the letter *Y*, with your thumbs pointed toward the ceiling.

5. Lower your arms to the ground.

6. Raise your arms so they're straight out and you look like a lowercase *T*.

TIP

You can throw in a *W* at the end of each rep for good measure. Pull your elbows toward your hips, keeping your thumbs pointed toward the ceiling, and bring your hands to shoulder-level before extending them back out and lowering them to the ground.

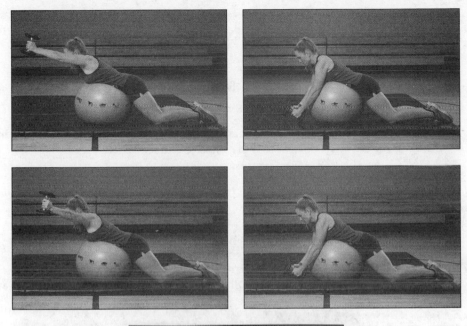

Zack McCrory

FIGURE 8-30:
Is, Ys, and *Ts.*

Do three sets of 10 reps each. If you're new to shoulder-strengthening exercises, start without any weights at all and work your way up.

EXAMPLE

Kettlebell pull-throughs

A kettlebell pull-through adds dynamic, 3D movement to a static plank, and it's great for building functional strength in your core. (Chapter 5 has details on 3D movements.) Just moving a kettlebell from side to side while you're performing a correct one-armed plank puts your core into overdrive. Here's how to pull it off (and you can see what it looks like in Figure 8-31):

1. Set up in a high plank position, engaging your front and back core, with a kettlebell by your left side.

2. **Keep your chest parallel to the floor and resist moving your hips while you slide your right arm under your body and grab the kettlebell's handle.**

3. **Drag the kettlebell under your body and place it on your left side.**

4. **Place your left hand back on the ground.**

5. **Reach your right arm under your body, grab the kettlebell, and drag it to your right side to complete one repetition.**

EXAMPLE

Do three sets of 10 to 12 reps, two or three times per week.

FIGURE 8-31:
Kettlebell
pull-through.

Zack McCrory

Internal, external, and elevated shoulder rotations

Internal, external, and elevated shoulder rotations can improve stability and provide you with extra strength to use on the LTK (and other ACFT events, as well as in your everyday life). Here's how to do them.

TIP

Keep your working elbow tucked in throughout each of these exercises, and avoid using momentum to execute the movements. Focus on using only your muscular strength, and don't be afraid to lighten the load to avoid injury.

Internal shoulder rotations (shown in Figure 8-32):

1. **Grasp a dumbbell or secured tube band in one hand with your thumb pointed toward the ceiling.**

2. **Tuck your elbow into your waist and place your forearm in front of you at a 90-degree angle from your body.**

3. **Slowly and deliberately hinge your arm to the side until it's on the same plane as your body; this movement looks like opening a door.**

4. **Slowly and deliberately hinge your arm back to the front so that it looks like you're closing a door.**

EXAMPLE

Aim for one or two sets of 10 reps on each side.

FIGURE 8-32:
Internal shoulder rotation.

Zack McCrory

External shoulder rotations (shown in Figure 8-33):

1. **Grasp a dumbbell or secured tube band in one hand with your thumb pointed toward the ceiling.**

2. **With your elbow at a 90-degree angle, fold your arm across your body so your palm is facing — and almost touching — the side of your abdomen to find your starting position.**

FIGURE 8-33: External shoulder rotation.

3. **Slowly and deliberately rotate your arm out to the opposite side in a half-circle, like it's a revolving door.**

4. **Return to the starting position slowly and deliberately.**

EXAMPLE

Do one or two sets of 10 reps on each side.

Elevated shoulder rotations (shown in Figure 8-34):

1. **Hold a dumbbell or secured tube band in one hand with your thumb pointed toward your body.**

2. **Raise your arm like one-half of a goalpost, maintaining a 90-degree bend in your elbow, to set up your starting position.**

3. **Slowly and deliberately lower your arm, hinging at the shoulder, until your forearm is parallel to the ground.**

4. **Slowly and deliberately raise your arm back to the starting position.**

EXAMPLE

Knock out one or two sets of 10 reps on each side.

FIGURE 8-34: Elevated shoulder rotation.

Zack McCrory

When My Granny Was 91: How to Improve Your Two-Mile Run Time

You run with your unit a few times a week for good reason: Running has been proven to improve physical and mental health. It can reduce stress, improve heart health, and boost your cardiorespiratory endurance, and all those things help you "be all that you can be." Although it's not always easy (I'm looking at you, division runs with that accordion effect) and it's not always fun, becoming a decent runner has plenty of benefits.

Now, with all that said, know that *too much* hard-surface running can be rough on your body. It may put you at risk for common running injuries, like IT band syndrome, shin splints, and plantar fasciitis. When possible, your best bet is to run on a surface designed for running, like a track, a natural trail, or even grass. Look at Sir Mo Farah, a legend of long-distance running; he runs about 130 miles each week, and 80 to 90 percent of that is on grass. You can't avoid running on pavement when you're doing PT with your unit, but you *can* make it a point to try different surfaces when you're training on your own.

Regardless of where you run, though, plenty of running-related exercises can help you improve your time, form, and endurance.

Sprint interval training

Sprint interval training is a great way to teach your body how to efficiently switch between aerobic exercise and anaerobic exercise. Sprinting is an anaerobic exercise, and having the ability to do it helps you on the ACFT. (And, if you're following the Army's line of reasoning, it helps you on the battlefield, too. *I'm up, he sees me, I'm down!*)

To perform sprint intervals, which you've almost certainly done before during PT as 30:60s or 60:120s, you need a watch that shows seconds or a few markers on your running surface. Whether you're doing 30:60s or 60:120s, they follow the same principle: You sprint like you stole something for the first (and lower) amount of time and then ease off into an active rest period by jogging for the longer period. When your active rest period is over, sprint again. Keep going until you've done five or six intervals — and do them every run day — and you should see your run time and cardiorespiratory endurance improve dramatically.

No watch? No problem. You can use markers along your running path to indicate where you should sprint. Sometimes I say to myself, "I'm going to sprint to that third light pole and then jog after that." (For the record, I don't always listen.)

TIP

When you run, whether you're sprinting or jogging, keep your arms at a 90-degree angle and make sure they're moving forward and back (rotating at your shoulder) rather than swinging side to side. Keep your trunk straight to give your lungs as much capacity as possible.

The key with sprint interval training is that you're doing it. You don't have to divide your distance or time into perfect segments. You just have to kick your anaerobic power into gear from time to time, and then shift back down to normal power for active rest. It doesn't have to be perfect.

EXAMPLE

Do six sprints, six active recoveries at a time — that's one set — each time you run.

Hill repeats

Hill repeats help you build strength, improve speed, and build resilience when you're running. Whether you're running up a slight grade or tackling one of the hills everyone remembers not-so-fondly from Basic Combat Training, the core principle is the same: You run up the hill fast, and you jog down it at a relaxed pace.

Try to find a hill that's about 100 meters long (or longer, if you're up for it). If you don't have a hill, make one on a treadmill at the gym by increasing your incline sharply. You have to go to flat-surface running rather than downhill, but it's still better than *not* doing hill repeats.

TIP

Don't stare at your feet or at the top of the hill. Look 10 to 15 feet in front of you so you don't get overwhelmed by the hill but can still stay focused.

EXAMPLE

Do hill repeats once or twice per week. Try to do at least three up and three down.

Walking lunge

Like regular lunges, walking lunges work all the major muscles in your lower body (your quads, hamstrings, glutes, and calves), but with the added benefit of challenging your core because you have to balance as you move. Pick a distance, like 25 meters, and follow these steps:

1. **Stand with your feet hip-width apart, your chest up, and your core engaged.**

2. **Take a big step forward with your left foot and lower your body so that both your knees are bent at a 90-degree angle.**

   Your left quad is parallel to the ground, and your right knee is hovering just above the ground. Don't overextend — you don't need to touch your knee on the ground to get the full benefits of this exercise.

3. **Push off with your right foot, bring it forward, and step straight into another forward lunge.**

TIP

Keep your torso upright and your core engaged with every move. You can put your hands on the back of your head, like you're doing a sit-up, or you can put them on your hips.

Check out Figure 8-35 to see what the walking lunge looks like in action.

You can vary this exercise by holding dumbbells while you lunge, or by wearing your IOTV (as long as it's not so tight that it restricts your breathing).

EXAMPLE

Aim for three sets of back-and-forth walking lunges a couple times a week, and increase the distance or the number of sets you do as you become stronger.

FIGURE 8-35:
Walking lunge.

Zack McCrory

Barbell squats

Barbell squats are a weighted version of standard squats. You can see a barbell squat in Figure 8-36, and then follow these instructions to perform your own:

1. **Holding a barbell across your shoulders behind your back, stand with your feet pointed out at about 30 degrees.**

You can choose a wide stance (shoulder-width or slightly wider) to strengthen your inner thighs and groin muscles a bit more or pick a narrower stance to put more focus on your quads.

2. **Push your knees out while moving your hips back, distributing your weight evenly throughout your feet.**

3. **Squat until your hips are slightly lower than your knees.**

4. **Use your leg muscles to push yourself back up to a standing position.**

   Keep your feet flat on the floor and distribute your weight evenly as you push yourself back up.

FIGURE 8-36:
Barbell squats.

Zack McCrory

You don't have to squat lower after you break parallel (that's what happens when your hips are slightly lower than your knees; your thighs are slightly angled past the parallel position). In fact, a lot of people get hurt by going too low. You still get all the benefits a squat has to offer if you break parallel and come right back up.

WARNING

This exercise has a few potential pitfalls:

>> Don't rest the bar against your neck. If you feel it on your cervical spine — the part of your spine that makes up your neck — it's too high. Lower it so it rests on your traps or between your traps and rear shoulders (at the top of your shoulder blades).

>> Don't let your lower back arch. Keep a neutral spine (which happens more naturally if you engage your core) to prevent your disks from getting squeezed under the bar's weight.

>> Don't let your knees collapse inward when you squat, and try to keep them in line with your toes. Generally, your knees should end up above the tops of your toes when you're at the lowest point of your squat; if they go much past your toes, your form is off.

>> During the squat, keep your chest up and look at a spot on the floor about 10 feet in front of you the whole time. If you're wearing a shirt with a logo on it, someone looking at you should be able to see that logo the whole time you're squatting. When you lean too far forward, you put a lot of strain on your lower back, take the load off your quads, and risk losing your balance.

EXAMPLE

Squat two or three times a week, doing three to five sets of 8 to 12 reps each time.

Calf raises

Calf raises are simple (you can do them with or without a loaded barbell or a set of dumbbells) and powerful. They work out your gastrocnemius, tibialis posterior, and soleus muscles. If you're locking your core and using your posterior chain, you'll also feel them up the backs of your thighs and in your glutes. A calf raise involves nothing more than standing flat-footed, raising your heels, and stopping on the ball of your foot. Check them out in Figure 8-37.

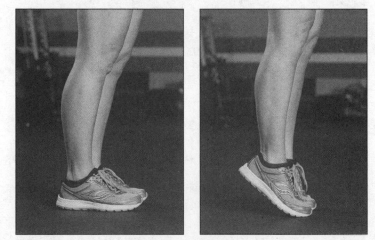

FIGURE 8-37: Calf raise.

Zack McCrory

You can vary your calf raises by doing them on a single leg at a time, bending your knees slightly, or holding weights in your hands.

Don't roll your ankles from side to side while you're doing calf raises. Go straight up and down.

Do three or four sets of 10 calf raises each a couple of times a week. When those become easy, add weight.

Glute bridges

Glute bridges engage your glutes, hamstrings, core, lower back, abs, obliques, and hip flexors, so a lot of moving parts need to work together. That's exactly what you want from an exercise, right? You can see what a successful glute bridge looks like in Figure 8-38 before you follow these instructions:

1. **Lie on your back with your knees bent and feet flat on the ground.**

2. **Place your arms at your sides with your palms facing down.**

3. **Lift your hips off the ground until your knees, hips, and shoulders form a straight line (you'll have a slight bend in your neck).**

   Flex your glutes at the top and keep your core engaged, and be careful not to hyperextend by pushing your hips too high into the air.

4. **Hold that position for three to five seconds before easing back down to the ground.**

You can do glute bridges very frequently — even several times a week. Squeeze them into your routine at least two or three times, and perform three to five sets of 8 to 12 bridges each.

FIGURE 8-38: Glute bridge.

Zack McCrory

Chapter **9**

Stretching for Recovery and Peak Performance

Recovery is an important part of athletic training because that's when the body repairs damaged tissues, restocks energy stores, and replaces fluid. You need between 24 and 48 hours to let your muscles recover between workouts. That doesn't mean you have to give your whole body a break, though — just the muscles you worked.

Without enough time to fix itself up, your body simply continues to break down, and you get results that are exactly the opposite of what you're looking for. When people overtrain (even professional athletes), they're setting themselves up for failure.

REMEMBER

You don't get stronger *during* a workout. You get stronger *between* workouts. It starts with immediate recovery, right after a workout, and continues until you start your next workout.

Stretching is a huge part both of recovery and of what I focus on in this chapter. I include some official Army recovery stretches; however, these stretches are limited, so I go into more detail on post-workout and recovery stretches for each part of your body as well.

WARNING

Don't stretch cold muscles. Doing so may decrease your strength and hamper your ability to move explosively. Worse, you can do damage. Before you stretch, do some light activity like walking or taking a short jog to get your blood flowing and make your muscles more pliable.

Bouncing Back Stronger through Recovery

Working out your muscles is only part of the battle. To become stronger, you have to allow your body to recuperate through recovery. You also have to eat the right foods, which I cover in Chapter 21, and watch out for overtraining, which can hold back your progress and cause injury

Short-term recovery is one of two types of recovery your body needs. (The other, as you may have guessed, is long-term recovery). Immediate short-term recovery involves getting into a low-intensity exercise after a workout to promote blood flow to your muscles so they can heal better and faster. The day after a workout is also part of short-term recovery.

Getting back on your feet after training with active recovery

You can recover actively or passively. Though some days it's fine for your body to be mostly inactive while you binge-watch your favorite shows (that's *passive recovery*), active recovery is actually good for your body. Active recovery can

>> Reduce delayed-onset muscle soreness (see the following section)

>> Promote blood flow to sore and stiff areas, which loosens things up

>> Elevate the heart rate without putting workout-level stress on joints or muscles

>> Help you avoid post-exercise fatigue after heavy training days

>> Improve your mood (and possibly even help safeguard your mental health)

>> Increase your cardiovascular fitness and endurance

Active recovery immediately following a workout is really about keeping your heart rate elevated (but not necessarily in the cardio exercise zone) so your muscles don't freeze up on you. Maybe you spend 15 minutes walking briskly on the treadmill with your heart rate between 120 and 140 beats per minute, swim a few laps, or go on a light hike. You also want to get up every hour and walk a bit throughout the day, regardless of which muscle group you worked. What matters is that you're moving around and getting your heart rate up a little, which does wonders for your whole body.

Active recovery the day after a workout is also incredibly important. Sometimes working another muscle group counts as active recovery, and sometimes heavy-duty cardio counts. However, other forms of active recovery include yoga, light resistance training, and dynamic stretching or mobility work. Even foam rolling and massage can count as active recovery between workouts. Check out *Yoga For Dummies* by Larry Payne and Georg Feuerstein and *Stretching For Dummies* by LaReine Chabut, both published by Wiley, if you need to boost your confidence in those areas.

Discovering delayed-onset muscle soreness

As a fitness instructor, one of my favorite things to hear is, "Angie, I've been thinking about you all weekend. Every time I moved, I got mad at you all over again." Sure, I want people to be sore; when they're sore, we both know growth is happening.

What these people experienced is *delayed-onset muscle soreness,* or DOMS. Although being sore is rough, it's a big sign that your muscles are doing what they're supposed to do after you've challenged yourself. This soreness is the result of micro-trauma to your muscles, which can become inflamed as they start to repair themselves. You don't experience DOMS if you aren't breaking down your muscles and making them stronger; you only become sore if you're challenging yourself and your muscles are trying to adapt.

Things you can do to minimize DOMS include stretching, which I cover throughout this chapter, and the following:

>> Stay hydrated before, during, and after workouts.

>> Engage in active recovery to increase circulation.

>> Get enough sleep so your body can produce adequate human growth hormone, or HGH, which kicks into high gear while you're in the deep stages of slumber.

DOMS VERSUS INJURY

Some types of pain aren't normal after a workout, but how do you know whether you're feeling plain old muscle soreness or you've experienced an injury? Typically, you look at when the pain starts, how long it lasts, what type of pain you're experiencing, and whether it's symmetrical (the same on both sides of the body). You don't feel DOMS while you're working out, but you're likely to feel an injury immediately. DOMS typically goes away (or at least improves significantly) within a few days, while pain from an injury is more likely to last. With DOMS, your muscles feel tight and achy, while injuries tend to produce sharper, more acute pain. Often, DOMS pain is symmetrical, and injury pain isn't.

If you suspect you're injured after a workout, "waiting it out" to see whether the pain improves on its own isn't worth it. The best thing you can do is go to sick call or schedule an appointment with your primary care provider (PCP). You should *never* try to push through the pain, because you're still going to come out on the other side in pain, and your injury will most likely be even worse. See Chapter 12 for tips on overcoming injuries and minimizing discomfort while you're waiting to see your PCP.

Building in recovery days and taking care of injuries

Someone who's new to working out may need two or three built-in recovery days per week, but if you're a soldier, your body is probably used to working out Monday through Friday. You may be fine with one day a week of active recovery (discussed in the earlier section "Getting back on your feet after training with active recovery"). However, the most important thing is to listen to your body. If you're getting burned out, feeling extreme exhaustion, feeling pain or persistent soreness that doesn't go away, seeing reduced performance, having problems sleeping, or noticing emotional changes, you likely need more rest than you're allowing yourself.

REMEMBER

I really can't stress this point enough: If you're injured while working out (or because of working out), basic recovery days aren't going to cut it. You need to go to sick call or make an appointment with your PCP. Some of the most common injuries people suffer, like sprains, strains, and inflammation, only get worse without treatment. If you notice an injury isn't getting better with time, you may need physical therapy — but you can't get that (or a profile) if you don't see your doctor first.

Avoiding overtraining syndrome

Overtraining and skipping recovery is harmful to your body — and it can lead to lower physical fitness levels, which is exactly what you want to avoid. Feeling like a rest day will set you back is normal, but going hard in the paint without resting can lead to overtraining syndrome. *Overtraining syndrome* is a real condition that's characterized by pain in the muscles and joints, a lack of energy or a washed-out feeling, headaches, decreased immunity, loss of enthusiasm for working out, increased incidence of injuries, and a compulsive need to exercise. You're more likely to develop overtraining syndrome if you don't build recovery days into your routine, so do yourself a big favor: Prevent it.

Here's more detail on what happens when you think rest days are a crutch:

>> You deplete your body's glycogen stores, which you need for energy.

>> You lose muscle mass because you're consistently breaking down your muscle fibers and they don't bounce back.

>> You experience extreme soreness, feel physically exhausted, and have a tough time getting moving (physically *and* mentally).

>> You can suffer negative mental health effects, like increased tension, likelihood for depression, irritability, and even anger.

>> Your corticosteroid levels increase. Cortisone and cortisol are no good for weight loss (in fact, they can even lead to belly fat retention), and they depress your immune system so you're more likely to get sick.

>> Your resting heart rate and exercise level heart rate both increase.

>> Your performance levels go down. Your muscles can't regenerate and come back stronger, so your performance declines.

Stretching Out Your Workout Recovery

Stretching after a workout helps your body cool down (and tells your heart to get back to your normal resting heart rate). Stretching between workouts, whether it's in the evening before bed or throughout the day on a rest day, is essential for overall fitness. It makes you more flexible and mobile, and it keeps your muscles strong and healthy. Work some type of stretching into your daily routine to lessen your risk of injury and feel better, too. If you're pressed for time, at least stretch your calves, hamstrings, hip flexors, and quads every day.

REMEMBER

Stretching's effects are cumulative. Your muscles didn't get tight overnight, and they won't loosen up completely overnight. Becoming more flexible can take weeks; you have to stretch over time and stay committed.

Stretching comes in many forms, including the following:

>> **Static stretching:** The most common form of stretching, *static stretching* just involves extending a muscle as far as you can (comfortably, of course) and holding the position for 20 to 30 seconds. Active static stretching involves pulling or pushing on the muscle to make the stretch more intense, and passive static stretching involves someone or something else (like an elastic band) applying force to the muscle. Most of the stretches I cover in the rest of the chapter are static stretches.

>> **Dynamic stretching:** *Dynamic stretching* involves continuous movement that puts your joints and muscles through a full range of motion. You can read more about it in the later section "Doing Dynamic Stretches for Multiple Muscles."

>> **Active isolated stretching:** You repeat these short, two-second stretches several times; at each interval, you try to increase your stretch by a small amount.

>> **Myofascial release:** Hard foam rollers are usually the weapon of choice for myofascial release. The roller applies gentle, sustained pressure on your connective tissues. You roll back and forth over the roller, which can help relieve tension and increase flexibility. If you're interested in learning more about this type of myofascial release, I recommend *Foam Rolling For Dummies*, by Mike Ryan (Wiley).

WARNING

Another type of stretching, *ballistic stretching*, uses your body's momentum to force it beyond its normal range of motion. It's essentially bouncing when you stretch, like when you sit on the floor and jerkily bounce your trunk forward to touch your toes. I (along with the American Academy of Orthopaedic Surgeons and the American College of Sports Medicine) don't recommend ballistic stretching because of the potential for injury, and science generally says that it has no benefits over other, safer forms of stretching, like dynamic stretching.

REMEMBER

In all the stretching sections in this chapter, I recommend holding a stretch for 20 to 30 seconds at a time. You can adjust this time to whatever works for you — if you want to hold a stretch longer, go for it! You should hold these stretches from 15 to 60 seconds. Any shorter than 15 seconds, and the stretch may not be effective; any longer than 60 seconds can make your muscle feel stiffer, according to the National Academy of Sports Medicine.

Attending to Army Stretches

When you're doing Army PRT with your unit, you perform highly regulated Army-style stretches. They're all good stretches and can help you with post-workout mobility, lessen the effects of DOMS (covered in the earlier section "Discovering delayed-onset muscle soreness"), and send a signal to your body that it can start to relax. I've left out the commands "Ready, Stretch," "Starting position, Move," and "Change position," as well as the technical aspects (such as "keep your fingers and thumbs extended and joined") in the Army stretches in the following sections because you're already familiar with them.

Overhead arm pull

The overhead arm pull is a tension-releaser for your triceps, and if you lean to the side like the Army prescribes, you stretch your lats, too. It can help increase your flexibility in your arms, shoulders, and trunk. Figure 9-1 shows the overhead arm pull.

FIGURE 9-1:
The overhead arm pull.

Zack McCrory

Here's how to do the overhead arm pull in accordance with PRT:

1. **Raise your left arm overhead, placing your left hand behind your head and as far down your back as you can reach.**

2. **Grasp above your left elbow with your right hand and pull your upper body to the right.**

   Lean your body to the side as if your back is against a wall. Don't lean back or forward as you tip.

3. **Hold the position for 20 to 30 seconds and then switch arms.**

Rear lunge

The rear lunge loosens up your hip flexors and increases flexibility in your trunk. Check out Figure 9-2 for a closer look at proper form on the rear lunge.

FIGURE 9-2:
The rear lunge.

Zack McCrory

The official instructions for the rear lunge go this way:

1. **Take an exaggerated step backward with your left leg, touching down with the ball of your left foot.**

   Keep your core engaged so your back stays straight throughout the stretch, and keep your feet facing forward.

2. **Hold the position for 20 to 30 seconds and switch legs, repeating the same step on the other side.**

Extend and flex

The extend and flex helps stretch out your hip flexors, abs, lower back, hamstrings, and calves if you're doing it with proper form. Figure 9-3 shows each position of the extend and flex in action. Because this stretch targets so many areas, it's a great one to do when you don't have a lot of time.

To do the extend and flex, follow these steps:

1. **Put your body in the front leaning rest position.**

   Keep your feet together throughout the stretch.

2. **Sag in the middle, moving slowly while you keep your arms straight and look upward (Figure 9-3a).**

   Let your thighs and pelvis rest on the ground, and relax your back muscles. Point your toes to the rear.

3. **Hold the position for 20 to 30 seconds.**

4. **Slightly bend your knees and walk your hands back toward your legs.**

5. **Straighten your legs and try to keep your heels together and on the ground (Figure 9-3b).**

6. **Hold the position for 20 to 30 seconds.**

Thigh stretch

Nothing beats a good, old-fashioned quad stretch, and that's what the Army's thigh stretch (shown in Figure 9-4) is all about. It gets your hip flexors, too, and you get to sit on the ground while you're performing the whole stretch.

(a)

FIGURE 9-3:
The extend and
flex.

(b)

Zack McCrory

FIGURE 9-4:
The thigh stretch.

Zack McCrory

Although this stretch has plenty of variations you can use on your own, these are the steps for the Army's thigh stretch:

1. **Sit on the ground with your feet straight out in front of you.**

   Engage your core so your trunk stays straight throughout the stretch.

2. **Roll onto your right side and put your right forearm on the ground, keeping it perpendicular to your chest.**

3. **Grasp your left ankle with your left hand and pull your left heel toward your buttocks while you pull your whole leg rearward.**

4. **Push your left thigh farther to the rear with the bottom of your right foot.**

5. **Hold the position for 20 to 30 seconds and then switch sides.**

Single-leg over

The single-leg over stretches your hips and lower back muscles, and it can help increase your mobility in those areas over time. Figure 9-5 shows the single-leg over, which is the last stretch in the Recovery Drill of PRT.

FIGURE 9-5:
The single-leg over.

Zack McCrory

To perform the single-leg over, follow these instructions:

1. **Turn your body to the right.**

2. **Bend your left knee to 90 degrees over your right leg and grasp the outside of your left knee with your right hand as you pull it toward the right.**

3. **Hold the position for 20 to 30 seconds before switching sides.**

Loosening up Your Legs and Hips

You use your legs and hips all day, every day, whether you're spending a lot of time sitting or you're always on the go. If you stretch nothing else in a day, squeeze some time in for these two areas.

TECHNICAL STUFF

When your hips are too tight, you're prone to aches and pains all over your body. Tight hip flexors even make properly rotating your pelvis difficult, which forces your lower back to over-compensate. That can lead to lower back injury.

Standing hamstring stretch

The standing hamstring stretch helps increase your pelvic mobility, which you need to walk, sit, and move in general. Strong, flexible hamstrings also provide a little extra support for your back. Figure 9-6 shows the standing hamstring stretch, but you don't have to reach all the way to the ground. Instead, reach as far as you can; over time, you'll find that the backs of your legs become more flexible. Eventually, you'll probably even be able to touch the ground with flat palms yourself.

FIGURE 9-6:
Standing hamstring stretch.

Zack McCrory

To perform this hamstring stretch, follow these steps:

1. **Cross your right foot in front of your left foot.**

2. **Slowly tip at the hip, lowering your upper body with your hands toward the floor while keeping your knees straight.**

3. **Hold the position for 20 to 30 seconds before switching sides.**

TIP

You don't have to cross your legs; you can keep them side-by-side in a natural position, too. You can also perform the hamstring stretch while you're sitting on the ground with your feet directly in front of you. Keep your toes pointed toward the ceiling and bend forward from your waist, keeping your legs straight.

Piriformis stretch

Your *piriformis muscle* is what helps you rotate your hip and turn your leg and foot outward. It starts at the lower spine and connects to the top of your thighbone, running diagonally over the sciatic nerve (which runs vertically right beneath it) It needs some TLC every day because a tight piriformis can cause pain, numbness, and tingling on the back of your leg all the way down to your foot if it irritates your sciatic nerve. If your piriformis is too tight, you can feel spasms and a literal pain in your butt. You can see a simple piriformis stretch in Figure 9 7.

Follow these steps to stretch your piriformis:

1. **Lie on your back with both knees bent and both feet flat on the floor.**

2. **Rest your left ankle over your right knee, like you're sitting in a chair and crossing your legs.**

3. **Use your hands to pull your right thigh toward your chest.**

4. **Hold the position for 20 to 30 seconds and switch sides.**

TIP

You don't have to cross your ankle over your knee to stretch your piriformis. You can simply lie on the floor and pull one knee up to your chest, then use your hand to pull it toward the opposite shoulder.

Frog stretch

The frog stretch is a yoga pose formally known as *mandukasana* that opens up your hips and groin muscles. It also targets the adductors (the muscles in your inner thighs) and core. Figure 9-8 depicts this stretch.

FIGURE 9-7:
Piriformis stretch.

Zack McCrory

FIGURE 9-8:
Frog stretch.

Zack McCrory

Start slowly with this stretch, and don't force your body into it if you're not ready:

1. **Start in a tabletop position with your hands beneath your shoulders and knees beneath your hips.**

2. **Slowly move your knees out toward each side.**

3. **Turn your feet out toward each side and flex your ankles so the insides of your feet, inner ankles, and inner knees are touching the floor.**

4. **Lower your body so you're resting on your forearms.**

WARNING

Don't try to force your knees apart to get closer to the ground. Stop lowering your body if you feel any pain — you just need to feel the stretch, nothing more.

5. **Hold the position for 20 to 30 seconds.**

Butterfly stretch

The butterfly stretch, which you can see in Figure 9-9, gives your groin and inner thighs a little relief after or between workouts.

These are the step-by-step instructions for the butterfly stretch:

1. **Sit on the floor with your legs in front of you.**

2. **Pull your feet in toward your groin and touch the bottoms of your feet together.**

3. **Hold your feet with your hands while you rest your elbows on your knees.**

4. **Keep your back straight and let your knees fall toward the ground.**

   You can apply gentle pressure on your knees if you don't feel your inner thighs stretching.

WARNING

   Don't bounce your legs up and down. Hold them still unless you're pushing them farther toward the ground. In that case, keep your movements slow and deliberate, and stop as soon as the stretch becomes uncomfortable.

5. **Hold the position for 20 to 30 seconds.**

FIGURE 9-9:
Butterfly stretch.

Zack McCrory

Lunging hip flexor stretch

Your hip flexors — a group of muscles that help manage your core stability and your gait — add support to your lower back and hips when they're functioning properly. When they're tense or tight, they can reduce your power and make you more prone to injury in that area of your body (including your lower back). These muscles are what pick up your legs when you run or go up a set of stairs. They need to be strong to perform their work, but you also need to stretch them. The lunging hip flexor stretch (see Figure 9-10) does just that.

FIGURE 9-10:
Lunging hip flexor
stretch.

Zack McCrory

Follow these steps to release your hip flexors and help them relax:

1. **Kneel on your right knee and bend your left knee in front of you with your left foot flat on the floor.**

   Both your knees should be flexed at 90-degree angles.

2. **Lean forward, pushing your right hip toward the floor.**

   Squeeze your glutes while you push your right hip toward the floor. If you don't put your knee down to the floor, that's okay.

3. **Hold the position for 20 to 30 seconds and repeat on the other side.**

Lying quad stretch

The lying quad stretch in Figure 9-11 is similar to the Army's thigh stretch (which I explain earlier in the chapter), but it doesn't require you to follow rigid rules or form unstretched body parts in potentially uncomfortable ways. You simply lie down and stretch your quads — it's that simple.

FIGURE 9-11: Lying quad stretch.

Zack McCrory

The lying quad stretch requires only that you lie on your side, prop your head in your hand, and grab the top ankle to pull it in toward your glutes. You can push your pelvis forward to get a deeper stretch, and you can rest the top knee on the bottom knee if it's easier.

TIP

Try to keep your legs together with this stretch. They don't have to touch, but keep them fairly close to get the right muscles.

Calf stretch

Your calves are responsible for a lot of hard work during the day. When you walk, the two muscles in them — the gastrocnemius and the soleus — kick into action. But if they're not flexible enough to support your everyday activities, the rest of your body has to compensate. That can lead to pain and even injury, so doing what you can to stretch your calves regularly is essential. Check out one example of a calf stretch in Figure 9-12 and try it out with the following steps:

1. **Stand near a wall with one foot back and the other foot forward.**

2. **Push your hands against the wall by leaning forward, flexing your forward knee.**

3. **Keep your rear heel flat on the ground and increase the angle of your ankle's flexion until you feel the stretch.**

FIGURE 9-12:
Calf stretch.

Zack McCrory

TIP Another great way to stretch your calves is to stand with both feet on a step or elevated surface. Drop one heel off the back of the step and put your weight on that side. You should feel your calf stretching as you increase your ankle's flexion.

Examining Essential Arm Stretches

Greater flexibility in your arms increases your range of motion, and some evidence suggests that it can prevent things like tendonitis and carpal tunnel syndrome. Even something as simple as reaching your hands over your head, opening your arms wide like you would with a chest stretch, or pushing your arms straight behind you can be beneficial to your arm muscles, but if you're like most people, you need a little extra — both after workouts and on recovery days.

Triceps stretch

Your triceps work together with your biceps to extend and flex your arms, and you probably use them more than you think you do. You can lengthen your triceps, prevent tension, and even loosen up connective tissue while improving your body's circulation easily through triceps stretches. Figure 9-13 depicts the simplest way to stretch your triceps.

FIGURE 9-13:
Triceps stretch.

Zack McCrory

This stretch is a variation on the Army's overhead arm pull (described earlier in the chapter), and you can do it anywhere. Stand with your feet shoulder-width apart and follow these steps to get a solid triceps stretch:

1. **Extend your right arm over your head and bend your elbow.**

Bring your palm as far down your back as you can.

2. **Grab your right elbow with your left hand and gently pull it to the left until you feel the stretch.**

3. **Hold the position for 20 to 30 seconds and switch sides.**

TIP

If you have shoulder mobility issues or a shoulder injury, you may still be able to stretch your triceps by bringing one arm across the front of your body and hugging it close with your other arm. Keep your stretched arm extended. (In the case of an injury, talk to your PCP or physical therapist about what kinds of stretches are okay for you to do before you try anything new.)

Standing bicep stretch

Whether you're feeling the curls you did during your last workout or you're on a recovery day, a good bicep stretch can lengthen your muscles and promote circulation, which helps your muscles repair themselves more efficiently. Check out Figure 9-14 to see one variation of a simple bicep stretch.

FIGURE 9-14:
Bicep stretch.

Zack McCrory

Stretch out both of your biceps at the same time by following these steps:

1. Extend your arms out to the side and put them parallel to the floor.

2. Turn your thumbs down so your palms are facing out behind your back.

3. Hold the position for 20 to 30 seconds and then switch sides.

TIP

For an added stretch, push your arms as far behind you as they'll comfortably go. You can make a handful of other modifications to the standing bicep stretch, such as pressing your forearm against the corner of a wall with your arm extended and then rotating your trunk away from it, or interlacing your fingers behind your back at the base of your spine, turning your palms facedown, and raising your arms up as high as you can.

Seated bicep stretch

The seated bicep stretch is a great flexibility exercise to work into your daily routine. You can see what it looks like in Figure 9-15.

FIGURE 9-15:
Seated bicep
stretch.

Zack McCrory

Follow these steps to perform the seated bicep stretch properly:

1. **Sit on the floor with your knees bent and your feet flat on the ground in front of you.**

2. **Put your hands on the floor behind you, with your fingers facing away from your body, and distribute your body weight evenly throughout each point of contact.**

3. **Slowly move your buttocks forward without moving your hands, and stop when you feel the stretch in your biceps.**

   You may also feel it in your anterior deltoids — the muscles on the fronts of your shoulders.

4. **Hold the position for 20 to 30 seconds.**

TIP

You can do this stretch without sitting on the floor if you place your hands on a table behind you and do a partial squat.

Wrist extension and flexion

Wrist extension happens when you raise the back of your hand, and *wrist flexion* happens when you bend your wrist so that your palm goes closer to your forearm. Both of these moves, which you can see in Figure 9-16, can stretch the muscles in your arms below the elbow.

FIGURE 9-16:
Wrist extension and flexion.

Forearm flexor stretch

Put a figurative twist on your wrist flexion to stretch out your forearms, which get plenty of work while you're training for the ACFT. Your lower arm works hard to grip things, ranging from the pull-up bar to kettlebells, so loosening it up is definitely important. Check out a simple forearm stretch in Figure 9-17.

Here's how to do it properly:

1. **Put one arm out straight in front of you with your palm facing up.**

2. **Use the other hand to pull your extended hand down so that your palm is facing outward and your fingers are pointing down.**

3. **Hold the position for 20 to 30 seconds and switch arms.**

FIGURE 9-17: Forearm flexor stretch.

Zack McCrory

Beefing up Your Neck, Shoulder, and Back Stretches

Stretching your neck, shoulders, and back can promote a healthy posture, prevent injury, and keep you from getting kinks, aches, and pains. Tight neck muscles feed into a cycle of poor posture. When your head and shoulders drift forward from sitting at your desk all day, standing around, or otherwise staying stationary for long periods of time, your neck muscles can shorten. The muscles in your chest can shorten, too, and when those two muscle groups are tense and shorter than they should be, poor posture becomes your default position. That leads to neck pain (including pinched nerves) and increases your chances of neck injury.

Seated shoulder squeeze

The seated shoulder squeeze, shown in Figure 9-18, helps loosen up your shoulders (and as a side benefit, your chest muscles). It gives those muscles extra blood flow and helps put your body in a proper position.

You can do the seated shoulder stretch in a backless chair or while you're seated comfortably on the ground. If you're on the ground, bend your knees and keep your feet flat on the floor. Then, follow these instructions:

1. Clasp your hands together behind your lower back.

2. Straighten your arms while squeezing your shoulder blades together.

3. Hold the position for 20 to 30 seconds.

Upper back stretch

Frequent computer and phone use don't do your upper back any favors. You may catch yourself with your head down, your shoulders hunched forward, and the middle of your spine curved from time to time — maybe because it starts to get a little achy. That means you're on the road to a stiff neck, upper or lower back pain, or persistent, nagging headaches. When you're in these positions for a sustained period of time, your upper back muscles can become tight and weak and you can't perform as well as you could if you spent some time stretching them. Figure 9-19 shows a good upper back stretch (technically, it's called a thoracic stretch).

You can do this upper back stretch just about anywhere. Here's how this stretch goes:

1. **Put your hands flat on your desk, a countertop, or even the back of a chair.**

   Your hands should be approximately shoulder-width apart.

2. **Slowly walk backward, keeping your hands in place, and lower your chest toward the ground.**

3. **Straighten your legs when your hips are behind your ankles, lifting your tailbone toward the ceiling.**

4. **Press your armpits toward the floor without moving your hands.**

FIGURE 9-19:
Upper back
stretch.

Zack McCrory

5. **When your upper body is at or just below the surface your hands are on, flip your hands over so your thumbs are pointing up or out.**

6. **Move your arms together and hold the position for 20 to 30 seconds.**

TIP

If you feel this stretch in your lower back, don't freak out. But do remember that the goal here is to stretch your upper back, so if you aren't feeling it there, raise the bottom of your rib cage as you press your armpits toward the ground.

Knee to chest stretch

Your lower back takes on a lot of stress when you work out, run, and even sit. Lower back pain is no picnic, but stretching can help prevent some causes of it. The knee to chest stretch in Figure 9-20 helps work out the muscles in your lower back (technically, your lumbar spine), and it can help your hips, too.

The knee to chest stretch is pretty straightforward. Just follow these instructions:

1. **Lie on your back with your legs on the floor in front of you.**

2. **Using both hands, gently pull your left knee toward your chest.**

   If you need to bend your right leg, that's okay, but try to keep it as straight as you can.

3. **Hold the position for 20 to 30 seconds before switching sides.**

FIGURE 9-20:
Knee to chest
stretch.

Zack McCrory

Seated back rotation

You may hear this stretch called the *seated back twist*, but rotation is more techni-cally accurate (and it just sounds healthier). This move can help your spinal mobility, and you may feel it all over your back. Figure 9-21 shows this powerful stretch.

FIGURE 9-21:
Seated back
rotation.

Zack McCrory

Follow these steps to perform a seated back rotation:

1. **Sit on the floor with your legs straight in front of you.**

2. **Cross your left leg over your right so that your left knee is at least at a 90-degree angle and your left foot is flat on the floor.**

3. **Straighten your spine and breathe in, placing your left hand on the ground behind you.**

4. **Exhale and rotate your trunk to bring your right elbow across your body, where you put it in front of your left knee.**

   Your elbow doesn't need to reach the other side of your knee. You can bring your right arm across your shin instead, or grab your thigh with your right hand. Be sure to keep your shoulders down, though.

5. **Hold the position for 20 to 30 seconds and then switch sides.**

Side-lying thoracic rotation

When you need to improve mobility in your thoracic spine, lumbar spine, and shoulders (and everyone does), the side-lying thoracic rotation can be the perfect stretch. Check it out in Figure 9-22.

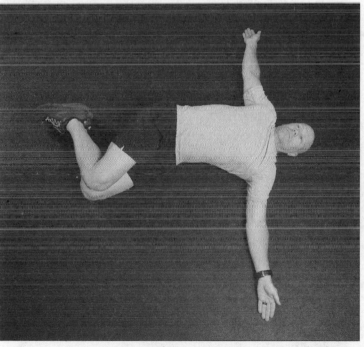

FIGURE 9-22:
Side-lying
thoracic rotation.

Zack McCrory

Despite its super-technical name, all you have to do for this simple stretch is follow these steps:

1. **Lie on your left side and bend your knees 45 to 90 degrees.**

   Keep your knees and hips in a fixed position throughout this stretch.

2. **Put your hands together at shoulder height in front of you with your arms straight.**

3. **Reach your right hand straight up, following it with your head, and put it on the ground behind your body.**

    Your upper body should look like a *T*, and your face should be turned toward your right hand.

4. **Hold the position for 20 to 30 seconds and then bring your right arm back over to put your hands together.**

5. **Switch sides.**

Upper trap stretch

Stretching your upper trapezius muscles, which run from the base of your head down into your thoracic spine and out to your shoulders, can help alleviate neck pain, headaches, and tension. It can also increase your shoulders' and neck's ranges of motion. Your upper traps do a lot of work, especially if you catch yourself slouching in front of a computer or you're extra-stressed (many people tense these muscles when they're under pressure). Figure 9-23 shows an upper trap stretch that you can do anywhere, seated or standing.

FIGURE 9-23: Upper trap stretch.

Zack McCrory

The key difference is that if you do the stretch while sitting, you use the arm that's not pulling your head to prop yourself up. Here's how to stretch this large, triangle-shaped muscle.

1. **Draw your head back so your ears are aligned with your shoulders and tuck in your chin.**

2. **Place one hand behind your back (or prop yourself up with it if you're seated on the ground) and place the other hand on the opposite side of your head.**

TIP

   Ultimately, do what feels right with the arm that's not applying pressure to your head. If it feels better when it's resting on your knee, then rest it on your knee.

3. **Gently pull your head toward the arm that's holding it.**

4. **Hold the position for 20 to 30 seconds and then switch sides.**

Cross-body shoulder stretch

The cross-body shoulder stretch in Figure 9-24 eases up the tension in your deltoid, teres minor, and supraspinatus (the busiest muscle in your rotator cuff), and you can do it any time it crosses your mind.

FIGURE 9-24:
Cross-body
shoulder stretch.

Zack McCrory

You can do this stretch standing or while seated. Just follow these steps:

1. **Grab one arm above your elbow with your opposite hand and pull it across your body (toward your chest) until you feel a stretch in your shoulder.**

   Keep your elbow below shoulder height

2. **Hold for 20 to 30 seconds and switch sides.**

Priming the Pecs: Chest Stretches

Your pectoralis major and minor (your pecs) need TLC regardless of whether you're training for the ACFT. Any time you're doing something in front of your body — reaching for a box of protein bars on a shelf, picking up a bag of dog food, or pushing a disabled vehicle — you're activating your chest muscles. Because they're some of your most commonly used muscles, they're usually tight. The chest stretches in this section can help lengthen these important muscles, provide you with a greater range of motion, and even improve your posture.

Lying chest stretch

The lying chest stretch lets you zero in on your pecs with a little bonus for your shoulders, and you can see it in Figure 9-25.

FIGURE 9-25: Lying chest stretch.

Zack McCrory

This simple stretch is best done on a yoga mat or padded surface:

1. **Lie in the prone position and place both your arms out to your sides, palms facing down, so you look like a letter *T*.**

2. **Slowly roll to your right side by pushing yourself with your left hand, lifting your left leg and bending the left knee.**

3. **Place your left foot behind you for stability and rest your head on the floor.**

   If putting your leg behind your body causes you discomfort, don't do it — just keep your legs together and stack your feet.

4. **Hold the position for 20 to 30 seconds and switch sides.**

Elbow-to-elbow grip

The elbow-to-elbow grip, a stretch that requires you to cross your arms behind your back (see Figure 9-26), isn't right for everyone. If you have shoulder mobility issues or a shoulder injury, stretching your chest using other methods (like the bent-arm wall stretch in the following section) is probably best.

You can perform this quick, simple stretch while you're sitting at your desk, after PT, or after a workout in the gym:

1. **Sit or stand with good posture.**

2. **Squeeze your shoulder blades together to broaden your chest.**

3. **Bring your arms behind your back and grip each elbow with the opposite hand; hold the position for 20 to 30 seconds.**

   Don't force your arms into this position. You have plenty of other chest stretch options if this one just isn't feeling right.

REMEMBER

Bent-arm wall stretch

The bent-arm wall stretch in Figure 9-27 is easy on your muscles and keeps some strain off your shoulders. You can do it whenever you're standing near the corner of a wall or a doorway.

FIGURE 9-27:
Bent-arm wall
stretch.

Zack McCrory

Though many people put their whole arm along the length of a wall or inside a door frame, I suggest you bend your elbow to protect your shoulder:

1. **Raise your hand halfway (like you would in a class setting) and place your forearm outside the corner of a wall or a door frame.**

2. **Step your opposite foot through the door until you feel your chest muscles stretching.**

   Don't twist your body. Step straight forward.

3. **Hold the position for 20 to 30 seconds and then switch sides.**

Stretching out Your Six-Pack

Your abdominal muscles are part of your core, and while you're awake (or at least while you're at work), they're almost always activated. Stretching your abs regularly helps increase your flexibility, improve your posture, enable you to strengthen your core, and decrease your risk of injury.

Sphinx

The sphinx stretch is also a yoga pose (and the more easygoing cousin of the cobra stretch). You can modify it based on how well your back adapts to it. Check it out in Figure 9-28.

FIGURE 9-28:
Sphinx stretch.

The sphinx can create some compression on your lower back, so choose a height that's right for your body:

1. **Lie on your stomach with your legs straight and toes extended.**

2. **Prop yourself up on your forearms and look straight ahead.**

   Keep your shoulders down and away from your ears.

3. **Hold for 20 to 30 seconds.**

TIP

You can turn a sphinx into a cobra by pushing yourself up onto your hands. You don't have to extend your arms all the way.

Child's pose against a wall

Child's pose is a wonderful stretch — and when you do it against a wall as shown in Figure 9-29, you get a great stretch in your thighs, hips, ankles, and lower back.

Zack McCrory

FIGURE 9-29:
Child's pose
against a wall.

Follow these instructions to loosen up with child's pose against a wall:

TIP

1. **Kneel down in front of a wall with your knees wider than hip-distance apart and your toes together.**

   Use a mat under your knees.

2. **Place your forearms or palms against the wall.**

3. **Let gravity pull your torso toward the floor and hold the position for 20 to 30 seconds.**

   Try to get your buttocks to touch your heels as you sink into the stretch. If you're having a hard time getting to that point, roll a towel and put it between your heels and your buttocks or between your thighs and calves to make it more comfortable.

TIP

Figure 9-29 shows a child's pose against a wall, but you can do the same thing on the floor for an even deeper stretch. Just change Step 2 by lowering your torso between your knees and extending your hands in front of you. Relax your shoulders toward the ground, put your forehead on the floor (or mat), and reach your arms out in front of you.

Doing Dynamic Stretches for Multiple Muscles

Dynamic stretches are movement-based, which makes them much different from the static stretches in the previous sections. Dynamic stretches help you use your own muscles to go through full ranges of motion, and most experts agree that you can use them to warm up or cool down after a workout. (That means they're generally safe to use before a workout.) The other benefit to dynamic stretches is that you can run through each one in the following sections on a rest day or to warm yourself up so you can safely perform static stretches.

Lunge with spinal twist

The lunge with spinal twist (shown in Figure 9-30) is a dynamic movement that can loosen up your quads, hip flexors, and back. *Remember:* If you usually only stretch after a workout, you may not start to become more flexible for a few weeks.

FIGURE 9-30: Lunge with spinal twist.

Zack McCrory

Grab a mat and follow these steps to do a lunge with a spinal twist:

1. **Take a big step forward with your right foot.**

2. **Bend your left knee so you drop into a lunge while you keep your right leg straight behind you, with your toes on the ground and heel up.**

3. **Put your left hand on the floor and rotate your upper body to the right, extending your right arm toward the ceiling.**

   Hold the position for a few seconds. You can then go back to the starting position or follow the next steps, which I recommend.

4. **Sit back on your left heel, extending your right leg in front of you with your toes pointed toward the ceiling.**

5. **Reach toward your right foot to stretch your hamstrings, holding the position for a few seconds.**

   If you can, grab your toes (or the ankle) on your right foot. But don't sweat it if you can't get your arm pointed all the way at the ceiling or reach your toes at first. Your mobility will improve with time!

6. **Go back to the lunge position and start over.**

   Repeat three to five times on each side.

90/90s

Tight hips can cause all kinds of problems, but a 90/90 stretch can help loosen things up. As an added benefit, this stretch targets your gluteus minimus and the muscles of your front leg. Check it out in Figure 9-31.

Here's how to do a 90/90 stretch:

1. **Sit on the floor (preferably with a mat) with your lead leg directly in front of you, bent inward at 90 degrees so your heel is aligned with your knee.**

   The outside of your thigh should touch the ground (or come pretty close).

2. **Move your back leg to another 90-degree angle with your inner thigh touching the ground and your heel aligned with your knee.**

3. **Slowly extend your back and lean over your forward leg.**

   Try to lie flat on your leg as you reach your arms over your head with your palms to the floor.

4. **Return to the upright position, repeat three to five times, and then switch sides.**

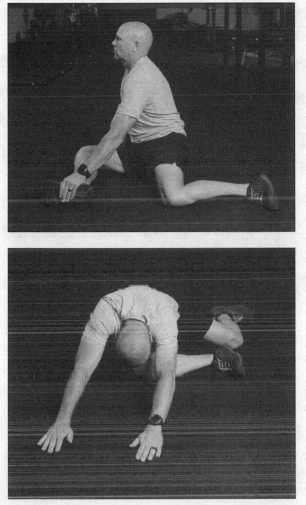

FIGURE 9-31:
90/90s.

Zack McCrory

TIP

When you sit up from a 90/90, you're in a great position to add a quad stretch. Just grab the ankle of the back leg and pull your foot toward your buttocks (you need to put the opposite hand down for support) as you push your pelvis forward.

Side bends

Side bends release tension from the muscles that attach to your ribs, including your lats and obliques, and they even stretch the muscles between your ribs. You can do them while standing or sitting, as Figure 9-32 shows.

FIGURE 9-32:
Side bend stretch standing and sitting.

Zack McCrory

REMEMBER

The rule of thumb with the standing or seated side bend is to go only as far as you comfortably can:

1. **Sit or stand with your spine neutral and your shoulders down and away from your ears.**

   If you're standing, place your feet about shoulder-width apart.

2. **Keep your hips, shoulders, and ears aligned as you raise one arm overhead, bending your upper body to the other side in a reaching motion.**

   Don't twist. Imagine that your back is touching a wall and that you have to keep your shoulder blades on it throughout the movement.

3. **Move slowly to the side until you reach your stopping point, and straighten as you lower your arm all the way back down to your side.**

4. **Repeat three to five times and then switch sides.**

Extended child's pose with sphinx stretch

Mixing an extended child's pose with a sphinx stretch is a great way to target your groin, back muscles, lats, and a few other muscles. Check out both positions — the extended child's pose and the sphinx — in Figure 9-33. Remember, too, that you can change out the sphinx for a cobra if you're limber enough.

FIGURE 9-33:
Extended child's
pose with sphinx
stretch.

Zack McCrory

Here's how to combine these two stretches seamlessly:

1. **Kneel on the floor with your toes together and your knees more than hip-width apart.**

2. **Lower your torso between your knees as you extend your arms over your head until your palms are touching the floor.**

   Try to sit back on your heels and rest your forehead on the floor.

3. **Hold the position for a few seconds and then raise yourself up on your forearms.**

   Alternately, you can extend your arms fully and rest on your palms so you're on all fours.

4. **Shift your body weight forward, keeping your knees in place, and lower the front side of your thighs and your hips to the ground.**

   Push your upper body up to stretch your abs and hold the position for a few seconds.

5. **Raise your hips and shift your body weight back, leaving your hands and knees in the same position, so that your buttock rests on (or near) your heels and you're back in child's pose.**

6. **Repeat three to five times.**

TIP

Some people find it easier to go into a cobra — the stretch where your arms are fully extended — than a sphinx. Try it both ways and do what's right for your body.

Standing figure 4

Your hips and glutes get some much-needed relief with a standing figure 4 stretch, and you get a little extra balance practice. This stretch, depicted in Figure 9-34, lets you choose whether to hold the position (making it a static stretch) or keep moving (making it a dynamic stretch).

FIGURE 9-34:
Standing figure 4.

Zack McCrory

To make the standing figure 4 a dynamic stretch, follow these instructions.

1. **Stand with your feet shoulder-width apart and drive your hips backward, like you're about to sit in a chair, as you raise your right leg and cross it over your left knee in one smooth motion.**

2. **Sit down into the stretch as far as you can comfortably go, resting your hands on your crossed leg or pressing them together in front of you.**

3. **When you reach your lowest position, use your left leg to push yourself back up to standing as you uncross your right leg and return your foot to the floor.**

4. **Switch legs and repeat Steps 1 through 3 three to five times.**

TIP

If you're using this exercise as a static stretch, hold the position in Step 2 for 20 to 30 seconds and switch legs.

Quadruped rotation

You can increase your T-spine mobility (that's your thoracic spine, which covers your upper back and abdomen) with quadruped rotations such as the one in Figure 9-35.

FIGURE 9-35:
Quadruped
rotation.

Zack McCrory

Here's how to tackle the quadruped rotation.

1. **Get on all fours with your knees under your hips and hands under your shoulders, keeping your spine in a neutral position.**

   This position is the *quadruped position*.

2. **Raise your right hand, rotating your spine so you're reaching toward the ceiling.**

Follow your reaching hand with your head, but don't turn your neck. If the reach is too much, you can also simply prop one hand behind your head with a light touch (like you would if you were doing sit-ups).

3. **After you reach your highest point, put your hand back on the floor and switch sides.**

4. **Repeat three to five times.**

Dynamic shoulder stretch from child's pose

Add a shoulder stretch to child's pose to target even more muscles. In addition to all the muscles a child's pose targets, this one gets your deltoids. You can see it in Figure 9-36.

FIGURE 9-36:
Dynamic shoulder stretch from child's pose.

Zack McCrory

Perform this stretch by following these instructions:

1. **Start on all fours with your hands below your shoulders and your knees below your hips.**

2. **Push your hips back.**

If you have the mobility for it, sit back on your heels. Otherwise, push back as far as you can.

3. **Walk your hands forward and rest your forehead on the floor.**

You can also rest your arms on a step.

4. **Thread your left arm under your body, pushing your hand between your right arm and right leg, as you press your shoulder to the floor.**

   It's okay if your shoulder doesn't touch the ground. Don't force it!

5. **Pull your arm back after you reach as far as you can and switch sides.**

6. **Repeat three to five times on each side.**

Cat/cow

The cat/cow gets your blood moving, helps increase spinal mobility and alignment, and opens the chest. As Figure 9-37 shows, you perform two moves with this stretch.

FIGURE 9-37: Cat/cow.

Zack McCrory

Perform the cat/cow by following these steps.

1. Start on all fours with your hands and wrists directly under your shoulders and your knees directly under your hips.

2. Point your fingertips forward and move your shins and knees hip-width apart while you keep your head in a neutral position.

3. Let your abdomen drop toward the ground as you lift your chin and chest; look up toward the ceiling to get into the cow pose.

4. Draw your abdomen in, arching your back toward the ceiling.

5. Release your head so that it simply hangs there to complete your transition to the cat pose.

   Don't force your chin to your chest.

6. Return to the cow pose and repeat the whole cycle three to five times.

Chapter **10**

Focusing on the ACFT for Females

When you look at physiology from the Army's standpoint — at least for the ACFT — it's all about athleticism with no regard for which style of Round Brown you wear or whether you wear trousers or a skirt with your dress uniform. The neutrally scored ACFT measures physical fitness in ways that indicate whether a soldier — any soldier — can perform on the battlefield. That means an 18-year-old male soldier fresh out of Basic Combat Training has the same set of standards as a female general who's been in the military for a few decades. Those standards are based on Physical Demand Categories, or PDCs, that tie into a service member's job. Depending on what you do for Uncle Sam, you have to perform at the Moderate (Gold), Significant (Gray), or Heavy (Black) category. Check out the PDC and scoring tables in Chapter 4.

REMEMBER

As of this writing, the Army officially recognizes only two genders. The Army's use of "gender-neutral" when referring to the ACFT refers to biological sex. Scientifically speaking, gender and biological sex are two different things, so for the purposes of this book, I use the terms *male* and *female* to refer to a person's biological sex.

Physiological differences exist, at least in a general sense, between males and females (Army or civilian). These differences can affect a person's performance on the ACFT. For example, the Army's own data showed that during the ACFT's rollout among initial entry training soldiers, males made more progress on events like the Leg Tuck (LTK) than female soldiers did. From the first week of basic to the time they began AIT, males went from doing five tucks to being able to do seven of them — but females went from doing less than half a full rep to being able to do just one full rep. For some females, one tuck doesn't cut it, though. That means working harder to hit three or five (the Significant and Heavy thresholds, respectively).

That doesn't mean females *can't* do certain things; it just means they may have to work harder and train more if they want to meet or exceed the standard. The bottom line is that even if you feel that the neutral scoring on the ACFT makes the test tougher for females to pass, it's still possible for them to do so. This chapter delves into what females can do (and what the Army says they should do) about physical training, including prepping for the ACFT.

Factoring Female Physiology into Common ACFT Challenges

Biological differences can explain why some Army females have a harder time doing the LTK than males do (and why some men found maxing out the sit-up event on the old Army Physical Fitness Test harder than many women did). Broadly speaking, science has shown that several physiological factors actually influence differences in athletic performance between male and female bodies, which you can see in Table 10-1.

TABLE 10-1 **General Physiological Differences between Biological Sexes**

Athletic Influence	Females	Males
Hormones	Primarily estrogen	Primarily androgen
Ratio of lean body tissue to fatty tissue	Less lean tissue and higher body fat	More lean tissue and lower body fat
Flexibility	Generally greater natural flexibility, laxity (looseness), and range of motion	Less natural flexibility and laxity
Bone structure	Wider pelvis and lighter bones	Narrower pelvis and denser bones
Musculature	Less muscle strength, which can be affected by ovulation*, and faster recovery from fatigue	Typically able to output more power

*Some studies have shown that a woman's VO$_2$ max and other measures of endurance are lower during two phases of the menstrual cycle — the follicular and menstrual phases. See the following section for more on menstrual cycle phases.

Cycling your way through workouts

The female menstrual cycle has four phases: menstruation, follicular, ovulation, and luteal. For many women, higher-intensity workouts may be more beneficial during certain phases of the menstrual cycle. For example, the data shows that saving high-intensity cardio until the end of the luteal phase can be advantageous. There aren't any significant changes in strength, but you may notice a difference in endurance. Table 10-2 outlines the four phases and offers suggestions on changing up your workout routines for each.

TABLE 10-2   ## Menstrual Phases

Phase	What's Happening	Duration	Working Out
Menstruation	Estrogen and progesterone production drop	3–7 days	Resting heart rate is typically a little lower than it is during the luteal phase; peak heart rate is typically lower; VO_2 max is generally lower. Exercise as you normally would, but expect your heart rate and caloric burn to be a little different than it is during other phases because your heart is working harder than normal. For many women, using shorter high-intensity workouts during this phase is best.
Follicular	Pituitary gland releases follicle-stimulating hormone, or FSH	Approximately 16 days	Resting heart rate is at its lowest point of the month, and peak heart rate is easier to reach. VO_2 max is normal.
Ovulation	Rise in estrogen levels, release of gonadotrophin-releasing hormone (GnRH), and rise in luteinizing hormone (LH), as well as increase in FSH	Approximately 1 day	This phase overlaps the follicular phase and the luteal phase, so exercise as normal.
Luteal	Production of human chorionic gonadotrophin (HCG)	11–17 days	Resting heart rate is typically higher; peak heart rate is typically lower; VO_2 max is significantly lower. Exercise as normal, but expect your heart rate and caloric burn to be a little different than it is during other phases. Your heart starts working harder than normal as you move into the menstruation phase.

You don't have to be a professional athlete to understand that your body's performance differs during the four phases of your cycle — it's really about the hormones your body is producing. They affect your workouts, and if you're the calendar-keeping type, you'll most likely notice. If you use a fitness tracker, have a look at your resting heart rate trends for each month over the past year; you can probably see some patterns (and predict what's coming up next).

Introducing the female athlete triad

When you're training for the ACFT, or when you're working toward a healthy and fit lifestyle, you're making smart choices that will most likely prolong your life and keep you mobile well into your golden years. People who play sports and work out regularly are less likely to experience depression or use alcohol or tobacco, and they even perform better on mental tasks.

But sometimes women get sucked into the female athlete triad — and it's not their fault. The *female athlete triad* (shown in Figure 10-1) outlines three big risks women face when training:

» **Low energy availability:** Wanting to lose weight to improve athletic performance is normal for women, but sometimes disordered eating is a result. In this context, disordered eating isn't only about anorexia and bulimia (although those are serious conditions on the triad that require treatment). In the triad, disordered eating refers to things that seem minor to most people, like eating too few calories to keep up with energy demands or avoiding certain types of food (such as foods that contain fat).

The bottom line is that sometimes female soldiers have low energy availability, which prevents peak performance because they're not consuming the fuels they need. I cover counting calories and balancing energy in Chapter 23.

» **Menstrual disturbance:** *Amenorrhea* occurs when your menstrual cycle becomes irregular or stops altogether. You may have experienced amenorrhea during Basic Combat Training or during other times of your life when you combined intense exercise and calorie deficiency.

» **Low bone mineral density:** Females who fall into the female athlete triad generally have lower estrogen production, and when that's combined with poor nutrition (especially poor calcium intake), a woman is more likely to develop osteoporosis. Women naturally have less-dense bones than men do (see Table 10-1 for other differences between females and males). Osteoporosis is a weakening of the bones due to the loss of bone density and improper bone formation — and women reach peak bone mass between the ages of 25 and 30. That means if you're under 30, your bones are still developing. Anyone else is naturally at risk for losing bone mass already developed.

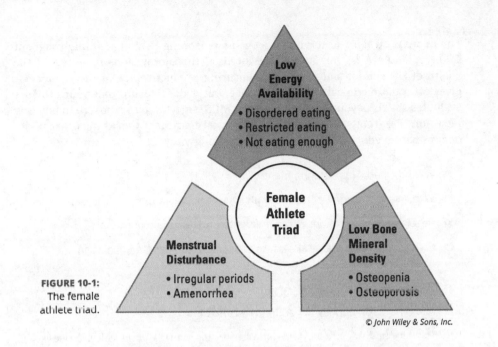

FIGURE 10-1:
The female
athlete triad.

Though some women never develop any of the conditions in the triad, some pick up one or two — or even all three.

Balancing Pregnancy and Physical Training

The Army takes protecting pregnant soldiers seriously, but it still needs to maintain them as soldiers as much as possible. The following sections break down some of the Army's policies on pregnancy as it relates to PT and the ACFT.

Profiling pregnant soldiers

If you're on a profile (any profile, not just one related to pregnancy) that prevents you from performing any of the events, you don't have to take the ACFT until that profile expires. But that doesn't mean you shouldn't be doing PT. In the Army, after your primary care provider, or PCP, determines you're pregnant (either by exam or by lab test), you get a physical profile that lasts until the end of your pregnancy. The profile lists activities your PCP feels are appropriate and any specific limitations your PCP feels you have. For normal pregnancies without complications, your PCP may say that appropriate activities include specific stretches, aerobic conditioning at your own pace, and lifting up to 20 pounds.

The Army is straight to the point about its reasoning behind profiling pregnant soldiers. DA PAM 40-502 says, "The intent of these provisions is to protect the health of the soldier and fetus while ensuring productive use of the soldier." It gives off a more clinical vibe than I'd use, but it does ensure that your provider evaluates the risks you face based on your MOS, such as your exposure to ionizing radiation, hazardous chemicals, and biological hazards. Other things that pregnancy profiles generally restrict include the following:

>> Wearing load carrying equipment

>> Wearing body armor, particularly after 14 weeks gestation

>> Receiving immunizations except influenza and tetanus-diphtheria

>> Being exposed to chemical warfare and riot control agents (such as gas chamber training)

>> Wearing JSLIST

>> Climbing on or working on ladders or scaffolding

>> Standing at parade rest or attention for longer than 15 minutes after 20 weeks of pregnancy

>> Participating in swimming qualifications and drown-proofing training after 20 weeks of pregnancy

>> Going to the field after 20 weeks of pregnancy

>> Participating in weapons training after 20 weeks of pregnancy

>> Riding in, PMCSing, or driving vehicles larger than light medium tactical vehicles after 20 weeks of pregnancy

TIP

Pregnancy and postpartum profiles (as well as those for nursing mothers) typically allow you to stop wearing permethrin-treated uniforms. For good measure, maternity uniforms aren't treated with this possibly risky chemical. If you're concerned about it, ask your PCP for more information or to ensure that it's included in your profile.

After 28 weeks of pregnancy, Army regulations say that leaders must provide female soldiers a 15-minute rest period every 2 hours. DA PAM 40-502 says that at this stage, duty weeks shouldn't exceed 40 hours, and the soldier shouldn't work more than 8 hours in one day. (The 8-hour workday *includes* time spent doing physical training.) If you have health concerns about working more than 40 hours in a week, it's okay to bring AR 40-502 or DA PAM 40-502 up to your leadership — and to use your commander's open-door policy if necessary. You can also let your PCP know that you're concerned.

You don't get quarters solely because of pregnancy, but if you have complications that preclude any type of duty performance, your physician may require you to stay home.

Usually when a profile exceeds 90 days, it must be a permanent profile, but that's not the case with pregnancy profiles. Because this type of profile is temporary rather than permanent, you don't qualify to take the modified ACFT (which I cover in Chapter 4). You have to wait until your pregnancy and postpartum profiles expire to take the ACFT.

TECHNICAL STUFF

Tuberculosis profiles are the only other temporary profiles that can last more than 90 days (you can find that exception in DA PAM 40-502).

Postpartum profiles dive into AR 600-8-10 territory because they involve convalescent leave, or con-leave. Con-leave after the completion of a pregnancy — including a miscarriage — is decided on a case-by-case basis. Your commander has no say in how long your post-pregnancy con-leave lasts; it's up to your physician alone. Sometimes doctors order longer con-leave for some females, such as when a soldier has had a C-section or was injured during delivery, than they do for others. A postpartum profile is supposed to last at least 45 days.

After any pregnancy that lasts longer than 20 weeks, you become exempt from taking a record ACFT for 6 months (but you can be given a diagnostic test). You're also exempt from a record weigh-in for the same duration of time.

Perusing the P3T program

Although the Army takes precautions for pregnant soldiers, as I outline in the preceding section, they aren't an automatic ticket to Fort Couch. After your health-care provider clears you for PT, which happens in most uncomplicated pregnancies, your command team enrolls you in the Army Pregnancy Postpartum PT (P3T) program. P3T is designed to help you maintain a base level of physical fitness during and after pregnancy, boost morale and reduce stress, and eventually reintegrate you into your unit's PRT program.

Army Regulation 40-502 and DA PAM 40-502, AR 350-1, and FM 7-22 all govern the Army's P3T program. Technical Guide 255X even outlines exercises you're supposed to do as part of the P3T program.

Every installation has a P3T program divided into at least four groups of soldiers who are

>> Fewer than 20 weeks pregnant

>> 20 to 28 weeks pregnant

» More than 28 weeks pregnant

» Postpartum (which can be divided into initial and advanced, if necessary)

The Army has really stringent rules that help soldiers in the P3T program, including ensuring that you're allowed to use the restroom as necessary and that you're allowed to run or jog only at your own pace. (You need written approval from your PCP to run or jog in the third trimester.) Likewise, you can't exercise to the point of exhaustion, breathlessness, or fatigue, and you can't perform exercises that require you to lie on your back if you're more than 20 weeks pregnant.

Your (Kid's) Mom Wears Combat Boots: Working Out Postpartum

In addition to P3T, you may find exercising on your own — outside the P3T program — necessary to recondition your body after delivery. Dozens of "mommy and me" workouts are available online, but before you start any of them, ask your PCP. Depending on your health, fitness level, and the type of birth you went through, your doctor may discourage certain exercises or movements (at least for a while).

REMEMBER

If you've had a C-section, you need to take it slow. You can start with small exercises, such as gently squeezing your abdominal muscles while concurrently squeezing your pelvic floor muscles. Your doctor may recommend waiting on any exercises until you've had a six- or eight-week checkup after a C-section. Even then, talk directly to your doctor about the exercises you can do safely. Don't depend on a P3T leader's (or anyone else's) guidance without discussing your body's individual needs with your PCP.

REMEMBER

About two-thirds of postpartum women experience *diastasis recti,* which you can see in Figure 10-2. That's the technical term for the separation of your rectus abdominis muscles. Some exercises make the condition worse, including sit-ups, push-ups, front planks, and even some yoga poses (like downward dog). Twisting movements are definitely a no-go. That means your ab exercises are going to be different from those of a woman whose abs aren't separated. The Army says you must splint your abdomen during abdominal exercises if you have a diastasis (separation) of more than two fingers in width.

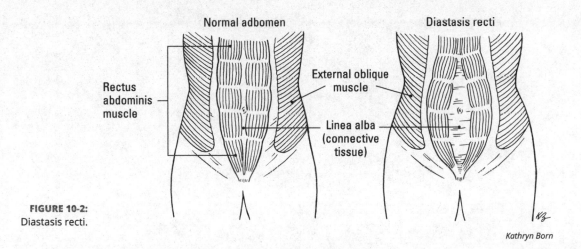

Normal adbomen

Diastasis recti

Rectus abdominis muscle

External oblique muscle

Linea alba (connective tissue)

FIGURE 10-2:
Diastasis recti.

Kathryn Born

You should absolutely talk to your PCP about modifying your profile to include prohibitions and restrictions on ab exercises — even with splints — if you have a split in your ab muscles.

TIP

You can do a self-test for diastasis recti before you talk to your PCP. Lie on your back with your knees bent and feet flat on the floor. Place your fingertips across your midline, parallel to your waist at your bellybutton. Put your other hand behind your head and lift your head up. At the same time, gently press your fingertips down. When you do, you should feel the space between your muscles narrowing. However, if that space doesn't narrow, or if your fingers sink into the gap, you may have diastasis. If you're not sure, make an appointment with your PCP to check for you.

You can do several exercises to help pull your muscles back together, including pelvic tilts and single-leg reaches while lying on your back. And if you're one of the fortunate women who *doesn't* have diastasis recti, or if you've successfully fixed the issue, several exercises can help you work on rebuilding your abdominal muscles. The core exercises in PRT (some of which you perform in P3T) are a great start, as are those I outline in Chapter 7, such as glute bridges, planks, kettlebell pull-throughs, and renegade row push-ups.

Chapter **11**

Surveying ACFT Training for Seasoned Soldiers

aving been around the block a time or two definitely has its advantages for leadership. If you're at the stage in your Army career when you can answer a question with "That's that 'new Army' for you," you know exactly what I'm talking about when I say you're a seasoned soldier. You probably also know what I'm talking about when I say an Army career isn't easy on your knees and your back. Whether it's from thousands of miles logged running on pavement or the performance of a specific job, everyone in the Army eventually feels the weight of the world on joints, disks, and connective tissues. Army years are like dog years; if you've been through more than a couple of enlistment contracts, your body probably feels like it's time for retirement. When things get bad enough, you see your primary care provider, or PCP, for a profile — but many soldiers leave that on the back burner for as long as they can.

Because you still need to pass the ACFT unless you're on a permanent profile that makes you a candidate for the modified test, this chapter is devoted to exercises you can do when you have knee and back problems.

Safety First: Taking Workout Precautions

You apply safety principles to everything you do in the Army, whether you're putting together a risk assessment for a land nav course or you're making sure privates are wearing their Kevlar helmets in Army vehicles. But exercise safety is equally important, especially if you're injured or have a chronic condition. Use these tips to stay safe and injury-free if you're starting to feel your age (and even if you're not):

>> **Be aware of your body.** If something doesn't feel right, or if it hurts, stop.

>> **Warm up and cool down, every time.** Prep your body for a workout by warming up every time. Don't forget to cool down and stretch, too, to promote recovery between workouts.

>> **Mix things up.** Don't stick to the same old exercises — switch up your routine to reduce the risk of overtraining injuries.

>> **Worry about your form — a lot.** Good form is always important, whether you're 18 or 45, but performing exercises properly is imperative for more seasoned soldiers. Muscles, bones, and connective tissues are less forgiving as they age.

>> **Think about braces and tapes.** Though you can't wear a brace or tape anything during Army PT without a profile giving you permission to do so, you certainly can utilize these aids when exercising on your own time. (And if something on you needs a brace or tape, stop putting it off — go see your PCP and get a profile. You're the one who has to live with your body for the rest of your life, so what anyone thinks doesn't matter.)

WARNING

You should always talk to your PCP about starting a new exercise program, and you should absolutely go to sick call or schedule an appointment if something hurts.

Kicking around Exercises for Knee Issues

Ideally, you'll talk to your PCP and get a referral to a physical therapist if your knees aren't feeling as good as they should. Your physical therapist will likely prescribe you plenty of exercises you can do to help the recovery process along and give you a list of things you can do to avoid injuring yourself further. Check out the knee-friendly exercises in the following sections that, depending on your condition, may help. Touch base with your PCP before you try any of them to make sure they're right for you. Before you do any of these exercises, warm up by taking a brisk walk while pumping your arms for at least two minutes.

Straight leg raises

Straight leg raises from the ground put little to no strain on your knees, but they help strengthen your quads (which support your knee) and the muscles surrounding your hips. Check out this exercise in Figure 11-1 and follow these instructions:

1. **Lie on your back with your hips square and both legs extended.**

2. **Bend one knee and keep that leg's foot flat on the floor.**

3. **Keep your other leg straight and raise it to the height of your bent knee by flexing your quadriceps.**

4. **Hold your straight leg up for 3 to 5 seconds.**

5. **Lower your straight leg to the floor under control.**

FIGURE 11-1: Straight leg raises.

Zack McCrory

EXAMPLE

Aim for three sets of 10 on each side.

Hamstring curls with dumbbells

Your hamstrings — the muscles on the back of your thigh — also help support your knees. Try these knee-friendly curls, shown in Figure 11-2:

1. **Lie on your stomach with your hands folded under your head while holding a light dumbbell between your feet.**

2. **Bend your knees to pull the dumbbell toward your backside.**

3. **Slowly lower to the starting position and repeat.**

FIGURE 11-2: Hamstring curls with a dumbbell.

Zack McCrory

EXAMPLE

Try to do three sets of 10 dumbbell curls in one sitting, with a minute of rest in between. If the weight is too light, pick a heavier dumbbell. You can also do them without the dumbbell altogether.

Wall squats

Runners use wall squats to improve quad strength while avoiding knee strain, and you can, too. Figure 11-3 illustrates a solid wall squat; here's how to do one:

1. **Stand with your back against a wall and your feet between 1 and 1.5 feet in front of you.**

   If you have long legs, your feet will be farther out.

2. **Slowly squat down while leaning into the wall for support, putting your arms out in front of you for balance if you need to.**

   Keep your feet flat on the floor during the entire exercise.

3. **Pause at the bottom of the squat for up to 10 seconds and then return to the standing position.**

EXAMPLE

Aim for three sets of 8 to 12 reps each.

FIGURE 11-3:
Wall squats.

Zack McCrory

Step-ups

Step-ups (shown in Figure 11-4) are a great way to exercise your legs, but the angle of flexion in your knee makes a huge difference safety-wise. If you're dealing with knee issues, you need to perform these exercises on the ground or with a very low step.

TECHNICAL
STUFF

At 10 degrees of knee flexion, taking a step creates pressure between your kneecap and thighbone that's equal to about half your bodyweight. At 60 degrees of knee flexion, the stress increases to 3.5 times your bodyweight, and at 90 degrees of flexion (or more), the pressure can be *eight times your bodyweight.* Under normal circumstances, that may be okay, but if you're dealing with a knee injury, you need minimal knee flexion as you work to strengthen the muscles that support it.

FIGURE 11-4:
Step-ups.

Zack McCrory

Ready to try step-ups? Follow these steps:

1. **Place your left foot on a step bench or platform that can support your weight.**

   Put your whole foot on the platform. Don't let your heel hang over the edge.

2. **Keep your pelvis level and press through the heel of your left foot to stand up straight, bringing your right foot on the platform.**

3. **Step down with your left foot and then your right, so that both your feet are flat on the floor, to complete one rep.**

EXAMPLE

Perform 15 up-and-down steps leading with your left foot and then 15 leading with your right foot to complete a full set of exercises. Aim for two sets in one sitting. If the steps become easier, don't increase the surface's height if you have knee issues. Instead, increase the number of reps you do on each side.

Side leg raises

Side leg raises benefit your hip flexors, thighs, glutes, hamstrings, calves, and obliques, which means they're a great addition to your workout regimen if you're dealing with knee problems. You can see a simple bodyweight-only leg raise in Figure 11-5 before tackling this exercise on your own.

1. **Lle on the floor on your side with your bottom arm propping up your head, folded beneath your head, or straight out above your head.**

   If you experience any neck discomfort, put your arm flat on the floor and rest your head on it. Use your top arm for support by placing your hand flat on the ground in front of your abdomen. Flex your bottom knee so that it has a 45- to 90-degree bend, while your entire body (down to your flexed knee) is in a generally straight line.

2. **Lift your top leg so it's at about a 45-degree angle from your body.**

3. **Lower your leg under control.**

FIGURE 11-5:
Side leg ralses.

EXAMPLE

Perform these exercises in sets of 8 to 12 reps each. Do three sets on each side. As you become stronger, you can add resistance with a resistance band or ankle weights.

Avoiding Certain Exercises for Back Issues

Show me a retired soldier who claims never to have had back pain while in the military, and I'll show you a grade-A fibber. According to the American Academy of Orthopedic Surgeons, spine impairment is a leading cause of disability in veterans — and many of those issues stem from injuries while serving. Repeated stress and trauma contribute to spinal damage you feel later in life, which means if you have a back problem, you need to see your PCP immediately. Don't try to tough it out, even if you think it's minor or "just a kink," because there are things you can do right now to minimize the long-term effects of an injury or damage.

WARNING

Never do any exercises you haven't cleared with your PCP or physical therapist when you have a back injury. Doing the wrong exercises can make your back pain worse or cause more severe damage.

A huge number of things can cause back pain in the military. Your spine is a column of 33 bones (called *vertebrae*) and tissue that extends from your skull to your pelvis. Between each vertebra is an *intervertebral disk* (a band of cartilage that works like a shock absorber). Your spine has five distinct sections, shown in Figure 11-6. The cervical section, which includes your neck, has 7 vertebrae, and your thoracic section has 12. The lumbar section in your lower back, below your ribs, contains five, while your sacrum and coccyx (tailbone) contain five and four that are fused together, respectively.

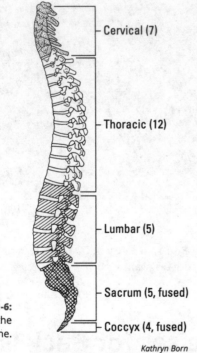

Cervical (7)

Thoracic (12)

Lumbar (5)

Sacrum (5, fused)

Coccyx (4, fused)

FIGURE 11-6: Sections of the spine.

Kathryn Born

Different types of back injuries require different treatments and rehabilitation exercises, which makes training for the ACFT tough. Prevention is the best medicine, and generally accepted medical advice says to develop a strong core to help avoid back injuries. However, if you're already injured or you're experiencing back pain, the best thing you can do is talk to your PCP about how to recover. *Remember:* Even with the strongest core and best diet, aging causes natural degeneration of bones and disks.

Injury aside, your PCP or physical therapist can recommend exercises designed to alleviate back pain, strengthen your core, and prevent future injuries. Because every back injury is different, and figuring out which exercises are right for you requires a professional diagnosis, I can't recommend specific exercises you should perform. I can, however, tell you which ones to avoid.

First things first: Avoid any exercise or movement that can aggravate your injury. As a general rule of thumb, if your pain is more than mild discomfort, you should stop what you're doing unless you're under the supervision of a medical doctor. For most people with back injuries, these exercises are on the no-go list:

>> Toe touches and windmills

>> Sit-ups

>> Leg lifts

>> Barbell exercises that put pressure on your spine (such as when you need the barbell on your back)

>> Cycling or exercises that require forward flexion for long periods of time

>> Contact sports or sports that involve quick movements and twisting (like tennis or golf)

>> High-impact exercise, such as running on pavement

Chapter **12**

Dealing with Injuries

P art of the Army brass's reasoning behind developing the ACFT was to prevent injury among the ranks. Because the test assesses a soldier's functional fitness level — that is, a soldier's ability to perform battle tasks rather than simply the ability to perform push-ups and sit-ups and run fast — the training that prepares you for it helps develop the muscles, flexibility, and endurance you use to stay healthy and be less prone to injuries. (Chapter 5 has more on functional fitness.) It's all in the revised edition of FM 7-22, *Holistic Health and Fitness*.

In this chapter, I explain how following the Army's Performance Triad can help you ward off injury. I also introduce some widespread Army injuries, weigh in on getting your ailments treated, and offer tips for taking care of minor injuries on your own.

An Ounce of Prevention: Avoiding Injury with P3

As the saying goes, "An ounce of prevention is worth a pound of cure." My grandma *and* my mom said that, and as a professional fitness trainer, I can tell you that it's absolutely true. The bottom line is that preventing injury is far better than dealing with the aftermath of one.

You can't prevent *all* injuries, but you can do what it takes to minimize their impact — both before and after they occur. Check out these basic injury prevention tips:

>> Stop an exercise if something doesn't quite feel right (even if you can't figure out why).

>> Stop an exercise if you feel pain (which is different from discomfort caused by work).

>> Take time off by building rest days into your schedule.

>> Wear the right gear, including supportive running shoes for your foot type.

>> Condition your muscles a little bit at a time to build strength and stability.

>> Improve your flexibility by stretching, which you should do after exercise and in between workouts.

>> Pay close attention to your form during every exercise you do.

>> Take breaks while you're exercising, including quick stops to hydrate.

>> Drink water, even when you're not working out, and skip drinks that sap your body's ability to help itself.

WARNING

That you need to go to sick call if you suspect an injury is serious should go without saying. I cover that in the section "Rub Some Dirt on It? Knowing When to Go to Sick Call" later in this chapter.

The Army's Performance Triad, or P3, is designed to help minimize injury. The triad includes sleep, activity, and nutrition, and you can see how these concepts relate to injury in the following sections. For more on the Performance Triad in general, head to Chapter 7.

Sleep and injury prevention

Lack of sleep is so prevalent in the Army that it's "normal," but it's not the best choice (for you or anyone else). In training and on the battlefield, lack of sleep slows you down. Getting enough rest is essential, even when you're not training up for the ACFT. That's because adequate sleep helps improve your reaction time, keeps you coordinated, and helps you make choices that prevent injury. A growing body of research says that more sleep can make you less injury-prone, while a lack of sleep can mess with protein synthesis, muscle recovery, and modulation of your body's inflammatory response, which can all lead to injury.

Use these tips from the National Sleep Foundation to make sure you're getting enough high-quality rest:

>> Stick to a sleep schedule that stays the same, even on weekends, to regulate your body's clock.

>> Practice a relaxing bedtime ritual that has nothing to do with blue lights or anything that causes stress or anxiety.

>> Avoid daytime naps if you have trouble sleeping at night — even quick power naps.

>> Design the right environment for sleep, including temperature (between 60 and 67 degrees Fahrenheit is ideal), noise (even a bed partner's snoring can disrupt your rest), and light (you shouldn't have any).

>> Exercise every day.

>> Sleep on a supportive and comfortable mattress, and make sure your pillows are firm enough.

TIP

Most mattresses have a life expectancy of 9 to 10 years. After that, they're less supportive and can lead to discomfort during the night.

>> Use bright light to manage your circadian rhythms, which means avoiding bright light in the evening and exposing yourself to natural sunlight as early as possible in the morning.

>> Avoid alcohol, nicotine, and heavy meals in the evening, which can all disrupt your sleep.

>> Spend the last hour before bed shifting into sleep mode by doing a calming activity, like reading.

>> Go into another room and do something relaxing if you can't fall asleep right away.

So how much sleep should you get? Sleep requirements vary slightly from person to person, but most healthy adults need between seven and nine hours of sleep per night to function at peak performance.

Actively preventing injury

Physical fitness and activity are essential in preventing injury (to the extent that it's possible). Working out safely strengthens weak muscles, helps you balance, and improves your biomechanics, which all work together to reduce your chance of injury. Your body's biomechanics — how your muscular and skeletal systems react to external forces and stimuli — improve with use, which is why activity is the second part of the Army's Performance Triad.

You don't have to work out to exhaustion every day. In fact, you shouldn't. You should work in one or two rest days each week to give your body a little extra time to recuperate. Use the fill-in-the-blanks workout calendar in the Appendix to set up your workout routines with built-in rest days.

REMEMBER

Being sedentary hurts more than it helps. That means even if you're doing PT with your unit in the morning or training on your own, sitting still for the rest of the day can be detrimental to your health. Standing all day isn't much better — you're still in a fixed position, which your body didn't evolve to do. The good news is that getting up even once an hour (twice an hour if you can) and doing a stretch or two from Chapter 9 helps keep your proverbial blood flowing and minimizes your chances of developing a dangerous health condition that stems from being too sedentary for too long. Don't tell anyone I told you this, but even getting up to grab a donut still counts as movement. You may want to look at Chapter 23, which is about your caloric intake, before you decide whether that's actually a good idea, though.

Fueling up for injury prevention

Eating — specifically, nutrition — is part of the Army's Performance Triad because it's an essential part of maintaining your body like a well-oiled machine. I'm not going to get into the "oiled" part, but if you want your body to run like it should, you need to give it the right fuel. Most people understand that good nutrition is important, but sometimes food's relationship with injury prevention gets overlooked. The right diet can help you become stronger and more stable, and it can help your body's tissues repair themselves if you do get injured.

Here are four nutritional principles you can't afford to forget if you're concerned about your body:

>> **Eat enough calories.** If your body doesn't get enough calories to meet all its maintenance and energy needs, it goes into a catabolic state. Without getting too gory, a body in a catabolic state eats its own muscles for fuel. As a result, you don't have any energy left to repair tissue damage from an injury. In fact, you don't have enough to repair tissue damage from a regular workout. Your muscle recovery rate slows way down, putting you at risk for further injury.

>> **Make sure your diet includes fat.** A lot of people look for fat-free and lowfat foods because fat has a bad rap, but your body needs some fat to create healthy cell membranes that can resist damage. Fat is helpful for repair, too, because some types of fats are parts of compounds that stop little injuries

from becoming big ones through inflammation. As a general rule, make sure that no more than 10 percent of your total daily calories come from saturated fat. Try to take in twice as much unsaturated fat as you do saturated fat (so about 20 percent of your total calories) each day. Also, try to get at least 3,000 milligrams of omega-3 essential fats every day. Check out Chapter 23 for more about good fats and bad fats in your diet.

>> **Eat within two hours of a workout whenever possible.** Most of the repair work your body does after a workout occurs in the first two hours, provided that you eat during that time. Protein is important when you eat after a workout, but it's even better when you pair it with carbohydrates. That's because carbs stimulate muscle protein synthesis (the repair process) and restock the glycogen stores in your muscles. That means post-workout is the perfect time for a turkey sandwich.

TECHNICAL
STUFF

In a study on Marine recruits, those who used a carbohydrate-protein supplement every day after working out during boot camp had 33 percent fewer total medical visits, 37 percent fewer muscle and tendon injuries, and less muscle soreness than recruits who didn't.

>> **Don't skimp on calcium.** Add a glass of lowfat chocolate milk (to keep your saturated fat intake under control) to that post-workout turkey sandwich so you can boost your calcium intake. The average adult needs between 1,000 and 1,300 milligrams of calcium a day because it's the most important nutrient for bone health. (Most adults only consume 500 to 700 milligrams of calcium each day, so coming up short is easy.) You can read more about minerals and other nutrients in Chapter 21.

Covering Common Injuries across the Army

Being a soldier is physically demanding, and it puts strain on your body in ways that most other jobs don't. According to the Army Public Health Center, or APHC, the biggest health problem facing soldiers is musculoskeletal injury. These injuries are soft tissue injuries caused by sudden impact, force, vibration, and unbalanced positions. They can affect muscles, nerves, ligaments, joints, blood vessels, and body systems. Some of the most common musculoskeletal injuries include the following:

>> Tendinitis

>> Carpal tunnel syndrome

>> Osteoarthritis

>> Rheumatoid arthritis

>> Broken bones

>> Dislocations

>> Muscle and tendon strains

>> Ligament sprains

>> Herniated disks

>> Back and neck conditions

That's just the short list. A soldier can suffer several other (and more specific) musculoskeletal conditions, but they all have two things in common: They lead to pain and restricted mobility. Musculoskeletal injuries need immediate treatment because if you let them go, the condition can become chronic or lead to disability through joint deformity or nerve damage.

The APHC says that almost 50 percent of military members experience at least one injury each year, resulting in more than 2 million medical encounters over the span of 12 months. Most are overuse strains, sprains, and stress fractures affecting the lower extremities (feet, ankles, lower legs, and knees). Even worse, more than half of these musculoskeletal injuries are related to exercise or sports — running in particular. (Need some running tips? Have a look at safer ways to run in Chapter 8.) Back and shoulder injuries are also common, but they're typically associated with lifting and carrying activities.

Injuries come in three main types: acute injuries, overuse injuries, and medical illnesses or conditions. Table 12-1 shows examples and symptoms of acute and overuse injuries and tells you when you need to go to sick call or schedule an appointment with your PCP.

WARNING

Some injuries are emergencies, such as concussions and broken bones. You need to see a doctor immediately for any emergency, even if it means going to the emergency room off post.

TABLE 12-1   **Musculoskeletal Injuries Common among Troops**

Injury Type	Examples	Symptoms	When to See Your Doctor
Acute	Sprains Strains Fractures Dislocations Torn cartilage Bruises Cuts Scrapes Pinched nerves Herniated disks	Pain that restricts activity or affects daily activity Swelling Bruising Deformity Spasms Restricted or locked joints Instability Numbness Tingling Shooting pains	Your joints swell, lock, or become unstable There's a visible deformity or mass in your arm, leg, or a joint You can't fully move a joint, arm, or leg You're unable to walk You have back or neck pain, especially when it's accompanied by numbness, weakness, or pain that runs down an arm or leg You have pain that doesn't go away after home treatment and rest You have pain that disrupts your daily activity or sleep
Overuse	Tendinitis Shin splints Stress fractures Tennis elbow Bursitis Fasciitis Nerve entrapment	Pain or other symptoms that get worse with activity and improve with rest* Tightness, popping, or grinding in joints Mild or localized swelling Weakness	You have localized pain that gets worse over time or increases with continued activity You have pain, swelling, stiffness, or weakness that prevents you from training You have pain or other symptoms that don't go away even with home treatments and rest You have pain that interrupts your daily activities or disrupts your sleep

*Overuse injuries are characterized by the way they develop. At first, symptoms are mostly only noticeable after vigorous activity. As the condition becomes worse, the symptoms start to occur with any activity. Eventually, the symptoms restrict activity.

Rub Some Dirt on It? Knowing When to Go to Sick Call

Conventional Army wisdom says that if you're hurt, you should rub some dirt on it and drink water. Well, it's not really Army wisdom; it's just something people say when a soldier gets injured. However, that's almost universally the wrong answer. Sure, you can walk it off if you get the wind knocked out of you when you're playing football at PT — but you can't do that with injuries.

Go to sick call or get emergency treatment if you're suffering an obvious injury, such as a broken bone that's sticking out of your skin or a swollen ankle that's turning more purple by the minute. Definitely go to sick call if your symptoms don't go away after rest and home treatment, like ice and heat (see the following section), or if an injury is holding you back from everyday activities, including PT or performing your job. As a soldier, you're entitled to go to sick call whenever you feel it's necessary, so please don't let anything hold you back if you feel like you're injured. I've said it before, and I'll say it again: You're the one who has to live in your body long after you leave military service, so take care of it. Going to the doctor now (and having your injuries properly documented) can save you weeks of frustration with the VA later, too.

When RICE Isn't a Carb: Treating Injuries at Home

RICE is an at-home treatment system that can help you determine whether an injury is serious — and at best, it can fix your issue and get you moving again. It's an acronym for rest, ice, compression, and elevation, each of which is important to help reduce swelling, ease your pain, and speed up the healing process. Most people can treat minor injuries, such as a slight sprain or strain, with RICE at home. Your doctor may also recommend it in conjunction with medical treatment for more serious injuries.

If you have any injury that's not getting better with RICE, or if it's substantial enough to cause pain that stops you from performing normal activities, see a doctor. You're in the Army, so all it costs you is the time you spend waiting to be seen. Besides, you need every injury to be documented in your medical file — just ask any senior NCO with back problems.

Rest as a home remedy

Pain is your body's way of telling you to knock off whatever it is you're doing. As soon as something hurts, stop it. Don't try to push through or work out despite the pain — there's nothing tough (or smart) about doing that. If you keep it up, you're risking further injury. You can even cause permanent damage, which is the last thing anybody wants.

If you have an injured extremity, rest it for at least 24 (but preferably 48) hours. Unless it happens on a Friday afternoon, that may mean going to sick call or making a same-day appointment with your PCP to get a temporary profile.

If you're new to the Army, you need to know that you can't just tell someone you're injured and expect that person to let you out of PT (or anything else, for that matter). You absolutely must have a physical profile to be exempted from any activity based on an injury.

Putting an injury on ice

Ice helps reduce pain and swelling, so it's the second component of the tried-and-true RICE home treatment. Apply an ice pack for 15 to 20 minutes every two to three hours during the first 48 hours after your injury. Wrap it in a towel to keep your skin comfortable and prevent frostbite injury (I personally use a soft pillowcase). If you don't have an ice pack, a bag of frozen vegetables or even loose ice in a zippered plastic bag works just as well. You should notice a little improvement in the way your injury feels after icing it for a while — but if you don't, that's a good sign you need to see a doctor, stat.

Keeping your injury under (compression) wraps

Swelling, also called edema, is the result of a rush of fluid and white blood cells (your body's own little soldiers) to the injured area. Sometimes it's also because small tears in the surrounding blood vessels cause fluid to leak into the area.

Swelling can be painful — and sometimes your body freaks out and swells too much. A compression wrap can minimize swelling and the pain that comes with it, provided that you wrap it correctly. Use an elastic medical bandage and wrap it snugly but not too tight. If it's too tight, it acts like a tourniquet and interrupts blood flow. If the skin below the elastic bandage turns blue or feels cold, tingly, or numb, loosen the bandage immediately. (And if the color doesn't return to normal, or if the area stays cold, tingly, or numb, you need to head to the ER.)

TIP

If you have an injury that results in swelling, go to sick call or set up an appointment with your PCP. You'll get a couple of ice packs and elastic bandages out of the deal, plus the standard 800-milligram bottle of ibuprofen to keep your tissues from going overboard with swelling. You may even get a profile that gives you enough time to recover properly.

Elevating an injured extremity

Gravity works against everyone — and in more ways than one. If you're injured, try to keep your injury elevated above your heart. Elevation reduces pain, swelling, and that uncomfortable throbbing feeling that comes with both. You can't prop your foot up on your battalion commander's desk while you're explaining how you sprained your ankle jumping off the maintenance bay's roof, but you can keep it propped up on a few pillows while you're watching TV at night. The Centers for Disease Control and Prevention recommends that you keep an injured area raised whenever you can, regardless of whether you're icing it or wrapping it.

3

Structure, Form, and Functional Fitness

Get in the know with tips and tricks for working out.

Put your muscles on the map so you know which areas need work (and what to do about it).

Pick up heavy-duty information on training with body weight, free weights, and machines.

Figure out how much cardiovascular exercise you need to improve your performance on the ACFT and how to measure heart health.

Tighten up your core knowledge and discover easy ways to strengthen your body's most essential muscle groups.

Make your workout work for you by tailoring it to your needs.

Chapter 13

Wising Up to Workout Wisdom

Working out effectively is a science. Sure, anyone can slap some weight on a bar and knock out a few reps, but everything you do in the gym, on the track, and even between workouts is important if you want to reap the full benefits. Your goals determine your path. For example, if you want to lose weight, you focus on getting your heart rate up and mixing in some strength training. If you want to build muscle, your primary focus sends you toward the weight machines at the fitness center. If you want to knock out a dozen leg tucks on the ACFT, you do the exercises that prep your body for the Leg Tuck (LTK) event. You get the picture.

Successful exercisers get into a routine that helps them maximize performance and reach their goals, and they know that the best path to achieving a goal is the shortest and simplest one.

Following Eight Habits of Highly Successful Exercisers

You didn't buy this book because you want to take your Two-Mile Run time down from 23 minutes to 22 minutes. You picked it up because you know you need to perform well and you want to get from Point A (where you usually hang out) to Point B (a fitter, healthier you) as quickly and efficiently as possible. (To find out just how well you need to do on the ACFT, check out the Physical Demand Categories in Chapter 4.) You can do that, barring injury, illness, or other physical limitations, by implementing the eight habits in the following sections.

Make health a lifestyle

You have to look at the big picture — and sometimes big changes are necessary. You're not going to diet for a month. You're going to skip temporary fixes and prioritize your workouts, rest days, and nutrition. That doesn't mean you can't slip up, but it does mean that if you try a crash course to prep for the ACFT or weight and tape, you're going to do just that: crash. And burn. And then crash and burn in six months when your next ACFT rolls around.

TIP

Even if you don't need to lose weight to stay within Army standards, make the dietary changes necessary to keep your body performing well.

Have fun with it

Working out is hard; no way around that. But you can make it fun by getting an "accountabilibuddy" or working out with friends. Do things you like to do, whether you're hiking or swimming laps in the sun, playing sports, or even participating in a group exercise program like MOSSA's Group Power or Cardio Blast. Try to find enjoyment in working out so it's not a chore that you dread.

Look at what you're doing as training, not exercising

When professional athletes train, they don't worry about what others are doing. They focus on doing their best during each workout. World record-holding sprinter Usain Bolt once said, "If you turn up worrying about how you're going to perform, you've already lost. Train hard, turn up, run your best, and the rest will take care of itself."

Get back on track as soon as you can

Everybody goes off the rails occasionally while they're training. Sometimes life gets in the way, and sometimes you just need a physical and mental break. Sometimes you just have to eat an entire cheesecake in one sitting. (Only me?) But when people who have made health a lifestyle get off-track, they get right back on. Try to remember that you're not just training for the next ACFT on the calendar. The work you're putting in now will help you on the next one, the next one, and the one after that, too.

Ask for help when you need it

When someone is woefully uninformed but thinks he or she knows it all, what happens is the *Dunning Kruger effect*. It's a cognitive bias that causes people with low ability to overestimate that ability. Don't be that guy. Highly successful exercisers and professional athletes defer to experts and are open to coaching. Use your unit's Master Fitness Trainer; that's what he or she is there for. And for Pete's sake, don't buy an expensive exercise machine after seeing it on a late-night infomercial.

Keep it simple

Don't overanalyze every workout, count every calorie, or try to plan every exercise on a rigid schedule. "From 0804 to 0807: Sit-ups. From 0807 to 0808: Rest. From 0808 to 0811: Bicep curls." That's too much to focus on, and it'll suck the joy out of every workout. (And if you're already struggling to *find* joy in your workouts, it'll be the last nail in the coffin.) Making things too complicated leads to burnout, frustration, and a sense of hopelessness, so keep your workouts as simple, manageable, and fun as you can.

Don't use weight loss as an indicator of your workout's effectiveness

Changes in diet drive weight loss, so gauge the effectiveness of your workouts on more than just what the scale says. Look at improvements in your strength and performance over time. If you need to, keep track of your progress in a notebook. Write down your run time each week, how much weight you lifted, or the number of reps you're able to do in a workout journal. Remember that muscle is denser than fat, so you may even gain weight when you commit to an exercise program, but it'll all shake out in the end because you'll pass tape.

WHAT ABOUT POPULAR WORKOUT PROGRAMS?

You've probably heard about a million popular workout programs during your time in the Army. Some are better than others, but some are downright harmful. As a general rule, steer clear of anything that encourages you to throw form out the window in exchange for knocking out more and more reps with more and more weight each time — no matter how many people won't shut up about it. Any exercise program that tells you that you should perform fast, difficult moves with weights when you're already fatigued is basically a recipe for injury. Likewise, if a workout program doesn't prioritize recovery, it should be a no-go. Watch out for programs that you can't customize by weight, reps, or other modifications, or that require you to perform "as many reps as possible" in a certain number of minutes. Exercise science just doesn't support these kinds of training. If you're interested in starting an exercise program, search the Internet for the program's name plus "fails" and talk to your PCP. That should tell you whether it's safe.

Mix endurance and strength training

Overall, you're better off if you do some endurance training and some strength training. Don't get tunnel vision about one or the other. They work together to make you healthier and fitter.

Optimizing Your Breathing for Your Activity

Breathing comes naturally to most people. It's one of the few things you never have to think about . . . except you *do* have to think about it when you're working out. If you breathe properly, you get more oxygen where your body needs it most. In turn, you perform better, burn more fat, and are able to relax more effectively after an intense workout.

The best way to breathe depends on what you're doing. The following sections break down a few breathing techniques for common activities.

Breathing while running

If you're anything like me, you're sucking wind after the first half-mile. When your breaths are short and rushed (like they naturally are when you sprint, and like most people's are during regular running), you keep more carbon dioxide in your body, which increases your heart rate and lactic acid production. In turn, your endurance decreases.

REMEMBER

Use the 3:2 inhale-exhale ratio instead. It goes like this: You inhale through your left, right, and left foot strikes on the ground. Then, you exhale fully on the right and left foot strikes. Try slowing your pace until you master the technique, and then give it a shot on a normal-speed run. You'll probably notice a lower heart rate.

Army cadences help you breathe properly while you're running because they're written to do so, but they don't follow the 3:2 ratio. Instead, they make you fully inhale and exhale forcefully as you sing — getting more oxygen into your body.

Breathing during strength training

Lifting, pushing, and pulling require you to breathe differently than you do when you aren't exerting yourself. Getting your breathing technique down for these activities is really important because if you do it incorrectly, you're inviting internal injuries (like hernias).

Here's the rule to follow: Always exhale on exertion. If you're pulling yourself up into a leg tuck, exhale. Inhale when you're on your way back down. If you're doing chest presses, inhale on the push and exhale when you lower the bar back to your chest.

Breathing to relax

Breathing can help you with stress management any time. Think about how you breathe when you first wake up in the morning, or how you breathe when you're binge-watching your favorite TV show. It's a lot different than it is when you're taking heat from your first sergeant or when you're working out.

Deep breathing is a great way to force your body to shake off stress. When you breathe deeply, your brain gets the signal that it's time to chill and sends that message to your body. You can use a couple of methods for deep breathing, but belly breathing is something simple you can do even while you're at work. Here's how:

1. **Sit in a comfortable position.**

2. **Put one hand on your abdomen, just below your ribs, and put your other hand on your chest.**

3. **Take a deep breath in through your nose, leaving your chest out of it so that your belly pushes your hand out.**

4. **Breathe out through your mouth as you feel your stomach move in with your hand (and use your hand to push all the air out).**

Take your time with each breath, and try to do it 5 to 10 times in one sitting. You'll find that you feel different — and probably better — when you're done.

Resting between Workouts

Working out breaks down your body tissues, so you have to give yourself time to repair and rebuild. You don't get stronger during a workout. You get stronger during recovery. That doesn't mean you work out one day and take the next day off, though. It means that you shouldn't work out and break down the same muscles back-to-back because they don't have enough time to get stronger in between bouts of exercise.

REMEMBER

Recovery is one of the most important aspects of training. It's right up there with doing the right exercises, using proper form, and taking in the right nutrients. I talk about recovery in a lot more detail in Chapter 9, but these are the main points to keep in mind here:

>> **You aren't going to lose gains you've made by taking a day off.** Or even a couple of days. It just doesn't work that way.

>> **Rest periods aren't really rest.** Your body is working hard to repair damaged tissues and come back stronger than before. That's part of the reason you burn extra calories after weight training.

>> **Downtime is good for you, but that doesn't mean you should turn into a couch potato on recovery days.** You should do active recovery, which I cover in Chapter 9.

Chapter **14**

Understanding Your Body's Muscular Structure

Your body is a complex machine, and you don't have to know how everything works in order to make it work for you. However, getting a good look at what you're developing to max out your ACFT score can help you tremendously.

The human body's muscular system includes three distinct types of muscle: skeletal, cardiac, and smooth. *Skeletal muscle* moves bones and other structures, *cardiac muscle* contracts your heart, and *smooth muscle* tissue changes shape so you can perform bodily functions (like digesting food and eliminating waste). You can't train your smooth muscle; its movement is involuntary. However, you can train your heart by way of building cardiorespiratory endurance, and you can certainly train your skeletal muscle.

Putting Your Skeletal Muscles on the Map

Minor differences aside, all human bodies are essentially the same when it comes to skeletal muscles. Though some bodies are larger than others are, some are more easily developed, and biological males and females produce different hormones that affect performance (as I discuss in Chapter 10), everyone is working with very similar equipment.

Getting to know your skeletal muscles

You have more than 600 skeletal muscles in your body. From the tiny muscle that stabilizes the smallest bone in your body to your gluteus maximus, skeletal muscles help you control movement, stabilize bones and joints, maintain posture, guard entrances and exits throughout your body, and generate heat. Most of these muscles are attached to your bones by bundles of collagen fibers that you know as *tendons.* Flip to Chapter 5 to get a closer look at your major muscles in the context of your whole body, including many that you use on the ACFT.

Skeletal muscle is *striated.* That means it features cells that are aligned in parallel bundles that form stripes when you view them under a microscope. This type of muscle is commonly called *voluntary muscle* because you can control its movement yourself. (Cardiac muscle is also striated, but its movement is involuntary; your brain controls that without any input from you.)

Skeletal muscles are made up of two main types of individual fibers. *Slow-twitch muscles* come into play when you're doing endurance activities. They can work for a long time without tiring. These marathon muscles are mainly involved in small, sustained movements and posture control. *Fast-twitch muscles* are good for quick and explosive movements, but they consume a lot of energy and tire quickly. They're the anaerobic powerhouses of skeletal muscle fibers.

All skeletal muscles are made up of a mixture of slow-twitch and fast-twitch fibers, but they come in different ratios depending on muscle function, extent of training, and even age. Average, nonathletic people have pretty close to a 50-50 combination of slow-twitch and fast-twitch muscle fibers. Power athletes, like Olympic weightlifters, have a higher ratio of fast-twitch muscle fibers, while endurance athletes, like long-distance runners, have more slow-twitch muscle fibers. For the ACFT, you need a good mix of both.

REMEMBER

As you may have guessed, you can develop slow-twitch muscle fibers with endurance training and fast-twitch muscle fibers with strength training. Resistance training increases the size of both, and some studies have shown that endurance training at high-intensity intervals can boost aerobic power. Developing one type of muscle fiber helps develop the other, which is why a well-rounded workout plan is essential if you want to perform your best on the ACFT.

Adding up antagonistic pairs

Skeletal muscles often (but not always) work in teams. One muscle is the primary mover and shaker for flexion, and the other is in charge of extension. For example, when you contract your biceps, your arm flexes at the elbow. When you contract your triceps, your arm moves back to an extended position. To keep your body operating properly, you should work out these teams — called *antagonistic pairs* — equally. You can even superset to make sure you're hitting it all in a short period of time, which I cover in Chapter 18.

The more you use your muscles, the more control you have over them and the more efficient they become at performing work. Strategically speaking, you can exercise your upper body's antagonistic pairs and get results in smaller muscles that don't work that often — and when you vary your exercise routine, you almost certainly hit everything you need. That's why trainers encourage you to do more than just bicep curls or squats, and it's another reason that muscle-based movement training, which you can read about in Chapter 5, is so important.

Antagonistic pairs of skeletal muscles in the upper body

The major antagonistic pairs of skeletal muscles in your upper body all control arm movements. Here they are:

>> Biceps (biceps brachii) and the triceps (triceps brachii)

>> Chest (pectoralis major) and back (trapezius)

>> Shoulders (deltoids) and back (latissimus dorsi)

Your biceps have the big job of moving your elbow and shoulder. Down toward your elbow, your bicep does all the heavy lifting; up toward your shoulder, it helps move your arm upward, forward, and sideways. Your triceps let you extend and retract your arm; when they're contracted, your elbow straightens and your forearm extends. These small-but-major muscles also help stabilize your shoulders.

One of your pectoralis major's main jobs is to control arm movements, while its antagonistic buddy, the trapezius, is responsible for moving, rotating, and stabilizing your shoulder. Both of these very large, fan-shaped muscles work together to help you do push-ups and a variety of battlefield tasks, like pushing a vehicle that's stuck in the mud.

The deltoid helps you rotate your arm, reach forward, throw an underhand pitch, elevate your arm, and reach to the side. The latissimus dorsi (commonly called lats) are in charge of arm extension, adduction, horizontal abduction, and internal rotation of the shoulder (and then some).

Antagonistic pairs of skeletal muscles in the lower body

Like your upper body (see the preceding section), your lower body has three major antagonistic pairs. These muscles work together to help you run, jump, play sports, squat, and perform a number of other functions. The major antagonistic pairs of skeletal muscles in your lower body are the

>> Gluteals and hip flexors (iliopsoas complex, or iliacus and psoas)

>> Front thighs (quadriceps) and back thighs (hamstrings)

>> Calves (gastrocnemius) and shins (tibialis anterior)

Your glutes are the biggest muscles in your body, and in addition to creating your backside's shape, they're responsible for raising your thigh to the side, rotating your legs, and pushing your hips forward. Your hip flexors (a combination of two muscles, the iliacus and the psoas) keep your core stable and maintain your gait.

The quadriceps extend your knee joint so you can walk, run, jump, and squat. Their counterparts, the hamstrings, are used for the same purposes, but they flex your knee joint so your legs bend.

Finally, your calves (gastrocnemius muscles) and shins (tibialis anterior) are a powerful antagonistic pair on your lower body. Your gastrocnemius muscle forms half your calf muscle, and its primary functions are to flex the foot at the ankle joint and flex the leg at the knee joint. Your tibialis anterior handles dorsiflexion — the action of pulling your foot toward your shin.

Zeroing in on the Cardiovascular System

Your *cardiovascular system*, which you probably know as your *circulatory system*, consists of your heart and a closed system of vessels — arteries, veins, and capillaries, to be exact. All the blood in your body flows through your cardiovascular system, which is driven by the cardiac muscle of your heart. Your heart is approximately the size of your clenched fist, but don't let its compact size fool you; just like your car's engine makes it go, your heart keeps your body going. Giving your heart plenty of exercise doesn't make it bigger (that would be dangerous), but it does make it more efficient. The more efficient your heart is, the better off you are. An efficient heart pushes out more blood with each beat, allowing it to beat more slowly and keep your blood pressure under control.

The heart has two sides, and each side has a pair of chambers. The chambers on top of each side are called the *atriums,* and the bottom chambers are called the *ventricles.* The right side pumps blood to your lungs, where it picks up oxygen, and the left side receives it on its journey back through. An electrical system in your heart controls your heart rate and coordinates the contractions it makes between the atrium and ventricle on each side.

Cardiorespiratory endurance, which is one of the things the ACFT measures, relies on fitness in your cardiovascular system, lungs, muscles, and blood vessels. This type of endurance reflects your body's ability to exercise your whole body for a sustained period of time without stopping. Distance running, swimming, and other aerobic exercises require cardiorespiratory endurance.

Keeping your heart healthy is imperative — not just so that you can perform on the ACFT but so that you can live longer and feel better as you age. The best ways to do that are to keep a healthy weight and follow a heart-healthy diet, which I cover in Chapter 21. And if you smoke, quit.

Chapter **15**

Strength Training to Get Army Strong

Muscle is denser than fat is, so it takes up less space in your body than fat does. But that's not the only reason you should focus on building your strength. Strength training has dozens of benefits; some of the most important (at least when training for the ACFT) revolve around how it helps you improve your balance, sleep better, and trim inches from your body that may be essential to passing tape on height and weight. Strength training ties into your stress levels and your overall fitness level, too. To strength train properly, you need to understand how to convey what you're doing in the gym or at home, how to stay safe when doing this specific form of exercise, where you're starting from, and what options you have to explore different kinds of training.

Bulking up Your Weight-Training Vocab

As you familiarize yourself with weight training, you'll hear these terms:

» **Rep (repetition):** A *rep* is moving a weight while doing one full movement of an exercise. For example, a full squat requires you to lower your body like you're sitting in a chair and then return to the standing position. That's one rep.

>> **Set:** A *set* is a group of reps. You may do two sets of eight reps, which means you've done a total of 16 repetitions with a break after the eighth.

>> **One-repetition maximum (1RM):** Your *1RM* is the amount of weight you can lift one time for a particular exercise.

>> **Intensity:** *Intensity* means how heavy a weight is in comparison to your 1RM. If your 1RM for a chest press is 150 pounds, using 100 pounds is more intense than using 99 pounds is.

>> **Volume:** In weight training, *volume* is the number of reps you perform. If you performed five chest flys with a ten-pound barbell last week and ten this week with the same weight, you increased the volume. (Contrast that with intensity, which would mean you increased the amount of weight you lifted but performed the same number of reps.)

>> **Frequency:** *Frequency* refers to how often you perform a particular workout, such as weightlifting or cardio, in a week.

>> **Density:** *Density* refers to how much work you do in a set period of time. If you're working out for an hour on Tuesday, when you do three sets of five different exercises and some cardio, and an hour on Thursday, when you do three sets of three different exercises and no cardio, your Tuesday workout is more dense than your Thursday workout is.

>> **Rate of perceived exertion (RPE):** Your *rate of perceived exertion* is exactly what it sounds like: a measurement of how much exertion you think you're, well, exerting. You measure it on the Borg scale (see Chapter 6 for details on the Borg RPE scale). Most weight training should put you between a 6 and a 10 on the Borg RPE scale.

>> **Muscle failure:** In practice, *muscle failure* training means you work out until each muscle group becomes unable to perform another rep. The idea is to overload a muscle to force it to adapt, and proper muscle failure training involves doing as many repetitions as you can with good form.

>> **Forced reps:** When you hit muscle failure but continue to work with the assistance of a spotter, you're doing *forced reps.* You should use these very sparingly; they can help with short-term gains, but they can hurt you over the long-term. (If you're on the fence about them, know that many powerlifters won't do forced reps.)

>> **Isolation exercises:** *Isolation exercises* are those that require only one joint to perform a full rep. A bicep curl is an isolation exercise because you only need to use your elbow joint.

>> **Compound exercises:** *Compound exercises* are those that require more than one joint to perform a full rep. A chest press is a compound exercise because it requires you to use your shoulder and elbow joints.

>> **Supersets:** *Supersets* require you to complete two exercises back to back with no rest between sets. For example, if you go straight from chest presses to push-ups, you're supersetting.

>> **Positive phase:** The *positive phase* of an exercise is the lifting part. If you're doing chest presses, the positive phase is when you push the weight away from your chest. If you're doing triceps extensions, it's when you extend the weight by straightening your arms.

>> **Negative phase:** The *negative phase* of an exercise is when you control the descent of your weight. In a bicep curl, it's when you bring the bar back down; in a leg tuck, it's lowering your body back down from the tucked position.

>> **Tempo:** *Tempo* refers to the pace of your exercise, including its positive phase and negative phase.

>> **Stress-recovery-adaptation cycle:** The *stress-recovery-adaptation cycle* is what your body goes through when you work out. When the stress of a workout is over, your body begins to recover. Then, your body tries to adapt so that if you put it under that stress again, it's better equipped to handle it. All well-planned workout regimens have this schedule in mind.

>> **Novice lifter:** A *novice lifter* is someone who can fully recover and adapt in 24 to 72 hours between workouts. That means you can add more weight to every workout without missing any reps.

>> **Intermediate lifter:** An *intermediate lifter* is a person who recovers and adapts weekly. That means you increase weight after a week of training at one weight.

>> **Advanced lifter:** An *advanced lifter* is someone who recovers and adapts monthly (or every few months). These lifters continue to use the same amount of weight for several weeks before increasing.

>> **Loading:** *Loading* is a planned period of time (typically one to three weeks) during which a lifter increases intensity, volume, or frequency and doesn't allow full recovery. Many lifters use loading to stress the body so much that it forces an adaptation response.

>> **Deloading:** *Deloading,* sometimes called *unloading,* is a one- to two-week period during which a lifter slows down in intensity, volume, or frequency to allow the body to recover.

>> **Over-reaching:** *Over-reaching* occurs when a lifter does too much — such as lifting weights too heavy for the number of reps performed — and can't recover by the next time a workout works those same muscles.

>> **Overtraining:** *Overtraining* occurs when someone puts too much stress on the body and doesn't allow adequate time to recover. It breaks the stress-recovery-adaptation cycle, and it can cause adverse effects. People who are too extreme on the exercise spectrum often overtrain and as a result are in a constant state of delayed-onset muscle soreness (DOMS; see Chapter 9) and have frequent injuries. Some popular workout programs encourage overtraining, particularly those that require people to do as many reps as possible with the heaviest possible weight (while throwing proper form out the window).

>> **Linear progression:** *Linear progression* refers to adding a little more weight to each workout, and it's especially helpful for novice lifters.

>> **Periodization:** Periodization is planned programming that includes a variation in volume, intensity, and frequency, and you use it when you go from being a novice to an intermediate lifter. You can read about periodization in the later section "Switching It up with Periodization."

>> **Circuit training:** Performing exercises without a significant period of rest between each is called *circuit training*. The Army uses circuit training in PRT (in its Strength Training Circuit), which starts with sumo squats and ends with leg tucks.

>> **Full-body training:** Training your whole body in one session is considered *full-body training*. Many popular programs, such as MOSSA Group Power, are full-body workouts in which you work everything from your calves to your shoulders.

>> **Split training:** In split training, a lifter works on one major section (like upper body or legs) and alternates each workout day. For example, you may work your biceps, triceps, shoulders, and back on Monday and Wednesday and your quads, hamstrings, and calves on Tuesday and Thursday.

>> **Body part training:** Some lifters work out only one body part per day. You may work out your back on Monday, your chest on Tuesday, your legs on Wednesday, your shoulders on Thursday, and your arms on Friday, for example.

Following Safety Principles

Effective strength training requires you to work out safely. You're not going to make any improvements if you're injured or using poor form.

Successful strength trainers know that the best time to train is after a warm-up. If your muscles are cold, your risk of injury increases. Start with a light jog and some dynamic stretching. Then, take things a little farther with a few short sets of isometric core exercises (think planks and dead bugs) — even if you're "only" working out your upper or lower body. The goal is to get your core ready to jump in and engage so you can perform all your exercises safely.

Proper form is absolutely essential in the gym. If you're doing exercises the wrong way, you're wasting effort on unintended movements — and you're probably going to work out the wrong muscles. Even worse, though, is that you significantly increase your risk of injury. Good form may look a little different on you than it does on your battle buddy, and that's largely due to differences in your physiology. Some variation is okay, especially when it stems from a person's body type or natural build, but there's a proper way to do every exercise (and thousands of ways to do them wrong). Invest a little time in learning proper form to keep yourself safe.

TIP

Nail down your form before you lift the heaviest possible weight you can handle. Start with light weights and plenty of reps so you can zero in on errors — and work deliberately and under control so you can figure out what "right" feels like.

Other checkpoints to use in the gym include the following:

>> **Breathe out when you're lifting or pushing and breathe in when you're releasing the load or weight.** That means you exhale on a bicep curl and inhale when you let the weight down. Never hold your breath when you're straining.

>> **Don't lock your joints.** Always leave a slight bend in your elbows and knees when you extend your arms or legs.

>> **Move under control.** When you move under control, you funnel stress to the right parts of your body rather than to the areas that can easily become injured. (Have you ever seen people throwing their backs into bicep curls? I have, and it makes *my* back hurt to watch.)

>> **Stop if something hurts.** Strength training exercises should cause muscle discomfort because they're hard, but they should never hurt.

REMEMBER

When you're in the gym, don't be afraid to ask how to use something properly. Getting instructions is always worth it, even if it means going up to the welcome desk and talking to the guy who watches you punch in your membership number. You can also talk to your unit's Master Fitness Trainer (MFT), who can help you nail down ways to minimize injury and use the most efficient body mechanics possible. (That goes for when you're out of the gym, too.)

Testing Your Strength

You've likely had "muscle failure" days during Army physical training (and they were probably on Tuesdays and Thursdays). The principle behind working out to muscle failure is solid — in some circumstances. Doing push-ups, sit-ups, or leg tucks until you just can't do any more is usually fine. And if you're trying to get bigger and more visible muscles, training to muscle failure with weights can be a good idea.

However, you shouldn't train to muscle failure with every set; a growing body of scientific evidence says that doing so may hinder your long-term growth. If you're into muscle failure, take this tip for a ride: Only use muscle failure on your last set of an exercise and see where that takes you in a month.

But you can use muscle failure in a different, productive way right now: to test out how you stack up to others and see how fit you're actually getting over time. Try the tests in the following sections now and then again in a month, after you've started an effective ACFT prep plan. If you use the principles and exercises in this book, you're on your way to more strength.

Checking out upper-body strength with push-ups

A simple way to measure how much your top half can handle is through push-ups. Don't time yourself, but see how many push-ups you can do before you reach muscle failure, and then compare it to the average for your age group in Table 15-1 or Table 15-2. Note that in this test, males do military-style push-ups and females do modified push-ups on their knees.

TABLE 15-1   **Push-ups for Males**

Rating	Age 20 to 29	Age 30 to 39	Age 40 to 49	Age 50 to 59	Age 60+
Excellent	55+	45+	40+	35+	30+
Good	45–54	35–44	30–39	25–34	20–29
Average	35–44	25–34	20–29	15–24	10–19
Fair	20–34	15–24	12–19	8–14	5–9
Low	0–19	0–14	0–11	0–7	0–4

TABLE 15-2 **Push-ups for Females**

Rating	Age 20 to 29	Age 30 to 39	Age 40 to 49	Age 50 to 59	Age 60+
Excellent	49+	40+	35+	30+	20+
Good	34–48	25–39	20–34	15–29	5–19
Average	17–33	12–24	8–19	6–14	3–4
Fair	6–16	4–11	3–7	2–5	1–2
Low	0–5	0–3	0–2	0–1	0

Crunching the numbers on abdominal strength

Your core strength is vital to passing the ACFT. The crunch test is a common way to see how you stack up against others and get a good overall idea of your abdominal strength. Grab a battle buddy and lie on your back on a mat with your knees bent. Rest your arms naturally at your sides (palms touching the floor) and have your buddy mark where the ends of your fingertips rest with hundred-mile-an-hour tape. Place a second piece of tape about 2.5 inches from the first piece, toward your feet.

When you're ready to start, align your fingertips with the first piece of tape. Crunch upward using your abdominal muscles, sliding your fingers along the mat to the second line. Lower your body back to the mat and do as many reps as you can without using momentum. Move in a smooth, controlled manner so you can get an accurate picture of your abdominal strength. Then, compare your number with those in Table 15-3 or Table 15-4.

TABLE 15-3 **Crunches for Males**

Rating	Age 35 and Under	Age 36 to 45	Over Age 45
Excellent	60	50	40
Good	45	40	25
Fair	30	25	15
Low	15	10	5

TABLE 15-4   Crunches for Females

Rating	Age 35 and Under	Age 36 to 45	Over Age 45
Excellent	50	40	30
Good	40	25	15
Fair	25	15	10
Low	10	6	4

Muscling your way through a leg strength test

One good measure of leg strength relies on how many squats you can do without resting. All you need is a chair and some fortitude to figure out how your abilities stack up to your peers and find your baseline. Do a light warm-up and then stand facing away from a chair with your feet shoulder-width apart. Squat down until your backside lightly touches the chair, stand up, and do it again. Keep squatting until you're unable to do any more (and then just take a seat until your legs stop wobbling and you can get up and stretch). Compare your numbers to those in Tables 15-5 and 15-6.

TABLE 15-5   Squats for Males

Rating	Age 18 to 25	Age 26 to 35	Age 36 to 45	Age 46 to 55	Age 56 to 65	Age 66+
Excellent	49+	45+	41+	35+	31+	28+
Good	44-49	40-45	35-41	29-35	25-31	22-28
Average	31-43	29-39	23-34	18-30	13-24	11-21
Poor	0-30	0-28	0-22	0-17	0-12	0-10

TABLE 15-6   Squats for Females

Rating	Age 18 to 25	Age 26 to 35	Age 36 to 45	Age 46 to 55	Age 56 to 65	Age 66+
Excellent	43+	39+	33+	27+	24+	23+
Good	37-43	33-39	27-33	22-27	18-24	17-23
Average	25-36	21-32	15-26	10-21	7-17	5-16
Poor	0-24	0-20	0-14	0-9	0-6	0-4

Switching It up with Periodization

When you're no longer new to the weight room, you may consider *periodization* training, in which you organize your workout regimen into different periods where you take a different approach to working out. Generally, these periods last anywhere from four weeks to two months. Periodization has been scientifically proven to help you avoid hitting a plateau, too.

TECHNICAL STUFF

In a study conducted at Penn State University, 30 women trained three times a week for nine months. Fifteen of the women did periodized training and changed their exercises, sets, and reps, while the other fifteen did circuit training with the same machines the entire time. The women who did circuit training hit a plateau about four months in, but the women who used periodization continued to make steady progress for the duration of the study.

Periodization is also one of the reasons group fitness classes change routines every four to six weeks — you need to switch things up for your body to make progress. In one period, you may choose to use only free weights, and in the next, you may use all machines. You may change the number of reps, sets, and even exercises you perform from one period to the next, too.

OVERTRAINING: IT'S JUST AS BAD AS POOR FORM

Motivation is an essential character trait if you want to excel in the military. But when you get so caught up in excitement about making gains and kick your workout regimen into overdrive, you're at risk for overtraining. Overtraining is an imbalance between exercise and recovery that occurs when you push your body so hard that it can't heal and adapt before you break it down again. When you're consistently sore, you have a hard time sleeping, you experience personality changes, you're extremely thirsty all the time, and your heart races when it shouldn't, there's a good chance that you're doing too much without adequate rest.

Overtraining is physically dangerous. Continual training can put you in a *catabolic state,* which means your body is burning muscle tissue rather than fat or carbohydrates as fuel. You can also run low on sodium, potassium, and magnesium because you're losing so much fluid through perspiration; in one of the worst-case scenarios, you can develop rhabdomyolysis. *Rhabdomyolysis* is a breakdown of skeletal muscle tissue, which then releases myoglobin into your bloodstream. If you have too much myoglobin in your blood stream, you're on your way to kidney damage. The takeaway? Give yourself a break. Build rest days into your routine. And if you're experiencing any of the symptoms listed here, stop what you're doing and talk to your doctor. It really may be a health emergency.

Appreciating the Real Worth of Free Weights and Weight Machines

Free weights, like dumbbells and barbells, are basic strength training tools that you can buy at your local big-box retailer. They're called *free weights* because they aren't attached to a machine; the only way to get them up and down is to use your own strength.

Dumbbells are short bars that are designed to lift with one hand, and they usually come in pairs so you don't have to work out one side at a time. Barbells are the long bars that you lift with two hands — the kind you see people doing bench presses with at the gym. Figure 15-1 shows a set of dumbbells and a barbell.

Zack McCrory

You can do hundreds of exercises with free weights. In fact, you perform nearly all of the exercises I describe in Chapter 8 with free weights. They're popular in functional fitness programs because they're so versatile, and you can use them in your own garage without buying an expensive machine that lets you do only a handful of specific exercises. Free weights are *amazing* tools for beginners, even if they seem intimidating at the gym.

Weight machines, like free weights, are definitely components of a well-rounded fitness regimen. And because they limit your range of motion and help encourage proper form, as well as enable you to isolate muscle groups, they're a great choice for beginners and experienced lifters. You can find several types of machines, including some that rely on plates you load up yourself, some with stacks of rectangular weight plates that you can adjust with a pin, and even some that use air pressure to provide resistance.

Weight machines do take a lot of the guesswork out of working out, but paying attention to your form is still important. If you're not sure how to use something in your gym, just ask; you can usually find plenty of people who love talking about working out. You can also ask your unit's MFT for guidance or work out with a battle buddy who has more experience with weights than you do. If all else fails, look at the side of the machine. Most feature illustrated instructions on proper use.

Looking at Group Strength Training

Group strength training is a wonderful way to find your groove at the gym — literally. Several great programs include choreographed moves to modern music, which creates several advantages for participants:

>> The music helps distract you from how tough the workout is, and it makes an hour feel like just a few minutes.

>> The choreographed moves take the guesswork out of what you're doing, and the instructor typically demonstrates unfamiliar moves before they come at you during the routine. You can watch the instructor (and your classmates) for a look at proper form.

>> You can choose your own weights and get one-on-one guidance from your instructor when you need it.

>> The group environment creates a sense that you're all in it together, so it's a fun way to get your workouts in (especially if you're short on time) and make new friends.

When you're choosing a group workout that's right for you, make sure it's a low-pressure environment — not one that demands you push yourself until you collapse, especially if you're a beginner. Find one that offers functional fitness exercises (see Chapter 5), blends body weight training with free weights, and includes balance training as well. For your body's sake, only choose a fitness program that prioritizes recovery, involves exercises that you're comfortable doing, and uses a variety of exercises so your body doesn't get used to what you're doing and plateau.

IN THIS CHAPTER

» Seeing how your cardiovascular system relates to exercise and endurance

» Testing your cardiorespiratory endurance

» Improving your fitness through cardio

Chapter **16**

Pumping Some Heart-Smart Aerobic Exercise

T he Army Combat Fitness Test is designed to measure your cardiorespiratory endurance, which is a fancy way of saying the military wants to know how well your heart, lungs, and muscles can work together for an extended period of time. The main event on the ACFT that measures your cardiorespiratory endurance is the Two–Mile Run, but you're not getting off that easily — the other events also get your heart pumping and your lungs working.

The best way to improve your cardiorespiratory endurance is to use it by running, cycling, swimming, and other cardio exercises, as well as being careful about your diet (which I cover in Chapter 24).

Understanding the Cardiovascular System's Role in Exercise

Your *cardiovascular system* consists of your heart; arteries, arterioles, and capillaries; and veins and venules. Your heart pushes oxygenated blood to your body through the arteries, arterioles, and capillaries, and the blood makes its return trip through venules and veins.

TECHNICAL STUFF

If you laid all the vessels in your cardiovascular system end-to-end, they'd extend for about 60,000 miles. Technically, they could wrap around the Earth twice with length to spare.

Arteries carry oxygenated blood away from your heart, while veins carry "oxygen-poor" blood back so it can get a refill. One exception: Your pulmonary artery brings oxygen-poor, waste-product-filled blood to your lungs (oxygen's main entry point into the body, and the point from which you exhale waste), and your pulmonary vein brings newly oxygenated blood back to your heart. Check out the heart in Figure 16-1.

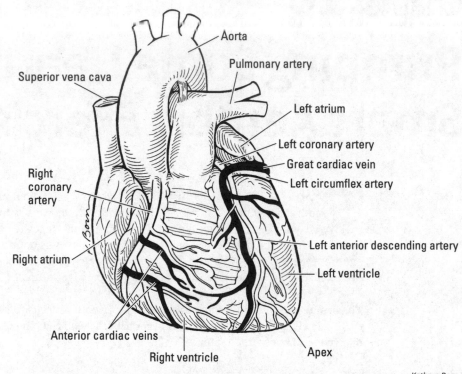

FIGURE 16-1:
The heart.

Kathryn Born

Your heart runs on an electrical system — it's the internal pacemaker you were born with. Electrical impulses that travel down a pathway through your heart trigger each heartbeat. That's why doctors can use electricity to restart your heart and electric pacemakers to keep it going if your own electrical system fails. Three major components make your ticker tick:

» **The sinoatrial (SA) node:** The *SA node* is a small bundle of specialized cells in your right atrium that serves as your heart's pacemaker. The electrical activity spreads through the walls of the atria, causing them to contract. That contraction forces blood into your ventricles.

» **The atrioventricular (AV) node:** The *AV node* is a group of cells in the center of your heart that slows down the electrical signal the SA node sends out. That way, the atria can contract before the ventricles do.

» **His-Purkinje network:** The His-Purkinje network is a pathway of fibers that send the electrical impulse to the walls of your ventricles, which causes them to contract. When your ventricles contract, they push blood out of your heart to your lungs and the rest of your body.

This one small electrical impulse is what keeps you alive, and it fires faster and faster when you exercise with increasing intensity.

Starting with resting heart rate

A normal heart beats between 50 and 99 times a minute at rest. Things like exercise, some medications, fevers, and stress can cause these electrical impulses to occur closer together, resulting in an increased heart rate.

When external factors aren't affecting your heart rate (when you're resting under normal circumstances), lower is better. That means your heart is so efficient that it doesn't have to work hard just to get blood and oxygen to the rest of your body. An extremely low or extremely high resting heart rate isn't good, though — either can be downright dangerous.

When your resting heart rate is too low, it's called *bradycardia.* "Too low" depends on the person, though. If you're a physically active person, a resting heart rate of 50 (or even lower — some professional athletes have resting heart rates in the 40s) is usually fine.

When your resting heart rate is too high, it's called *tachycardia.* "Too high" also depends on the person, but usually, more than 100 beats per minute (bpm) means your heart is working too hard when you're at rest. If your heart rate stays too high for too long, your heart muscles are being starved of oxygen; eventually, those cells can die and cause a heart attack.

Linking heart efficiency and exercise

Exercise strengthens your whole body — including your heart. The more you exercise, the stronger and more efficient your heart becomes. A strong heart doesn't need to beat as often because it pushes out more blood with each beat. In that way, it's like every other muscle in your body. If you can carry two sandbags in one trip, you're more efficient than you'd be if you could only carry one.

The more efficient your heart becomes, the better it can supply oxygen to your body, which enables you to exercise harder and for longer periods of time. When you exercise regularly, your body also gets better at pulling oxygen out of your blood and using it as fuel. That improves your athletic performance across the board.

Identifying why the Army measures cardiorespiratory fitness

When the Army uses the ACFT to measure your cardiorespiratory fitness, it's really measuring how efficiently your body works with oxygen. That lets the military know how likely you are to be able to hold up to the rigors of combat.

From a longer-term standpoint, encouraging all its soldiers to reach high cardiorespiratory fitness levels is in the Army's best interests. Physical activity makes you generally healthier (now and in the future), so the Army and the Veterans Administration will have to worry about helping you through fewer physical ailments. Exercise can

>> Allow better blood flow in the small blood vessels in your heart, which helps prevent clogs that cause heart attacks

>> Increase your levels of HDL cholesterol (the good kind of cholesterol that lowers your risk of heart disease by flushing the bad kind of cholesterol — LDL — out of your system)

>> Keep your weight down

>> Improve your mood

>> Lower your risk for some types of cancer

>> Reduce your risk of osteoporosis

>> Give you more energy and help you sleep better so you function better

Finding Your VO₂ Max

VO₂ max is an important measurement of your cardiorespiratory fitness. This number shows your *maximal oxygen uptake*, the maximum rate of oxygen you can use while you're exercising at your hardest. The more oxygen you can use at that point, the more energy you can produce. This reading is important because your muscles need oxygen when you're performing prolonged aerobic exercise (like running), and your heart has to be able to pump enough blood throughout your body to meet its demands. Most experts consider VO₂ the best indicator of cardiovascular fitness and aerobic endurance.

Professionals test cardiorespiratory endurance by measuring a person's VO₂ max. You can set an appointment at an Army Wellness Center to have your resting oxygen intake and your VO₂ max measured. You can also test yourself by using *submaximal* tests (which don't require you to hit your maximum capacity) like the Astrand Treadmill Test, the 2.4-km Cooper Run Test, and the Multistage Beep Test. You can read about these tests in the following sections; for more on ways to improve your VO₂ max, check out the later section "Queuing up the Cardio."

REMEMBER

Don't get caught up in the numbers. Figuring out what your VO₂ max is right now can give you a baseline so you can measure your improvement over time, but VO₂ isn't the only component of fitness.

Astrand Treadmill Test

The Astrand Treadmill Test is a way to measure your aerobic fitness by using a treadmill that has an adjustable speed and gradient, a stopwatch, and a battle buddy (if you want help). This method requires a little math, but when you're finished, you can compare your results to those listed in the tables later in this section to see how your results stack up.

USING THE ARMY WELLNESS CENTER FOR FITNESS TESTING

When you go to an Army Wellness Center and take its tests, you get a printout that tells you where you are as of that day. You can go back every month and ask the folks there to retest you. Over time, they build graphs and charts that show you how your fitness levels are improving. The first time I went to an Army Wellness Center, I was surprised to learn that my body fat percentage was higher than I physically felt like it was, but my VO₂ max and metabolic equivalent were pretty similar to what my fitness-tracking watch was telling me. (You can read more about metabolic equivalents in Chapter 23.)

The longest the Astrand Treadmill Test can take you is 17 minutes, but you may stop before you run the full amount of time. That's okay; the test is designed to allow you to figure out your VO_2 max, even after a short period of time on the treadmill. You don't change the speed at any point during the test. You change only the incline.

Here's how to perform the test:

1. **Get on the treadmill and set your speed to 5 miles per hour.**

2. **Have your partner start the stopwatch as soon as the treadmill starts moving.**

3. **Move at 5 miles per hour for three minutes and then set the treadmill's incline to a grade of 2.5 percent.**

4. **Continue to add 2.5 percent to the treadmill's incline every two minutes thereafter until you're unable to continue.**

   Your partner can tell you to increase the grade every two minutes. Table 16-1 has a breakdown of the time you spend in each stage and the inclines you need.

5. **Have your partner stop the stopwatch as soon as you hit "Stop" on the treadmill.**

6. **Calculate your VO_2 max by using this formula, where *time* is time in minutes:** $VO_2 \ max = (time \times 1.444) + 14.99$

If you stop the test after 12 minutes and 30 seconds (that's 12.5 minutes), your formula will look like this:

$$VO_2 \ max = (12.5 \times 1.444) + 14.99$$

When you run these numbers through a calculator (remember to do what's in the parentheses first — hey, I'm all about mental workouts, too), the results come out to 33.04. That's your VO_2 max.

Write down your own VO_2 max and find it in Table 16-2 if you're a male or Table 16-3 if you're a female to see your projected level of cardiorespiratory fitness.

TABLE 16-1

Astrand Treadmill Test Stages

Stage	Speed	Time in Stage	Incline
1	5 mph	3 minutes	0%
2	5 mph	2 minutes	2.5%
3	5 mph	2 minutes	5%
4	5 mph	2 minutes	7.5%
5	5 mph	2 minutes	10%
6	5 mph	2 minutes	12.5%
7	5 mph	2 minutes	15%
8	5 mph	2 minutes	17.5%

TABLE 16-2

VO$_2$ Max Cardiorespiratory Fitness Levels (Males)

Rating	Age 13 to 19	Age 20 to 29	Age 30 to 39	Age 40 to 49	Age 50 to 59	Age 60+
Superior	55.9+	52.4+	49.4+	48.0+	45.3+	44.2+
Excellent	51.0–55.9	46.4–52.4	45.0–49.4	43.8–48.0	41.0–45.3	36.5–44.2
Good	45.2–50.9	42.5–46.4	41.0–44.9	39.0–43.7	35.8–40.9	32.3–36.4
Fair	38.4–45.1	36.5–42.4	35.5–40.9	33.6–38.9	31.0–35.7	26.1–32.2
Poor	35.0–38.3	33.0–36.4	31.5–35.4	30.2–33.5	26.1–30.9	20.5–26.0
Very poor	<35.0	<33.0	<31.5	<30.2	<26.1	<20.5

TABLE 16-3

VO$_2$ Max Cardiorespiratory Fitness Levels (Females)

Rating	Age 13 to 19	Age 20 to 29	Age 30 to 39	Age 40 to 49	Age 50 to 59	Age 60+
Superior	41.9+	41.0+	40.0+	36.9+	35.7+	31.4+
Excellent	39.0–41.9	37.0–41.0	35.7–40.0	32.9–36.9	31.5–35.7	30.3–31.4
Good	35.0–38.9	33.0–36.9	31.5–35.6	29.0–32.8	27.0–31.4	24.5–30.2
Fair	31.0–34.9	29.0–32.9	27.0–31.4	24.5–28.9	22.8–26.9	20.2–24.4
Poor	25.0–30.9	23.6–28.9	22.8–26.9	21.0–24.4	20.2–22.7	17.5–20.1
Very poor	<25.0	<23.6	<22.8	<21.0	<20.2	<17.5

2.4-km Cooper Run Test

The 2.4-km Cooper Run Test requires you to run 2.4 kilometers (1.49129 miles, but you can round up to 1.5) as fast as you can. Your time goes into a formula that gives you your VO_2 max. All you need is a stopwatch and a 2.4-kilometer hard running surface, such as a track. You can time it yourself or have someone time it for you.

Start the timer as soon as you start running and stop it as soon as you hit 2.4 kilometers. Then, put your time (in minutes) into this formula:

$$VO_2 \max = (483 \div time) + 3.5$$

Plug your numbers into a calculator, doing the math inside the parentheses first. If you run the 2.4 kilometers in 8 minutes, 30 seconds, you get 60.3. A time of 10 minutes means your VO_2 max is 51.8, and if it took you 15 minutes, it would be 35.7.

Find your numbers in Tables 16-2 and 16-3 in the preceding section to see how you measure up to the average person.

Multistage Beep Test

The Multistage Beep Test is a bit more complex than the Astrand Treadmill Test and the 2.4-km Cooper Run Test in the preceding sections. It involves running between two lines that are 20 meters apart, in time to recorded beeps that sound every minute. Each beep means the subject must run faster, and the test continues for several minutes until the runner can't keep up with the beeps any longer. Because setup (and calculating a VO_2 max) is more complicated for the Multistage Beep Test, I don't go into details here; for an individual, performing one of the other two tests is much simpler. (Usually, the Multistage Beep Test is used for athletic teams.)

Queuing up the Cardio

If you want to improve your cardiorespiratory fitness, the best way to do it is through exercise that gets your heart pumping. You can't really do much to make your lungs bigger, but you can make them more efficient by understanding your VO_2 max and doing exercises that can help increase it. I cover VO_2 max in the earlier section "Finding Your VO_2 Max."

Some of the best things you can do to improve your VO_2 max include 30:60s, 60:120s, and hill repeats, which I cover in Chapter 8. But even if you're not doing those exercises specifically, any cardio can help make your heart healthier, stronger, and more efficient. Running, cycling, swimming, and dancing are all great ways to boost your cardiorespiratory fitness level.

Hitting your target and max heart rates

When you exercise, knowing your maximum heart rate is important. Your max heart rate is the average maximum number of times your heart should beat in one minute. The simplest way to calculate your max heart rate is to subtract your age from 220. That means if you're 40, your max heart rate should be somewhere around 180 beats per minute.

You need to know your max heart rate because in order to significantly improve your cardiovascular fitness for the ACFT, you want to spend most of your cardio exercise time with your heart beating at 70 to 85 percent of that number. (Even an increase of 50 percent provides you with some benefits, as I cover in Chapter 6, but to noticeably improve, 70 to 85 percent should be your target.) If you're 40 and your max heart rate should be around 180 beats per minute, you want to exercise at a level that gets your heart beating in the range of 126 to 153. Table 16-4 gives you a quick look at target heart rate zones by age group, thanks to the American Heart Association (which places people from ages 20 to 30 in the same heart rate zones), and you can use it as a guideline when you're planning exercises.

TABLE 16-4

Average Target and Maximum Heart Rate Zones

Age (in years)	Target Heart Rate Zone (70 to 85%)	Average Maximum Heart Rate (100%)
20	140–170 bpm	200 bpm
30	133–162 bpm	190 bpm
35	129–157 bpm	185 bpm
40	126–153 bpm	180 bpm
45	122–149 bpm	175 bpm
50	119–145 bpm	170 bpm
55	116–141 bpm	165 bpm
60	112–136 bpm	160 bpm
65	109–132 bpm	155 bpm
70	105–128 bpm	150 bpm

As I discuss in Chapter 6, you can reap some benefits from even slightly elevating your heart rate. If you're generally sedentary or are on a permanent profile that's prevented you from doing much cardio, starting small and performing exercises that make your heart beat at 50 percent of its max capacity is okay. But if you want to see significant improvement, regardless of where you fall on the physical fitness spectrum, aim for exercises that really get your blood pumping.

Going beyond minimum cardio recommendations

The American Heart Association (AHA) recommends at least 150 minutes of moderate-intensity physical activity each week, so anyone doing 30 minutes of moderate cardio a day, five days a week, meets that requirement. But most Americans don't; a study by the Centers for Disease Control and Prevention found that only 20.6 percent of people get the recommended 150 minutes. The average adult does only 17 minutes of activity that qualifies as "fitness" per day.

Just by being in the Army, you're ahead of the curve (PT is required Monday through Friday), so that's good news. When you run three times per week for PT, you meet or exceed the AHA's recommendations. But those targets are just a baseline; if you want to improve, you have to do more. Advanced cardio training, which involves HIIT workouts and group cardio classes, can be extremely beneficial if you're trying to get an edge.

High-intensity interval training, or HIIT, has become trendy, and for good reason. These types of workouts are rigorous and fast, and they're efficient and effective because they include short bursts (usually three to five minutes) of incredibly intense, heart-pounding cardio exercise followed by a few minutes of lower-intensity exercises, which slow your heart rate down. Typically, your heart rate ranges between 50 and 85 percent of your max throughout a HIIT routine. A well-planned HIIT workout lets you increase your heart rate a little, bring it back down, and increase it higher with each successive exercise. You reach your highest heart rate toward the end, just before you cool down.

Many popular group cardio classes follow a similar track, and you can find them at gyms all over the country (and even overseas). Some involve low steps you can use to move your feet in time with music, while others blend music and lights in a dance club-like setting. Some of the classes I teach are the former, and believe me — you don't need rhythm to increase your heart rate and see almost immediate benefits. (You'll have a lot of fun, too.)

Chapter 17

Trying Functional Fitness Concepts for Your Core

N early everything you do in your day-to-day life — sitting at your desk, running in formation, picking up your kids, walking your dog — puts your core to work. Your core stabilizes your whole body. It helps you balance on two feet and move in any direction and helps prevent your muscles from doing things on their own. Though many people look at core work as a means to getting sculpted abs, its real importance lies in strengthening those muscles to keep you mobile and your body functional.

Introducing Your Core Muscles

Your *core muscles* are all over your body's trunk. They're in the front, on the sides, and in the back. Figure 17-1 shows your front core muscles, which include the transversus abdominis, the internal abdominal oblique, the rectus abdominis, and the external abdominal oblique.

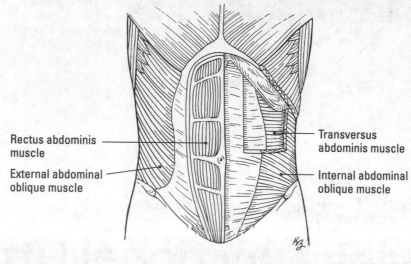

Rectus abdominis
muscle

External abdominal
oblique muscle

Transversus
abdominis muscle

Internal abdominal
oblique muscle

FIGURE 17-1:
Muscles of the
front core.

Kathryn Born

These muscles have specific functions:

>> **Transversus abdominis:** The *transversus abdominis* (or *transverse abdominal muscle*) is the deepest of your abdominal muscles, and it wraps around your spine to protect it and keep your body stable.

>> **Internal abdominal oblique:** Your *internal obliques* function on both sides of your body to flex your trunk, and *unilaterally* (on only one side or the other) to flex your trunk and rotate it to the same side.

>> **Rectus abdominis:** The *rectus abdominis* flexes your trunk forward, and it creates your six-pack.

>> **External abdominal oblique:** You have a pair of these important core muscles, and they help rotate the trunk, pull your chest downward, and support your spine when you rotate it.

Your *abdominal fascias* are sheets of connective tissue that attach, stabilize, enclose, and separate your muscles. They aren't actually muscles themselves, but they're also important.

Your back core is equally important because it directly supports your spine. The muscles of your back core include your erector spinae, multifidus, gluteus medius, gluteus minimus, which you can see in Figure 17-2, and latissimus dorsi, which you can see in Chapter 4.

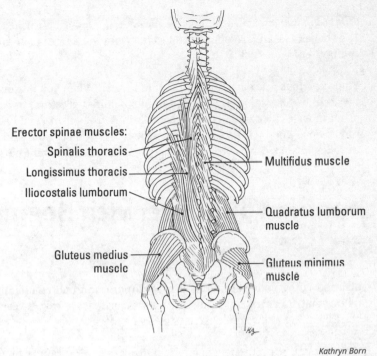

Erector spinae muscles:

Spinalis thoracis

Longissimus thoracis

Iliocostalis lumborum

Gluteus medius
muscle

Multifidus muscle

Quadratus lumborum
muscle

Gluteus minimus
muscle

FIGURE 17-2:
Muscles of the
back core.

Kathryn Born

Your back core muscles each have important jobs:

>> **Erector spinae:** These nine large muscles run almost vertically on either side of
your spine and stabilize your entire spinal column. Together, they help you bend
your back backward (like you do when you're looking directly over your head),
bend to the side (like you do when you're stretching the muscles on your side),
and rotate to either side (like you do when you're turning to look behind you).

>> **Multifidus:** This super stabilizing muscle looks out for your *lumbar spine*
the part that holds up your lower back — by working with the transversus
abdominis and your pelvic floor muscles.

>> **Gluteus medius:** Your *gluteus medius,* which lies partly under your gluteus
maximus muscle, helps move your hip joint so you can stay steady when
you're walking.

>> **Gluteus minimus:** The *gluteus minimus* helps you walk by managing the way
your *femur* (thighbone) moves and stabilizing your pelvis in relation to your
femur.

>> **Latissimus dorsi:** Your *latissimus dorsi* (lats) are the largest muscles in your
upper body; they wrap from your spine around your ribs. They connect your
arms to your vertebral column and help protect and stabilize your spine while
they provide back and shoulder strength.

Thoracolumbar fascia is a connective tissue that supports the muscles in your back. It's shaped like an arrowhead and located from the tops of your glutes to about the midpoint of your back.

Your core muscles work together automatically. When you do something like pick up a child, for example, your abdominals, spinal erectors, and a whole host of other muscles kick into action to contribute to the effort (and keep you from tipping over). When you do a leg tuck on the ACFT, you use your latissimus dorsi, the muscles in your front core, and other muscles from different parts of your body.

Strengthening Your Core with Beginner Core Exercises

Strengthening your core helps prevent injury and makes moving easier. It also helps you trim down, so fitting into your favorite jeans may be easier, too. You can start by doing a few core exercises every day.

Whether you're pretty new to physical fitness training, you're bouncing back after an injury or childbirth, or you're concerned about working your core, a handful of "beginner" core exercises can help you build strength. Before you dive into dedicated exercises, though, make sure you're making core-smart choices throughout the day, such as the following:

>> **Hold your stomach in whenever you think of it.** Don't suck it in — just tighten your muscles so your tummy becomes flatter and your bellybutton gets closer to your spine while you breathe normally.

>> **Walk in place while you're watching TV.** If you're counting steps, try to get a thousand during each episode (it'll take about 10 minutes to get them all).

>> **Swap out your work chair for an exercise ball for a half-hour a day.**

>> **Sit on the floor cross-legged (and with a straight back) when you're going to be in one place for a while.**

Strengthening your core does require some work on your part. You can check out the simple at-home core exercises in the following sections to get started.

Hip lifts

Hip lifts can loosen your joints and help strengthen the muscles that control your hips' movement. Check them out in Figure 17-3; they're great whether you're new to core work or you're a seasoned pro.

FIGURE 17-3:
Hip lifts.

Here's how to do hip lifts:

1. **Lie flat on your back with your knees bent at about a 90-degree angle.**

   Keep your arms at your sides and make sure your spine is neutral.

2. **Press your feet into the floor and lift your hips toward the ceiling.**

   Tighten your entire core while you make this move.

3. **Hold that position for three to five seconds.**

4. **Lower your hips back down under control, returning to a neutral position on the floor.**

Repeat this exercise 10 times.

Crunches

Crunches (shown in Figure 17-4) work out your abs, your internal and external obliques, and the transversus abdominis. All four of these muscles need regular workouts if you want to keep them strong (and keep your stomach as flat as possible).

FIGURE 17-4:
Crunches.

Zack McCrory

Performing crunches is pretty simple:

1. **Lie on your back with your knees bent, fingertips lightly touching the back of your head or neck, and feet flat on the floor.**

   Keep space between your chin and chest by looking up at the ceiling.

2. **Raise your shoulder blades off the floor by using your core muscles.**

3. **Slowly lower yourself back to the floor.**

If you're new to crunches, repeat this exercise 5 to 10 times. Then, add more reps when you're ready.

Bicycle kicks

Your obliques and abs get plenty of work with bicycle kicks, which you can see in Figure 17-5.

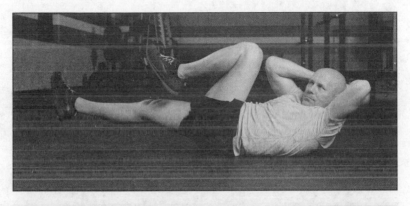

FIGURE 17-5: Bicycle kicks.

Zack McCrory

You can modify the height of your legs to change the intensity you feel with each bicycle kick — just follow these directions:

1. **Lie on your back with your knees bent so your calves are parallel to the floor.**

Touch the back of your head lightly.

2. **Raise your shoulders off the floor and straighten your left leg while you pull your right knee in toward your chest.**

3. **Alternate so you straighten your right leg while you pull your left knee in toward your chest, like you're riding a bicycle.**

Don't lower your shoulders to the floor or relax your torso.

Repeat this exercise 15 times on each side and add more reps when you're comfortable.

The Superman

Your back core muscles get stronger with use, and the Superman exercise in Figure 17-6 is one way to make sure they get plenty of action.

FIGURE 17-6:
The Superman.

Zack McCrory

Here's how to do a Superman:

1. **Lie facedown on the ground, stretching your arms out above your head and letting the tops of your feet rest on the ground.**

2. **Raise both hands and feet at the same time, trying to get 6 inches between them and the floor.**

Keep your head straight and look at the floor.

3. **Hold the position for three to five seconds and then return to the starting position.**

Repeat this exercise 10 times.

TIP

You can modify this exercise by putting your arms straight out to the side rather than overhead, or you can even pull your arms down to your sides with your elbows bent while you hover your arms off the ground.

Pulling Your Own Weight During Core Training

When you're doing core work, many exercises let you add weight to increase the challenge and put more stress on your muscles. For example, you can do crunches while holding a weight plate on your chest, hold a dumbbell in your hands while you do Russian twists, or even try Supermans while holding a light medicine ball between your feet. And many other core exercises already include weights, such as renegade rows and kettlebell pull-throughs (which I cover in Chapter 8).

Bodyweight alone is extremely effective, too. Exercises like V-ups, scissor crunches, and side planks can give you just the right challenge; if you need more intensity, add more reps. These may feel a little more difficult (and require a bit more coordination) to perform than the core exercises in the preceding section, but they're absolutely okay for beginners who want to give them a shot.

V-ups

V-ups, which you've probably done during PT a time or two, challenge your rectus abdominus, your obliques, and your back core muscles. They even help work your quads and hamstrings, too. Figure 17-7 shows a V-up.

FIGURE 17-7:
V-ups.

Zack McCrory

Here's how to tackle the V-up:

1. **Lie on your back with your legs and arms extended forward.**

2. **Simultaneously raise your upper and lower body while trying to touch your fingers to your toes.**

3. **Return to the starting position and repeat.**

TIP

Don't forget to breathe. Exhale while you raise your body and inhale while you lower it.

Scissor kicks

Scissor kicks, which you most likely know as flutter kicks, work your hip flexors and transversus abdominis. Even if you're an experienced exerciser, you're going to feel multiple reps of these moves (shown in Figure 17-8) in your hip flexors.

FIGURE 17-8:
Scissor kicks.

Zack McCrory

Although you've probably done scissor kicks plenty of times, step-by-step instructions never hurt:

1. **Lie on your back with your arms by your sides (or beneath your buttocks) and your legs extended out in front of you.**

2. **Press your lower back toward the mat and tuck in your pelvis.**

3. **Lift both your legs 6 to 12 inches off the ground.**

   You can lift them higher if you're not ready to keep them close to the ground.

4. **Lift your left leg up and slightly lower your right leg to the floor.**

5. **Lower your left leg so it's 6 to 12 inches from the floor (or wherever you started) while simultaneously raising your right leg.**

6. **Continue making scissoring motions with your legs as straight as you can keep them.**

Try two sets of 12 to 20 reps, and if you're not feeling challenged enough, add more sets.

Side planks

Side planks put a big target on your obliques, which don't really get much attention during normal crunches or other exercises that require your abs to move back and forth. They're very simple to do, whether you choose to rest on your forearm or your palm. Figure 17-9 shows a good side plank.

FIGURE 17-9:
Side plank.

Zack McCrory

The side plank is simpler than it feels:

1. **Lie on your right side with your legs extended and stacked from your hips to your feet.**

   Prop your right elbow directly beneath your right shoulder.

2. **Engage your abdominal muscles as you lift your hips and knees from the ground.**

   Keep your torso in a straight line — don't sag or bend. As soon as you start to sag, or to roll, come out of the plank so you don't get a strain injury.

3. **Hold the position with a goal of 60 seconds (but don't stress if you don't make it that long).**

4. **Switch sides and repeat the process.**

When you have the balancing aspect down and can hold a side plank on your forearm for 60 seconds, graduate to resting on your palm with your arm fully extended.

You can modify this exercise by bending the knee on the ground (or both knees) behind you.

Trying Out the Army (Core) Ball — No ASUs Necessary

A stability ball can really help strengthen your core, and you can use it for a huge variety of exercises. Even taking 30 minutes out of your day to sit on a stability ball can work wonders for your muscles. You don't have to be an experienced exerciser to use a ball in your workouts; they're good for anyone who wants to work on core stability, balance, and strength. Check out these exercises you can do with a stability ball.

Ab rolls

Ab rolls require you to kick your core muscles into high gear because you have to balance while using your abs to stabilize your body. Figure 17-10 shows an ab roll in action.

Follow these steps to do an effective ab roll (or a dozen):

1. **Place your hands on a stability ball in front of you with your arms parallel to each other.**

2. **Slowly roll forward, rolling the ball out as far as you can without arching (or straining) your back.**

3. **Push your elbows into the ball and squeeze your abs to pull your body back to the starting position.**

Repeat this exercise for 12 to 16 reps.

FIGURE 17-10:
Ab rolls.

Zack McCrory

Stability ball knee raises

Balancing on the ball with your core braced to do knee raises is great for every part of your core. Check out this exercise in Figure 17-11.

Here's how to do these knee raises.

1. **Balance on the ball with your buttocks barely hanging from the edge.**

2. **Lightly touch your hands to the back of your head.**

3. **Lift your right foot off the ground and bring your knee toward your chest.**

4. **Return your foot to the ground under control and repeat with your left leg.**

Zack McCrory

Do 12 to 16 of these moves, and you'll be feeling it in your core.

TIP

Turn this exercise into a bicycle crunch by trying to meet your knee with your opposite elbow. That works your obliques, too.

Stability ball hip thrusts

The stability ball hip thrusts in Figure 17-12 share the load with your glutes and hamstrings while you work your core muscles.

Grab a stability ball and try these for yourself:

1. **Lie faceup on the floor with your heels resting on a stability ball, hips lifted off the floor, and legs almost straight.**

2. **Engage your core and pull the ball toward your glutes by bending your knees.**

   Squeeze your glutes and hamstrings during the entire movement.

3. **Extend your legs and return to the starting position.**

FIGURE 17-12: Stability ball hip thrusts.

Zack McCrary

Perusing Core Exercises for Pregnancy Profiles

Working out during pregnancy — with special emphasis on your core — can help you feel better and even bounce back faster post-pregnancy. Keeping a strong core can help you

>> Steer clear of back pain

>> Increase the amount of oxygen flowing through your system while you're exercising

>> Improve digestion

>> Push harder during delivery

>> Lose baby weight and recover after delivery

REMEMBER

Before you start a new exercise program, talk to your obstetrician to make sure you're cleared for certain activities. After you get the green light, some of the best things you can do for your core while you're pregnant, from the first trimester to the third, include walking, swimming, and moving around in general (so if the rhythm finds your feet while you're brushing your teeth, playing with your other children, cooking dinner, or doing anything else, just go with it!). You can also try — with your doctor's clearance — the exercises in the following sections.

Cat/cow

Although I discuss the cat/cow pose as a stretch in Chapter 9, it's also a great pregnancy exercise:

1. **Get on the floor on all fours, keeping your hands directly under your shoulders and your knees directly under your hips.**

2. **Relax your back while you inhale so that your baby bump gets closer to the floor, lifting your tailbone and eyes toward the ceiling.**

3. **Hold the position for a few seconds and then release back to your starting position.**

4. **Arch your back, pressing your spine up toward the ceiling while you contract your abdominal muscles.**

5. **Hold the position for a few seconds and then release back to the starting position.**

Repeat this exercise four to six times.

Modified side plank

A modified side plank is a good way to engage your core — particularly your obliques — when you're expecting. Check out this modified pose in Figure 17-13.

Here's how to do the modified side plank:

1. **Lie on your side with your bottom arm bent so your elbow is directly below your shoulder.**

    Don't tense your shoulders and neck; try to keep them in a neutral, relaxed position.

FIGURE 17-13:
Modified side
plank.

Zack McCrory

TIP

2. **Stack your legs on top of each other and bend your knees so that your feet are behind you.**

   You can decrease the intensity of this exercise by staggering your feet or putting one in front of the other.

3. **Engage your core and raise your hips off the ground, being careful not to sag.**

   Keep your body as straight as possible.

4. **Hold the position for 10 seconds and then rest.**

Repeat two or three times and then switch sides.

Side lunges

Side lunges are a lot like the forward lunge in PRT except, well, you move to the side rather than forward. The side lunge can strengthen your pelvic floor while working your abdominals, glutes, quads, hamstrings, and more. Step out at a 45-degree angle from the starting position, which you can see in Figure 17-14.

Follow these steps to do a side lunge:

1. **Stand with your feet about shoulder-width apart and your knees soft.**

2. **Take a large step out at a 45-degree angle from your body.**

3. **Slowly push yourself back to the starting position by using your leg and core muscles.**

Switch sides after you go one way and do 10 reps with each leg.

Zack McCrory

Pregnancy core stretch

Your doctor may clear you for the pregnancy core stretch depicted in Figure 17–15 (as well as some of the ab stretches I describe in Chapter 9).

The pregnancy core stretch can help release tension from your back (and may even give you some relief from back pain). You can use it after you work out or when you start to feel discomfort in your lower back. Here's what to do:

1. **Stand with your feet hip-width apart behind a chair (or near a counter, table, or other belly-height surface).**

2. **Hold the back of the chair and bend your knees while simultaneously rounding your back.**

   Tuck your chin toward your chest, and tuck in your pelvis.

Hold for 10 seconds and repeat several times if you want to.

FIGURE 17-15:
Pregnancy core
stretch.

Stretching and Toning Your Core with Pilates and Yoga

Pilates and yoga are healthy ways to stretch, strengthen, and tone your core. Both put a lot of emphasis on core engagement, but they use very different methods. People sometimes use them together because they complement each other; yoga helps improve flexibility (even in your joints) and balance, and Pilates strengthens and relaxes your muscles. I recommend *Pilates For Dummies*, by Ellie Herman, and *Yoga For Dummies*, by Larry Payne and Georg Feuerstein (both published by Wiley), if you want to explore these powerful ways to change your body for the better.

Pilates

Pilates is a low-impact exercise regimen that strengthens muscles and promotes mobility. Many of its moves target the core but work other muscles as well. Your options range from Classic Pilates and Mat Pilates to Reformer Pilates and Clinical Pilates; you can explore which version is right for you.

For many people, Pilates offers several health benefits, such as

>> Improved flexibility

>> Increased strength and muscle tone, particularly in the core

>> Better spine stabilization

>> Improved posture and balance

>> Increased body awareness

Yoga

Yoga is a mind and body practice that's been around for ages and has several styles that combine breathing techniques, physical postures, and meditation or relaxation. Yoga encourages flexibility and muscle strength, with many poses focused on the core. One of yoga's biggest benefits when it comes to a healthy core is that it helps strengthen your abdominal muscles so they can support the muscles in your back core — and as a result, they improve your posture, which can help eliminate back pain and related issues. Some styles of yoga focus more on spiritual aspects, while others are tied more into physical aspects. For that reason, yoga isn't one-size-fits-all:

>> *Hatha yoga* is a slower-moving class that requires you to hold specific poses for the space of a few breaths.

>> *Vinyasa yoga* connects movement and breath (and sometimes the pace is quick).

>> *Iyengar yoga* uses props like blocks and blankets to help you work on your range of motion.

>> *Ashtanga yoga* uses the same six poses in every class.

>> *Bikram yoga* uses 26 poses in a hot room over 90 minutes.

>> *Hot yoga* uses more than 26 poses in a hot room.

>> *Restorative yoga* is a slow-moving class with longer positional holds and focuses on deep relaxation.

Chapter **18**

Personalizing Your Workout Routine

A good workout routine covers all the areas you need improvement in and then some. You can't neglect the areas you're already strong in or you'll lose the progress you've made, so keeping your workout regimen as well-rounded as possible is a good idea. You're getting at least the minimum from conducting PT with your unit every morning, but making time to work out on your own — even if it's just a half hour every day — leads to bigger, better benefits (including enhanced performance on test day).

Building Your Own Workout Routine

Your workout routine should reflect what your body needs to gear up for the ACFT. That probably means running through each event (if you haven't already) to see where you need some improvement. Then, start looking at exercises that support your efforts in those events. No matter what you work on, though, make sure to include plenty of core work, cardio, and stretching.

TIP

Overcomplicating the process of creating a workout routine is easy, so keep things simple. Choose a handful of exercises that you like (or at least that you don't *hate*) and stick with them for a while. You can change things up in four to six weeks. And if you really don't want to create your own workout routine, think about signing up at a gym that offers group cardio and strength classes, working with your unit's Master Fitness Trainer to develop something, or downloading an app like MOSSA MOVE, which offers a 14-day free trial at `https://mossa.net/mossa-move`.

Identifying your personal goals and resources

Before you can get down to the business of creating a workout routine that works for you, ask yourself these questions:

>> **What are my goals?** You're probably reading this book because you're prepping for the Army Combat Fitness Test, but you may also want to lose weight, bulk up, or get ready for a half-marathon. Your goals shape how you build your workout routine.

>> **How much time do I have before or after work to dedicate to exercise?** Maybe you can only squeeze in an extra 30 minutes per day while you're juggling family responsibilities, or maybe you want to spend 2 hours in the gym after work because you can. No matter how much time you have, developing an efficient workout that hits all your hot spots is essential.

>> **What kind of equipment do I have access to?** If you want to work out at home and you don't have much — or any — fitness equipment, you may have to change your expectations and hit the gym a few days a week. If the thought of working out at home makes you cringe (like it does yours truly), you may consider hitting the circuits outside your office or heading to the Fitness Center on post. You may even want to invest in a gym membership off-post to take advantage of classes and personal trainers.

When you know your goals, how much time you can spend, and what kind of equipment you can work with, you can start setting up your workout plan. The bottom line is that the best workout plan is the one you can actually stick to long enough to see results, so choose a handful of exercises that you can use (see Chapter 8 for exercises matched to specific ACFT events).

Weight a minute: Figuring out your reps and intensity

Your goals help you decide how much — and at what intensity — you should be performing the exercise you choose. And if you already know your *one-repetition maximum* (1RM, the maximum amount of weight you can lift for an exercise), you can make smart choices about how much weight you need to lift. (If you don't already know your 1RM, check out the following section.)

You have to evaluate your needs for every exercise you choose, so give yourself a week or so to work out the kinks. As you become more familiar with your body and how it responds to this type of training, you can fine-tune your plan.

Finding your 1RM

To figure out your 1RM, the American College of Sports Medicine recommends that you first get familiar with the movement you're about to do. Then, do a light warm up consisting of five to ten reps at 40 to 60 percent of what you think will wear you out (so if you're pretty sure 100 pounds is your limit, warm up with 40 to 60 pounds). Rest for a minute and do some light stretching. Then, perform three to five reps at 60 to 80 percent of your perceived maximum resistance (so three to five reps with 60 to 80 pounds if you believed 100 pounds was your 1RM). Rest for up to five minutes and then add 5 to 10 pounds to the bar. If you can successfully lift that weight, rest for another three to five minutes and add 5 or 10 more pounds. Keep going (being sure to observe the rest periods after each lift) until you can't perform the exercise; the weight that's on your bar at that point is your 1RM.

Breaking down reps and weight levels for various goals

Table 18-1 shows the number of reps most people should do, and with what percentage of weight, to achieve specific results. The ranges are wide because every person's body is different; a weight you're comfortable with may not work for me, and a number of reps you can do may not be the same as what I can do.

TABLE 18-1   ## Goals, Rep Ranges, and 1RM Percentages

Goal	Number of Reps	Percent of 1RM
Endurance	13–20	60–70 percent
Strength	7–12	70–85 percent
Power	1–6	85–100 percent

For many people training for the ACFT, doing some exercises in each group makes sense. Each is important to a well-rounded exercise routine, too.

Don't stress over whether you should schedule yourself three sets of five reps with a heavy weight or five sets of 12 reps with a lighter weight! Try starting with a lighter weight and higher reps while you nail down your form. Give yourself a week or two to adjust. Then, revisit your schedule based on your goals and make adjustments as necessary.

You don't have to train in one rep range (or with the same weight) all the time.

Supersetting

Supersets are a form of strength training that requires you to move quickly between exercises without taking a big rest break. Supersets can help you cram more into your time at the gym, but they also can help you build stamina, give your muscles adequate rest time between sets, and give your heart a workout.

Some people get the best results from planning supersets that work with antagonistic muscle pairs, which I cover in Chapter 14. You may work biceps and triceps together, or you may mix things up even more, such as alternating squats with chest presses. These workouts are yours, and you have the freedom to create them however you want!

Making time to stretch

Never, ever leave stretching out of a workout routine. Give your body plenty of time to cool down and loosen up while your muscles are still warm from training. In fact, build stretching into your workout schedule. For more on stretching (and why your body absolutely needs it), check out Chapter 9.

Marking training days on your calendar

When you've planned your exercises, start putting them on your calendar. Check out Table 18-2 for some inspiration and then use the fill-in-the-blank calendar in the Appendix to get started. Remember, you can mix things up as much as you want, but try to fit in practice for each ACFT event throughout the week.

TABLE 18-2   ## Sample One-Week Workout Calendar

Monday	Tuesday	Wednesday	Thursday	Friday	Saturday	Sunday
Cardio: Run	Sumo squats	Cardio: Hill repeats	Leg Tuck practice	Cardio: Sprint-Drag-Carry practice and 60:120s	Practice for additional ACFT event	Recovery
Standing Power Throw practice	3 Repetition Maximum Deadlift practice	Hand Release Push-Up –Arm Extension practice	Squats	Tricep presses	Power jumps	
Bicep curls	Romanian deadlifts	Tuck jumps	Bent over rows	Rows	Deadlifts	
Triceps extensions	Lunges	Medicine ball power jumps	Kettlebell swings	Incline bench presses	Weighted squats	
Zercher carries	Pull-ups	Chest flys	Hang cleans	Bicep curls	Hang cleans with overhead presses	
Dips	Calf raises	Standing front shoulder raises	Overhead push presses	Mixed-grip pull-ups		
Planks	Bent over rows	Renegade rows	Lunges	Scissor kicks	Weighted lunges	
Side planks	Crunches	Shoulder raises	Deadlifts	Sit-ups	Supermans	
	Medicine ball throws	Sit-ups	V-ups	Planks	Stability ball knee raises	
					Side planks	

REMEMBER

Don't train the same muscle groups back-to-back when you're creating your workout calendar. Doing squats on one day and tuck jumps the next is okay, but try not to do squats two days in a row. Remember that you get stronger between workouts as your muscles recover, and although some people (like Olympic weightlifters working under a coach's supervision) can safely train back-to-back, overtraining one muscle group without enough recovery time can lead to overuse injuries. The exceptions are cardio and core; most people can do cardio and core work every day (within reason).

Scheduling recovery days into your routine

Everybody needs a break. Although the workout calendar in Table 18-2 shows only one day — Sunday — as a rest day, you can take more than one rest day per week (and should, if your body needs it). When you're a few days into your new workout routine, take some time to listen to your body. If you're achy, your joints hurt, or you show up and you're physically unable to complete some exercises, a rest day may be in order. Don't mistake muscle soreness, which I cover in Chapter 9, for achiness, though. You're most likely going to get sore, so you're going to have to embrace the suck on that one.

Aim for active recovery on the days you're not going to the gym. That means walking, doing a little yoga, making time for dynamic stretches (see Chapter 9), or otherwise getting your body moving without putting too much strain on your muscles.

Charting your progress

One of the best things you can do for yourself is to keep track of your performance. As you progress in your workout routine (and before you change things up in four to six weeks), write down how much weight you're able to lift in each workout, how many 60:120s you can do, how far and how fast you can run, and other big metrics that help you visualize your improvement over time. You can use a calendar app on your phone, a paper notebook, or even a single sheet of paper that you keep in your wallet. See the sample chart in Table 18-3 to get inspired to create your own workout log.

TABLE 18-3   **Sample Workout Log**

Exercise	1RM/Best Time	Date, Sets, Reps, and Weight	Date, Sets, Reps, and Weight	Date, Sets, Reps, and Weight	Date, Sets, Reps, and Weight
Chest press	200 lbs.	Jan. 1: 3 sets of 8 @ 145 lbs.	Jan. 8: 3 sets of 8 @ 150 lbs.	Jan. 15: 3 sets of 8 @ 150 lbs.	Jan. 22: 3 sets of 8 @ 155 lbs.
Dumbbell curls/biceps	65 lbs.	Jan. 2: 2 sets of 10 @ 35 lbs.	Jan. 9: 2 sets of 10 @ 35 lbs.	Jan. 16: 3 sets of 12 @ 35 lbs.	Jan. 23: 3 sets of 13 @ 35 lbs.
2-mile run	16:30	Jan. 3: 16:47	Jan. 10: 16:49	Jan. 17: 16:38	Jan. 24: 16:35

TIP

Make use of the Army Wellness Center on your installation. Before (or shortly after) you begin your workout plan, set up an appointment to have your body composition, VO_2 max (more on that in Chapter 16), and resting metabolic rate (Chapter 23) measured. Before you leave the Wellness Center, set your next appointment a month out.

Sneaking in Daytime Workouts You Can Do Anywhere

The five small-but-mighty exercises in the following sections can help improve your ACFT score, and the best part is that you can do them while you're standing around the motor pool on Monday morning, waiting for formation, or even at your desk. These mini workouts go hand-in-hand with the full-scale workouts you're doing before or after work. (Remember, too, that nobody's stopping you from dropping down into the front leaning rest position and knocking out a handful of push-ups or doing some Iron Mikes!)

Chair dips

Chair dips (shown in Figure 18-1) are simple — all you need to sneak in a quick triceps, traps, pecs, and serratus anterior workout during the workday is a chair.

Zack McCrory

FIGURE 18-1:
Chair dips.

Here's how to do chair dips in the office:

1. **Sit on a sturdy, stationary chair.**

   For obvious reasons, don't do this exercise with a rolling chair. (And if you do, please make sure someone is recording — and that you send it to me.)

2. **Scoot your buttocks toward the edge of the chair and grasp the front edge of the seat with your hands, right next to your hips.**

   Put your feet flat on the floor and keep them hip-distance apart.

3. **Move your torso forward off the chair so that your arms are holding your body up.**

   Your buttocks should hover over the floor, and your knees should have a slight bend in them. Your heels should be just a few inches forward of your knees.

4. **Slowly lower your body, using your elbows like a hinge until each makes a 90-degree angle.**

   Keep your shoulders down and away from your ears, your elbows straight behind you (don't wing them out), and your buttocks as close to the chair as possible. If you need a little more heat in your triceps, extend your legs out farther.

5. **Push yourself back up to the starting position and start again.**

Calf raises

If you learn one thing in the Army, it's the art of waiting. But you can put that time to good use with calf raises, which you can see in Figure 18-2.

FIGURE 18-2:
Calf raises.

Zack McCrory

Follow these steps to squeeze in a handful of calf raises while you're at work. If you're up for it, you can do it with something in your hands — say, a pair of fuel cans — but you can also do them empty-handed.

1. **Stand with your feet hip-width apart.**

2. **Push through the balls of your feet and raise your heels until you're standing on your toes.**

   Don't roll your ankles in or out; just go straight up and down.

3. **Lower back to the ground.**

Single-leg squats

Single-leg squats put laser-focus on each leg, blasting your quads, hamstrings, and glutes. See what they look like in Figure 18-3.

FIGURE 18-3:
Single-leg squats.

Zack McCrory

Here's how you perform single-leg squats while you're at work (or any other time you have a few minutes to spare):

1. **Stand on your left foot with your right leg extended in front of you so that your foot is off the ground.**

2. **Bend your left leg and sink into a squat by pushing your hips backward, like you're sitting in a chair.**

3. **Squat as low as you can without sacrificing form or tipping over and then pause for a brief moment.**

4. **Push back up through your whole foot, squeezing your glutes the whole way to the top.**

Do an entire set on one leg (aim for five to ten reps) before you switch to the other.

TIP

If you're balance-challenged, try propping your right foot behind you on a chair or a shorter surface. Don't put any weight on it; just rest your toes on it as you squat with your left leg. You may know this variation as the Bulgarian split squat.

Bicep presses

When your arms are free and you're sitting at a desk, you can put some tension on your biceps with presses:

1. **Bend your elbows and put your forearms under your desk (or a heavy table) with your palms facing up.**

2. **Push up against the underside of the desk with your biceps flexed, like you're going to lift it up.**

   The key here is creating tension. Don't press upward so hard that you flip your desk.

3. **Hold the tension for 10 seconds before you relax your muscles and repeat.**

Seated hip thrusts

Seated hip thrusts, depicted in Figure 18-4, are a lot tougher than they look.

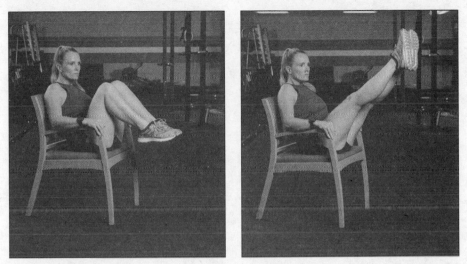

FIGURE 18-4: Seated hip thrusts.

But don't let that toughness stop you from trying them for yourself:

1. **Sit on the edge of your chair and bend your knees at a 90-degree angle.**

2. **Hold the seat or armrest with your hands for support and lean back about 45 degrees.**

3. **Pull your legs toward your chest, knees still bent.**

4. **Extend your legs straight out.**

5. **Pull your legs back in to your chest and then drop your feet without letting them touch the floor.**

ADDING MORE STEPS TO YOUR DAY

Walking is a full body exercise, and squeezing in a few more steps can make a big difference in your overall fitness level. According to the Mayo Clinic, the average American walks only about 3,500 steps per day (that's between 1.5 and 2 miles). But to fall into the "low active" category, you need between 5,000 and 7,499 steps a day. My advice? Aim for at least 10,000 steps per day, which puts you solidly in the "active" category.

You can add steps to your day without really noticing them. Try taking the stairs, walking the long way around to get into work, parking as far as you can from wherever you're going, and taking active breaks where you get up and walk in place (or out to the smoke pit to say hi to your friends; just don't light up yourself). Walk your dog in the evening or take a stroll with a walking buddy. You can even set a timer to go off every 30 minutes to remind yourself to get up and take some steps.

4

Nutrition and the "Whole Soldier" Concept

IN THIS PART . . .

Get a good measure of the Army's standards for height and weight.

Pick up nutrition basics, explore vitamins and minerals, and discover the downside of dehydration.

Give yourself the best shot by understanding how your consumption choices (good and not so good) add up.

Chapter **19**

Surveying Army Standards for Height and Weight

I f you've ever taken an Army physical fitness test, you've been measured and weighed; you may have even been taped to find out whether you meet the requirements in Army Regulation 600-9, *The Army Body Composition Program*. Meeting these Army standards isn't optional. You have to fit within them or you get enrolled in the Army Weight Control Program (AWCP), effective the same date you're counseled for your body composition. If you fail to make satisfactory progress in the AWCP, AR 635-200, *Active Duty Enlisted Administrative Separations*, and AR 600-8-24, *Officer Transfers and Discharges*, say that the Army can send you packing for Fort Couch, time now.

But to understand the Army's standards for height and weight — and why it gives you the coyote brown boot if you don't meet them — you have to know how the Army calculates BMI and what allowances it makes for soldiers. You also need to know what to do to get within an Army-acceptable weight range, which I cover in more detail in Chapter 24.

Taking Stock of Army Height and Weight Requirements

The Army requires you to maintain a certain weight relative to your height and body composition. Acceptable weights are listed in AR 600-9 as well as in Tables 19-1 and 19-2. These charts correlate directly to a soldier's BMI.

TABLE 19-1   ## Weight Requirements for Male Height

Height (in Inches)	Minimum Weight (in Pounds)	Max Weight: Age 17 to 20	Max Weight: Age 21 to 27	Max Weight: Age 28 to 39	Max Weight: Age 40+
58	91	n/a	n/a	n/a	n/a
59	94	n/a	n/a	n/a	n/a
60	97	132	136	139	141
61	100	136	140	144	146
62	104	141	144	148	150
63	107	145	149	153	155
64	110	150	154	158	160
65	114	155	159	163	165
66	117	160	163	168	170
67	121	165	169	174	176
68	125	170	174	179	181
69	128	175	179	184	186
70	132	180	185	189	192
71	136	185	189	194	197
72	140	190	195	200	203
73	144	195	200	205	208
74	148	201	206	211	214
75	152	206	212	217	220
76	156	212	217	223	226
77	160	218	223	229	232
78	164	223	229	235	238
79	168	229	235	241	244
80	173	234	240	247	250

TABLE 19-2	**Weight Requirements for Female Height**				
Height (in Inches)	Minimum Weight (in Pounds)	Max Weight: Age 17 to 20	Max Weight: Age 21 to 27	Max Weight: Age 28 to 39	Max Weight: Age 40+
58	91	119	121	122	124
59	94	124	125	126	128
60	97	128	129	131	133
61	100	132	134	135	137
62	104	136	138	140	142
63	107	141	143	144	146
64	110	145	147	149	151
65	114	150	152	154	156
66	117	155	156	158	161
67	121	159	161	163	166
68	125	164	166	168	171
69	128	169	171	173	176
70	132	174	176	178	181
71	136	179	181	183	186
72	140	184	186	188	191
73	144	189	191	194	197
74	148	194	197	199	202
75	152	200	202	204	200
76	156	205	207	210	213
77	160	210	213	215	219
78	164	216	218	221	225
79	168	221	224	227	230
80	173	227	230	233	236

If you don't meet the height and weight requirements for your age, designated personnel measure the circumference of certain parts of your body and use those measurements to determine your body fat. Men are measured at the neck and waist, while women are measured at the neck, waist, and hips over the "greatest protrusion of the gluteal muscle." Each part is measured three times to generate an average to the nearest half inch, and the totals are recorded on a DA Form 5500, which you can see in Figure 19-1.

BODY FAT CONTENT WORKSHEET *(Male)*

For use of this form, see AR 600-9; the proponent agency is DCS, G-1.

Name *(Last, First, Middle Initial)*			RANK		NOTE:
HEIGHT *(to nearest 0.50 inch)*		WEIGHT *(to nearest pound)*		AGE	½" = .50
STEP	FIRST	SECOND		THIRD	AVERAGE *(to nearest 0.50 in.)*
1. Measure neck just below level of larynx *(Adam's apple.)* **Round up** to the nearest 0.50 inch. *Repeat three times, then average to the* nearest 0.50 inch.					
2. Measure abdomen at the level of the navel *(belly button.)* **Round down** to the nearest 0.50 inch. *Repeat three times, then average to the* nearest 0.50 inch.					
3. Enter the average neck circumference.					
4. Enter the average abdominal circumference.					
5. Enter circumference value *(step 4 - step 3)*.					
6. Enter height in inches to the nearest 0.50 inch.					
7. Find the Soldier's circumference value *(step 5)* and height *(step 6)* in figure B-1 *(Percent Fat Estimation for Men)*. Enter the percent body fat value that intercepts with the circumference value and height. This is Soldier's Percent Body Fat.					

© *John Wiley & Sons, Inc.*

FIGURE 19-1:
DA Form 5500,
Body Fat Content
Worksheet (Male).

The person filling in the DA-5500 must then perform mathematical calculations outlined in AR 600-9 (although most people use an online calculator) to figure out the soldier's body fat percentage. Table 19-3 has allowable body fat percentages.

TABLE 19-3

Allowable Body Fat for Male and Female Soldiers

Age	Males	Females
17–20	20%	30%
21–27	22%	32%
28–39	24%	34%
40+	26%	36%

If you fail the tape test by going over your allowable body fat percentage, you're enrolled in the Army Body Composition Program (ABCP), which I discuss in the following section. You can also be put in the ABCP for weighing too little.

REMEMBER

Although a pretty decent amount of controversy surrounds whether the Army's body fat-testing method is accurate and effective, that method is what the organization uses, and commanders have to abide by it when they're recommending people for the ABCP. But nobody will measure your body fat unless you weigh more than the allowable amounts in Tables 19-1 and 19-2.

Going into the Army Body Composition Program

The Army Body Composition Program, which used to be called the Army Weight Control Program, is a mandatory program for soldiers who don't meet the height and weight standards I cover in the preceding section. When a soldier fails height and weight, the Army requires a counseling statement within 48 hours. This counseling statement includes the soldier's

>> Authorized screening weight

>> Current weight

>> Current number of pounds overweight

>> Authorized body fat percentage

>> Current body fat percentage

>> Current number of percentage points over authorized body fat

The counseling is necessary to enroll a soldier in the ABCP, but it also comes with certain requirements, including unfavorable actions:

>> A flag in accordance with AR 600-8-2, which suspends all favorable personnel actions (including tuition assistance, promotions and awards, and enrollment in military schools)

>> Nutrition counseling, either at the post's medical center or its Army Wellness Center, within 30 days

>> Enrollment in remedial physical training

>> Maintenance of satisfactory progress, which is a weight loss of 3 to 8 pounds per month

>> Monthly weigh-ins until the soldier meets the appropriate body fat percentage

You can request a medical exam if you believe you have an underlying condition that is directly causing your weight gain or inability to lose weight or body fat.

You must also read U.S. Army Public Health Command's Technical Guide 358, *Army Weight Management Guide*, within 14 days of enrollment and schedule your appointment with a dietitian or other healthcare provider. Additionally, you have to complete and return a Soldier Action Plan to your commander within 14 days.

WARNING

After you're in the ABCP, you can't be removed until you meet the appropriate body fat percentage. If you don't make satisfactory progress within six months of your enrollment, you can be involuntarily separated from the military. Likewise, if you make it out of the ABCP and are put back in the program within 12 months, or if you're reenrolled after 12 months but within 36 months, your command can initiate the separation process.

Distinguishing BMI from Body Fat Measurements

As of this writing, the Centers for Disease Control and Prevention estimates that nearly 40 percent of American adults over the age of 20 are obese. The Army uses body fat measurements to get a look at whether soldiers are overweight, but those body fat measurements aren't necessarily an indicator of your body mass index, or BMI. Although you don't see your BMI recorded on your PT scorecard, the Army uses it (through weight-for-height standards) to ensure you meet BMI requirements for service. BMI can be (but isn't always) an important indicator of your overall fitness and risk for health conditions. Some doctors use it as an individual screening tool to assess a person's risk for some diseases that are associated with a higher BMI, such as type 2 diabetes, heart disease, and cancer. You can have your BMI measured at an Army Wellness Center if you're interested.

A high BMI tends to indicate a high level of body fat, while a low BMI can indicate that a person doesn't have enough body fat for optimal health. Table 19-4 shows where people fall on the body mass index based on a mathematical formula where $BMI = 703 \left(\dfrac{\text{weight in pounds}}{\text{height in inches}^2} \right)$. (The number 703 comes from the conversion from the metric system.)

As an example, a 6-foot male who weighs 200 pounds has a calculated BMI of 27.13, which puts him squarely in the overweight camp. If he gains 50 pounds, he's in the obese range, but if he loses 20 (reaching a weight of 180 pounds), he's a healthy weight.

TABLE 19-4

Adult BMI Ranges

BMI	Weight Range
<18.5	Underweight
18.5 to 24.9	Healthy
25.0 to 29.9	Overweight
>30	Obese

REMEMBER

If you're pregnant, you're very muscular (like a bodybuilder, not just toned), or you're over the age of 60, BMI may not be an accurate reflection of your body fat. However, the Army's adjusted BMI table seeks to address that.

The Army's BMI requirements are different from civilian BMI classifications; it accounts for potentially higher muscle mass of soldiers by slightly increasing the allowable body fat percentages for women (particularly those in higher age brackets) and changing the requirements for men who would be in a civilian "overweight" range. The Army took these steps to prevent soldiers from engaging in excessive weight-loss efforts, which can increase the risk of injury and other health problems. Check out the Army's version of allowable BMI by age and biological sex in Table 19-5.

TABLE 19-5

Army's Max BMI

Age	Men	Women
Under 21	25.9	25.0
21 to 27	26.5	25.3
28 to 39	27.2	25.6
Over 40	27.5	26.0

TECHNICAL STUFF

BMI assumes that you have an average amount of body fat, which includes fat deep inside your stomach cavity surrounding your organs (rather than the fat that's visible under your skin). Intra-abdominal fat is closely linked to type 2 diabetes and heart disease risks.

Chapter **20**

Becoming a Lean, Green, Fighting Machine: Principles of Nutrition

"I always maintain my arms, my equipment, and myself." Sound familiar? That line of the Soldier's Creed refers to your weapons, your TA-50, and your overall fitness level — and if you lose sight of the fitness part, you're subject to involuntary separation from Uncle Sam's family. Nutrition is an important component of fitness; a well-balanced diet can help you get all the calories and nutrients you need to fuel your body. In fact, many experts say that nutrition is *the* most important part of fitness. Eating right alone won't help you pass the ACFT, but your scores depend on your filling up with the right kinds of fuel.

Proper nutrition helps you reduce body fat (and lose a few pounds), reduces your risk of illness and injury, and makes you healthier overall. But it's about more than just choosing veggies over donuts — it's about eating plenty of lean proteins, healthy carbohydrates, essential fats, and antioxidants. It's also about knowing the difference between *needing* food and *wanting* food.

Dishing on Hunger and Appetite

Appetite and hunger aren't the same thing, and being aware of the differences between the two can help you get back in touch with your body's hunger and fullness cues. The following sections break down these differences and give you the scoop on some of the hormones tied to eating and satiation.

Distinguishing hunger from appetite

Hunger is your body's way of telling you, "Hey, we're running on fumes here." It's that uncomfortable feeling you get when your stomach is growling (which it's far more likely to do when you're giving a briefing or sitting through mandatory training, isn't it?). When you're hungry, you may feel light-headed or crabby, or you may slow down and feel tired.

No matter how you feel, it's your brain that's to blame. When your stomach finishes processing the food you eat, one of the hormones your body excretes is *ghrelin* (often called the hunger hormone). Research has shown that ghrelin travels through your bloodstream to tell your brain that you need more calories for energy, and then your brain tells you to start foraging in the fridge. (For more on ghrelin and other eating-related hormones, check out the following section.)

Signs of hunger are really similar to thirst cues, which also means that many people think they're hungry when they're really on the path to dehydration. Headache, fatigue, difficulty concentrating, and even lightheadedness are all symptoms of hunger *and* thirst. I cover hydration in Chapter 22.

REMEMBER

Hunger isn't something that you should try to control; it's your body's way of telling you that you need fuel.

Appetite, on the other hand, is the *desire* for food even when you don't need it (that is, when you aren't hungry). Lots of factors can influence your appetite, like your blood sugar levels and hormones, your mood or emotions, and sensory cues such as the smell of cookies baking. To be clear, your appetite increases when you're physically hungry, too.

TIP

How do you tell the difference between hunger and appetite, especially when you can experience them both at the same time? Ask yourself whether you'd eat a food that you weren't excited about. If you had the option to reach for a carrot stick right now, would you do it? What about an MRE's Snack Bread? If you wouldn't eat something you weren't excited about, you're probably not hungry. Your appetite is just on the rise.

Hobnobbing with hunger hormones

Your body produces several hormones to deal with hunger and satiation (being full). Ghrelin, the hunger hormone I mention in the preceding section, makes you consume more food, take in more calories, and store fat. The higher your ghrelin levels are, the hungrier you get; the lower they are, the fuller you feel. But ghrelin isn't the enemy. It's the signal that travels through your personal comms to let you know it's time to eat. After you start eating and your stomach expands, your body stops producing so much ghrelin, and your hunger diminishes.

When you're full, your body releases *leptin*. This powerhouse of a hormone is produced in fat cells located in *adipose tissues* (commonly known as body fat); the more fat cells you have, the more leptin your body produces. Leptin tells your brain that you have enough energy stored up to engage in "expensive" metabolic processes, like exercise and even puberty and pregnancy. Because the amount of leptin you produce is directly tied into how much body fat you have, it should technically regulate your weight by lowering your appetite and causing your body to feed itself with energy from your fat cells. But if you're overweight or obese, you may have too much leptin in your blood. That can cause *leptin resistance* — a condition in which you keep producing more and more leptin and lose sensitivity to it.

Leptin does a lot more than regulate your appetite, though. It's also responsible for regulating bone mass, activating immune cells, increasing your heart rate, and driving up your blood pressure.

Other important hormones include the following, shown in Figure 20-1:

>> Insulin-like peptide 5, or ILP-5, which is mainly produced in the colon and can stimulate hunger

>> Cholecystokinin, or CCK, which is produced in the upper small intestine in response to food and helps give you a feeling of fullness

>> Peptide YY, glucagon-like peptide 1, oxyntomodulin, and uroguanylin, which are all produced in the lower part of the small intestine in response to food and also give you a feeling of fullness

>> Amylin, insulin, and pancreatic polypeptide, which are all produced in the pancreas and can inhibit hunger

These hormones usually peak between 30 and 60 minutes after a meal, which is why eating until you're overstuffed is so easy. Everything usually returns back to normal within three to four hours.

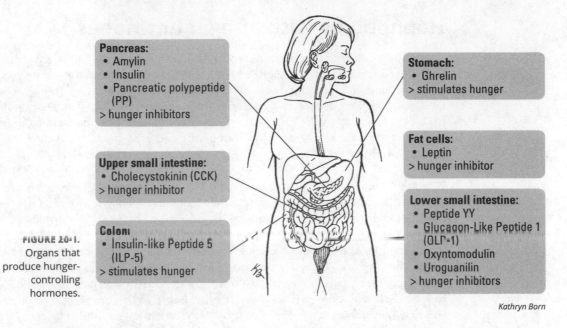

Pancreas:
- Amylin
- Insulin
- Pancreatic polypeptide (PP)

> hunger inhibitors

Stomach:
- Ghrelin

> stimulates hunger

Upper small intestine:
- Cholecystokinin (CCK)

> hunger inhibitor

Fat cells:
- Leptin

> hunger inhibitor

Colon:
- Insulin-like Peptide 5 (ILP-5)

> stimulates hunger

Lower small intestine:
- Peptide YY
- Glucagon-Like Peptide 1 (GLP-1)
- Oxyntomodulin
- Uroguanilin

> hunger inhibitors

FIGURE 20-1. Organs that produce hunger-controlling hormones.

Kathryn Born

TECHNICAL STUFF

When you eat, your brain — the hypothalamus specifically — gets signals through "pleasure pathways" that use dopamine, serotonin, and endocannabinoids that can influence your eating behavior.

Eating Pre- and Post-Workout

Good nutrition can help you perform better and recover faster, so knowing what to eat (and when) is an important component of working out.

Fueling up before working out

When you work out on an empty stomach, you force your body to dip into its energy reserves (hopefully those stored in fat cells) to keep you going. Exercising without eating first isn't the ideal solution to weight loss, though. You may end up having less stamina than you would've if you'd eaten a light meal (or even a snack). Your blood sugar levels can drop, too, leaving you feeling lightheaded, shaky, or even nauseous — none of which is conducive to a good workout.

If you can, eat a complete meal that contains carbs, protein, and fat between two and three hours before you exercise. The closer you get to your workout, the smaller and simpler your meal should be. For example, if you're eating an hour before you work out, pick foods that contain mostly carbs and some protein — and that are easy to digest. The best foods to eat before you work out depend on what kind of workout you're doing and your personal goals; for example, protein-rich foods can help your muscles recover but likely won't help you much if you're running.

Carbohydrates

Your muscles use the glucose from carbohydrates as fuel. Your body processes and stores glucose in glycogen (both in your muscles and in your liver), which it then uses as a ready source of energy if your blood glucose levels go down. Some good pre-workout foods with carbs include

>> Bananas, which are packed with simple carbs, natural sugars and potassium.

>> Toast (or bread), which offers you complex carbohydrates.

>> Oats, which are so full of fiber that they release carbs slowly and help you keep consistent energy levels through a workout. (As a bonus, they contain vitamin B, which can help convert carbs into energy.)

Protein

Pre-workout protein consumption can help improve your athletic performance; several studies have shown that it increases muscle protein synthesis. Protein can also help your body produce a better *anabolic response* (how your body turns simple molecules into larger and more complex ones, which it needs to do to grow muscle), as well as improve your muscle recovery and increase your strength and lean body mass. Some of the best protein-packed foods to eat before working out include the following:

>> Chicken, which is full of protein and is generally easy to digest. (You may also want to know that dark-meat chicken has more of the good fats you need than white meat does. Chapter 24 has more on healthy fats.)

>> Eggs, which have high-quality proteins. If you eat the yolk, too, you give your body some essential amino acids, which I cover in Chapter 21.

>> Greek yogurt, which has about 17 grams of protein in one serving — and which tastes great with fruit, so you can get your carbs in, too. (For more on pre-workout carbs, see the preceding section.)

WHAT ABOUT SUPERFOODS?

Nutrient-dense foods — sometimes called *superfoods* — include lean proteins, healthy carbs, and healthy fats. They're great sources of vitamins, minerals, and antioxidants, all of which I cover in more detail in Chapter 21. Sometimes superfoods contain compounds (like capsaicin) that boost your metabolism and help you burn body fat faster, too. But beware of gimmicky superfood pills; the real superfoods are options like avocado, fish, berries, leafy greens, whole grains, and beans. Nothing can replace a balanced diet with lots of fruit and veggies (and regular exercise). If you're not eating a balanced diet and exercising, there isn't a superfood in the world that can bail you out.

Fat

Fat in and of itself isn't an enemy of fitness; your body needs certain kinds of fat to work properly. When you're performing low- to moderate-intensity exercise, your body gets its fuel from fat. Some of the best fat-containing foods to eat before you hit the gym include

>> Avocados, which are full of monounsaturated fats that help lower bad cholesterol and keep you moving.

>> Nuts, which give you a dose of protein, too. Try peanuts (or peanut butter).

>> Olive oil, which you can drizzle over a salad or veggies.

Getting the right foods after your workout

Eating after a workout is pretty important, too. If you're going for muscle mass, for example, you want to take in some protein within 30 minutes; that gives your body the amino acids it needs to repair and rebuild, plus build new muscle tissue.

Try dishing up some of these tasty post-workout options:

>> Eggs and whole wheat toast, which can help replenish your energy, keep your blood sugar levels stable, and pack in some amino acids to rebuild muscle.

>> Greek yogurt and fruit, which give you protein, energy-boosting carbs, and antioxidants (if you use the right fruits, like blueberries) that can help tone down muscle inflammation after an intense workout.

>> Chicken, brown rice, and vegetables, which provide you with protein, lots of vitamin B-6 to boost your immune system, and carbs to replace your spent energy.

Making ACFT-Smart Dietary Changes

Not all dietary changes are created equal. The following sections explain why fast-fix options aren't going to help you meet your ACFT goals and show you some more appropriate approaches.

Promoting fitness by avoiding diets

Dieting can be the kiss of death for fitness. When you diet instead of developing healthier eating habits, you're setting yourself up to fail from the start.

When you're on a diet, your appetite increases and your levels of leptin drop. (For details on leptin, check out the earlier section "Hobnobbing with hunger hormones.") Your metabolic rate may decrease, too, especially if you restrict calories for a long period of time. That's because you're eating less and your fat cells are losing some of their padding; you don't produce the same amount of leptin that you did before, so your brain goes into starvation mode. It essentially says, "I don't have the same energy available as I once did, so my body must be starving."

I discuss diets in more detail in Chapter 23, but know that the healthy way to lose weight (or maintain what you have) is to avoid fad diets that promise to help you shed pounds quickly. Instead, swap out unhealthy foods loaded with empty calories (as I note in the following section) and change your eating habits permanently.

TECHNICAL STUFF

When you diet and your brain thinks you're starving, several processes in your body begin, and they're all designed to drive your leptin levels back up. One of the more notable processes is the stimulation of the *vagus nerve*, which runs between your brain and your abdomen. The vagus nerve makes you hungrier so that you take in extra calories and store them in your body's fat.

Incorporating healthier eating habits (without dieting)

TIP

Don't go on a diet. Instead, change out some of the things you eat for healthier options (and make sure you're eating for the right reasons). You can make these ACFT-smart dietary changes right now:

>> **Fill half your plate with fruits or vegetables at every meal.** The Academy of Nutrition and Dietetics recommends that you load up on these vitamin-, mineral-, and fiber-rich foods each time you sit down at the table.

>> **Pick the right kinds of fats.** Steer clear of saturated and trans fats, which can raise your cholesterol levels and increase your risk of heart disease. That means taking it easy on fatty beef, pork, poultry with skin, butter, and cheese. Trade them out for skinless chicken, low-fat dairy products, fish, and nuts.

>> **Swap out your soda or energy drink for good, old-fashioned water.** Sports drinks, mixed coffee drinks, and juices are usually loaded with sugar that you don't need. I cover the importance of water in Chapter 22 and useless calories in Chapter 23.

>> **Get more fiber.** Fiber can help reduce belly fat, give you more energy, and lower your risk of all kinds of diseases (including heart disease, type 2 diabetes, and even some types of cancer). If you're filling half your plate with fruits and veggies, you're well on your way to a healthy fiber intake. You can also replace refined breads with whole grain breads, trade in white rice for brown rice, and eat whole-wheat pasta.

>> **Keep an eye on your portions.** You can trick your brain into eating less when you use a smaller plate. Other ways to manage portion control include using a plate or cup (and never eating right out of the bag), steering clear of TV snacking, and eating slowly.

Chapter 24 covers what your body's ideal diet looks like in more detail.

IN THIS CHAPTER

» Taking a general look at food groups to eat and to watch

» Getting the skinny on vitamins

» Making a case for minerals

» Demystifying carbs

» Discovering antioxidants and amino acids

Chapter **21**

Identifying the Building Blocks of Nutrition

Throughout history, human bodies have evolved to eat plants and animals. Together, these types of foods create a balanced diet that provides people with the nutrients they need. So why do about half of American adults have one or more preventable, diet-related chronic diseases, like obesity, heart disease, and type 2 diabetes? There's no simple answer, but over the last century, the food industry has added things like refined grains, concentrated sweeteners, and artificial ingredients to foods people eat every day. Unfortunately, a lot of those additives can lead to long-term health problems.

Choosing the Right Food Groups

You may not be able to avoid every health problem, but you can improve your long-term health by skipping "junk" foods with empty calories (at least most of the time, anyway) and eating

>> A variety of vegetables and legumes (beans and lentils)

>> Whole fruits

>> Whole grains

>> Fat-free or lowfat dairy

>> Proteins

>> Healthy oils

Setting the table with MyPlate

MyPlate, the U.S. Department of Agriculture's most recent initiative on healthful eating (the one that replaced the Food Guide Pyramid), divides foods into these five categories:

>> Fruits, which the USDA considers any fruit or 100 percent fruit juice. These foods can be fresh, canned, frozen, or dried.

>> Vegetables, which can be whole veggies or 100 percent vegetable juice. They can be raw or cooked, fresh or frozen, canned, or dried.

>> Grains, which are any food made from wheat, rice, cornmeal, oats, barley, or any other cereal grain. Grains are divided into two subgroups: whole and refined.

>> Dairy, which includes all fluid milk products and solid foods made from milk, provided that the foods retain their calcium content.

>> Protein foods, which include meat, poultry, seafood, legumes and peas, eggs, processed soy products, nuts, and seeds.

The *Dietary Reference Intake*, or DRI, is the amount of a vitamin or mineral you need to stay healthy. (DRIs are the U.S. Department of Agriculture's replacement for the old Recommended Dietary Allowance, or RDA.) DRIs are tailored to men and women as well as to specific age groups. Every vitamin and mineral has a *Tolerable Upper Intake Level*, or UL, as well; that's how much of either you can take without risking an overdose or dangerous side effects. When you're looking at food labels, you see *Daily Value*, expressed as %DV. That's a measurement of how much of each vitamin or mineral you should get if you're eating a 2,000-calorie-per-day diet. You can read more about the DRIs and ULs for specific vitamins and minerals later in the chapter.

Keeping less healthy options in check

Limiting your intake of saturated fats and trans fats, added sugars, and sodium goes a long way to keeping you healthy and encouraging your body to perform its best. Though you don't have to count every calorie, try to stick to the following guidelines:

>> **Oils, including vegetable oil, margarine, salad dressing, nuts, olives, avocados, and some fish:** Less than 31 grams (7 teaspoons) per day.

>> **Saturated fat:** Less than 27 grams per day.

>> **Sodium:** Less than 1,500 milligrams per day.

>> **Added sugars:** Less than 25 grams (about 100 calories or 6 teaspoons) per day.

Many candy bars and even "healthy snacks," like granola, have more added sugar than you think. High-fructose corn syrup in particular gets a lot of bad press because it's higher in fructose than table sugar is; while glucose goes to your bloodstream and gets burned up as energy, fructose goes to your liver and gets stored as fat.

Added ingredients can matter, too. Foods like shredded cheese and lowfat ice cream often contain *cellulose*, which is a calorie-free ingredient made from wood pulp, cotton, or other vegetable matter that adds bulk to "diet" foods. Cellulose isn't generally harmful to your body, but some other additives cause researchers concern, including sodium nitrite, carrageenan, trans fats, and some artificial food coloring. If you can, try to steer clear of processed foods and go straight to fruits, vegetables, and meats. That way, you know exactly what you're putting into your body.

Taking Vitamins for a Spin

Vitamins are essential substances that your body needs. Specifically, you need vitamins A, C, D, E, and K, as well as the B vitamins. (Thiamin, riboflavin, and niacin are B1 through B3, while pantothenic acid is B5, pyridoxal is B6, and cobalamin is B12). You also need biotin and folate (or its human-made cousin, folic acid).

REMEMBER

Nearly half of all American adults report taking multivitamins, many of which contain most or all of these essential vitamins, but multivitamins (or any vitamin supplements, for that matter) can't replace eating a good variety of foods that contain natural vitamins.

Getting vitamins the old-fashioned way

Table 21-1 spells out which vitamins are in common whole foods, as well as what scientists know they do for your body and what can happen if you're deficient. (*Note:* Your body can synthesize vitamin D from sunlight as well as absorb it from foods.) A lot of foods have added vitamins (for example, fortified cereals), but they can have added sugars, too, so check the labels.

TABLE 21-1 **Vitamins and What They Do for Your Body**

Vitamin	What It Helps With	Foods Containing It	Signs of Deficiency
A	Formation of healthy teeth, bones, soft tissues, and skin Defense against viral and bacterial infections Healthy hair and nails Prevention of night blindness	Carrots Sweet potatoes Winter squash Cantaloupe Apricots Spinach Kale Collard greens	Night blindness Vision problems Dry, scaly, or thickened skin Impaired immunity that leads to gastrointestinal or respiratory infections Slow growth (in children)
B group	Nerve function Healthy blood cells DNA production Healthy brain function Metabolism and metabolic processes	Meat, poultry, and fish Eggs Milk Leafy green vegetables Legumes Avocados Bananas Whole grains	Anemia Skin disorders Tingling or numbness in hands and feet Irritability, confusion, and forgetfulness Unsteadiness and poor muscle coordination
C	Cell health Iron absorption Healthy teeth and gums Wound healing Immune system Collagen production	Citrus fruits Papaya Strawberries Bell peppers Broccoli Brussels sprouts Dark leafy greens	Rough, bumpy skin Spoon-shaped fingernails with red spots or lines Dry, damaged skin Slowly healing wounds Swollen and painful joints Bleeding gums and tooth loss Poor immunity

Vitamin	What It Helps With	Foods Containing It	Signs of Deficiency
D	Healthy bones Calcium absorption Immune system Potential lowering of colo-rectal cancer risk	Seafood such as salmon, herring, catfish, and trout Milk Eggs Shiitake mushrooms	Poor immunity Fatigue Bone and back pain Depression Bone loss Hair loss Muscle pain
E	Cell health and protection against damage Vitamin K absorption Muscle cell repair	Sunflower seeds Almonds Leafy greens Bell peppers Asparagus	Problems with coordination Numbness and tingling Muscle weakness Vision problems Inability to absorb fat Poor immunity
K	Formation of blood clots	Leafy greens Brussels sprouts Broccoli Asparagus	Easy bruising Excessive bleeding Heavy menstrual periods Bleeding in the GI tract

Gauging DRIs and ULs for vitamins

Check out Table 21-2 to see recommended DRIs and ULs for people consuming a 2,000-calorie-per-day diet, which applies to adults age 19 or over (and doesn't count for women who are pregnant or breastfeeding, because they have different nutritional requirements). The abbreviations are mcg for micrograms, mg for milligrams, and IU for international units.

Overdoing it on vitamins can be dangerous, too. Your body can eliminate some of the extra vitamins you take in, but high doses of vitamins can build up in your system and eventually become toxic. Some vitamin supplements come pretty close to your body's UL, so getting too much is easy, especially if you're eating a healthy diet. Consult with your primary care provider to make sure you're making the right vitamin supplement choices, and check out the latest edition of *Nutrition For Dummies* by Carol Ann Rinzler (Wiley) for more about zeroing in on the nutrients you need.

TABLE 21-2   **DRIs and ULs for Vitamins**

Vitamin	DRI for Females 19–30	DRI for Males 19–30	DRI for Females 31–50	DRI for Males 31–50	DRI for Females over 51	DRI for Males over 51	UL
A	700 mcg	900 mcg	700 mcg	900 mcg	700 mcg	900 mcg	3,000 mcg
C	75 mg	90 mg	75 mg	90 mg	75 mg	90 mg	2,000 mg
D	600 IU	600 IU	600 IU	600 IU	600 IU	600 IU	4,000 IU
E	15 mg	15 mg	15 mg	15 mg	15 mg	15 mg	1,000 mg
K	90 mcg	120 mcg	90 mcg	120 mcg	90 mcg	120 mcg	N/A
B1 (Thiamin)	1.1 mg	1.2 mg	1.1 mg	1.2 mg	1.1 mg	1.2 mg	N/A
B2 (Riboflavin)	1.1 mg	1.3 mg	1.1 mg	1.3 mg	1.1 mg	1.3 mg	N/A
B3 (Niacin)	14 mg	16 mg	14 mg	16 mg	14 mg	16 mg	35 mg
B6	1.3 mg	1.3 mg	1.3 mg	1.3 mg	1.5 mg	1.7 mg	100 mg
B12	2.4 mcg	2.4 mcg	2.4 mcg	2.4 mcg	2.4 mcg	2.4 mcg	N/A
Choline	425 mg	550 mg	425 mg	550 mg	425 mg	550 mg	3,500 mg
Folate	400 mcg	400 mcg	400 mcg	400 mcg	400 mcg	400 mcg	1,000 mcg

Source:https://health.gov/our-work/food-nutrition/2015-2020-dietary-guidelines/guidelines/appendix-7/

WARNING

Most supplements you see on the grocery store's shelves don't have a DRI or UL (at least not for every ingredient). That's because the U.S. government has set levels for only a small number of vitamins and minerals available — and experts just don't know how much is good or how much is too much.

Considering special conditions for vitamins

Some people need more vitamins than others do. You may be one of them if you

>> **Take certain medications:** You may be short on important vitamins that the medications prevent your body from absorbing. You should check with your doctor about testing your levels periodically.

>> **Smoke cigarettes:** Your blood is probably low in vitamin C. Additionally, you most likely have more free radicals in your body than nonsmokers do (which vitamin C can fight). You can read more about free radicals in the later section "Addressing Amino Acids and Antioxidants."

>> **Follow a vegan diet:** You may need more vitamin C to help your body absorb iron from the plants you eat. You may also need to eat more grains that have been enriched with vitamin B12, which only comes from fish, poultry, milk, cheese, and eggs.

>> **Are pregnant:** You need more vitamin C, D, E, B2, folate, and B12 than your nonpregnant, non-breastfeeding battle buddies do.

>> **Are breastfeeding:** You need more vitamin A, E, B1, B2, and B3 than women who aren't breastfeeding do so you can produce healthy milk.

>> **Are approaching menopause:** You may be a little low on vitamin D.

>> **Avoid the sun (or just don't spend enough time in it):** You probably need more vitamin D.

Minerals: Mining for Your Body's Essentials

Like vitamins, your body needs a whole host of minerals to keep things running smoothly and perform a huge range of functions, including transmitting nerve impulses and making the necessary hormones to regulate your heartbeat.

Many of these minerals are absolutely essential for health. The two main kinds of minerals are macrominerals and trace minerals. Your body needs larger amounts of macrominerals, such as calcium, phosphorus, magnesium, sodium, potassium, chloride, and sulfur, than it does trace minerals.

Eating your major minerals

Like vitamins, you should strive to get most of your minerals from the foods you eat. Table 21-3 shows the minerals your body needs, what they do, where to get them, and what happens if you're deficient.

TABLE 21-3   **Minerals and What They Do for Your Body**

Mineral	What It Helps With	Foods Containing It	Signs of Deficiency
Calcium	Healthy bones and teeth Nerve impulses and communication Blood clots Immune system Energy production Muscle contraction	Dairy products Leafy green vegetables	Muscle spasms or cramps Numbness and tingling Confusion, memory loss and depression Weak, brittle nails Easy fracturing of bones
Chloride	Fluid and electrolyte balance Production of digestive juices	Salt Seaweed Rye Tomatoes Lettuce Olives Celery	Weakness or fatigue Dehydration Fluid loss Difficulty breathing Diarrhea or vomiting (caused by fluid loss)
Magnesium	All biologic processes Glucose utilization Protein synthesis Cellular energy production	Leafy green vegetables Fish Nuts Beans Whole grains	Muscle spasms or cramps Numbness and tingling Abnormal heart rhythms Seizures

Mineral	What It Helps With	Foods Containing It	Signs of Deficiency
Phosphorus	Strong bones	Dairy	Loss of appetite
	All cellular functions	Fish	Bone pain
	Cell membrane health	Meat	Stiff joints
		Poultry	Fatigue
		Vegetables	Irregular breathing
		Eggs	Numbness
			Weight changes
			Irritability
Potassium	Muscle contraction	Bananas	Muscle cramps
	Nerve impulses	Oranges	Muscle twitching
	Protein synthesis	Raisins	Fatigue
	Energy production	Spinach	Constipation
	Nucleic acid synthesis	Broccoli	Weakness
		Potatoes and sweet potatoes	Abnormal heart rhythm
		Mushrooms	
		Cucumbers	
Sodium	Water balance in tissues	Salt	Table or sea salt
Sulfur	Sulfur-containing amino acids, which help cells detoxify toxic compounds and manage free radicals	Onions	Arthritis
		Garlic	Brittle nails and hair
	Inflammation response	Eggs	Depression
	Metabolization of food	Meat	Memory loss
		Dairy	Gastrointestinal problems
			Slow wound healing

Moderating minerals: DRIs and ULs

You need a wide range of minerals in your body to support healthy function, but you don't need tons of all of them. As a general rule, here's what you need to consume under normal conditions, regardless of biological sex or age (unless otherwise noted), based on the most current data from the U.S. Department of Health:

>> **Calcium:** The DRI is 1,000 milligrams per day, unless you're a woman over 51; then you need 1,200 milligrams per day. The UL for calcium is 2,500 milligrams.

>> **Magnesium:** The DRI is 310 to 320 milligrams per day for women and 400 to 420 milligrams per day for men. The UL is 350 milligrams for women and 420 milligrams for men.

>> **Phosphorus:** The DRI is 700 milligrams per day with a UL of 4,000 milligrams.

>> **Potassium:** The DRI is 4,700 milligrams per day, with no upper limit yet established.

>> **Sodium:** The DRI is 1,500 milligrams per day for those under 50 and 1,300 for those between 51 and 70. The UL is 2,300 milligrams per day.

Recognizing who needs more minerals

Some people need more minerals than others do, even when they're eating a balanced diet that has plenty of fruits and vegetables. You may be one of them if you

>> **Follow a vegetarian or vegan diet:** You may be low on iron and calcium, which you may be able to get through fortified foods.

>> **Are pregnant or nursing:** You need a little more of everything in both of those cases, but most prenatal vitamins contain enough to get you through.

>> **Are a human:** Seriously! Men who are extremely sexually active may need more zinc in their diets because they lose it during ejaculation. Women aren't off the hook, either: They lose iron during their monthly cycles. If you use an intrauterine device (IUD), you may also need a little extra.

Chewing on Carbs

Carbohydrates are your body's biggest source of fuel. When you digest carbs, your body breaks them down into simple sugars that your bloodstream absorbs. That's your *blood sugar*, or *glucose.* Glucose then works its way into your cells with a little nudge from insulin, and like I discuss in Chapter 6, that glucose is available for fuel during anaerobic exercise.

Breaking down simple and complex carbs and dietary fiber

Digestible carbs can be simple or complex. *Simple carbohydrates* break down faster in your body than complex carbohydrates do, which means you digest the simple ones more easily. The energy you get from simple carbs fizzles out quickly and can cause a crash. Simple carbs are in foods like table sugar and syrup as well as in milk and fruit. *Complex carbs* are what give you lasting energy; you find them in breads, oats, rice, wheat, barley, and cornmeal as well as in vegetables, beans, and nuts.

Fiber is a kind of carb, but it's one you can't digest. Your body doesn't break these carbs down into sugar molecules; in fact, they pass right through your body undigested. Dietary fiber is incredibly important because it helps regulate the way your body uses sugar, and it helps keep your hunger (and blood sugar) under control.

Fiber comes in two types: *soluble,* which dissolves in water and can help lower your glucose levels (and your cholesterol), and *insoluble,* which doesn't dissolve but helps food move through your digestive system. Soluble fiber is hidden away in oatmeal, nuts, apples, legumes, and a handful of other foods. Insoluble fiber is in wheat, brown rice, beans, carrots, cucumbers, and tomatoes.

You need at least 20 to 30 grams of fiber every day. If you're 50 or younger, shoot for 38 grams of fiber a day (for men) or 25 grams (for women). Men and women 51 and older should aim for 30 grams and 21 grams per day, respectively.

TECHNICAL STUFF

Having a high intake of dietary fiber has been linked to a lower risk of heart disease and metabolic syndrome, and it lowers your cholesterol. Scientists also say it lowers your risk of *all* cancers and helps you achieve (and maintain) a healthy weight. Diets with very little fiber but plenty of foods that spike blood sugar increase your chance of developing type 2 diabetes.

Putting your carbs to work for you

You don't see DRIs for carbohydrates or fiber because if you're meeting your body's dietary needs, you're most likely getting enough of all the good stuff. Most people should get between 45 and 65 percent of their daily calories from carbs, so that means if you're working with a 2,000-calorie-per-day diet, between 900 and 1,300 calories should come from carbohydrates. That works out to somewhere between 225 and 325 grams.

Use these tips to add the right carbs to your daily diet:

>> Kick off your day with whole grains, such as steel-cut or old-fashioned oatmeal (not instant), or a cold cereal that has "whole grain" listed first on its ingredient list.

>> Switch to whole grain breads, and consider eating foods like brown rice or quinoa.

>> Skip fruit juice and have a piece of fruit instead.

>> Have beans rather than potatoes when possible (potatoes promote weight gain, anyway).

>> Strive to fit nutritionally dense foods into your diet. That means skipping the soda or energy drink.

WARNING

Most medical professionals will tell you to steer clear of low-carb diets for long periods of time. These programs can be helpful when you want to lose weight in the short term, but they're associated with increased risk of death from a variety of causes — especially when they involve lots of red meat and fatty, processed, or salty foods.

Addressing Amino Acids and Antioxidants

Two important nutritional elements are amino acids and antioxidants. *Amino acids* are organic compounds that combine to form proteins; when proteins are digested or broken down, the amino acids hang around to

>> Break down food

>> Repair body tissue

>> Synthesize hormones and neurotransmitters

>> Help your immune system

>> Transport nutrients

Your body can't make essential amino acids, so you have to get them from food, such as lean meat, fish, dairy, eggs, legumes, grains, and nuts and seeds. (Your body can make nonessential and conditional amino acids.)

Antioxidants are substances your body needs to prevent or slow down cell damage caused by *free radicals* (unstable molecules that your body makes in response to your environment or other issues; they're cells' waste products). You find antioxidants in foods like berries, cherries, citrus fruits, dark leafy greens, tomatoes, and olives. Antioxidants are also in fish, nuts, vitamins E and C, green tea, melatonin, onion, garlic, and cinnamon. (I don't recommend eating these foods all together, though.)

Getting antioxidants is so important because if your body can't clear out free radicals, you're subject to *oxidative stress.* Oxidative stress can lead to all kinds of problems; it's been implicated in diabetes, atherosclerosis (hardening of the blood vessels), high blood pressure, heart disease, neurodegenerative diseases, and even cancer. It even contributes to aging.

TIP

In addition to eating antioxidant-rich foods, watch your sugar, fat, and alcohol intake. Those who eat diets high in these items are more exposed to free radicals than those who don't. So are smokers and people who spend time around smokers.

TECHNICAL
STUFF

You can also prevent oxidative stress and free radical damage in other ways, such as exercising regularly (which, coincidentally, is a good idea if you're taking the ACFT), being careful with chemicals and radiation exposure (don't worry, 74Ds — your CBRN cage is probably fine), wearing sunscreen, avoiding overeating, and getting plenty of sleep.

Chapter **22**

Drink Water: It's More Than a Basic Training Chant

Water is essential for all life on Earth, but in this chapter I focus on how it impacts yours specifically. You have to maintain a good balance between getting too waterlogged and becoming dehydrated. Almost all the foods you eat contain water that counts toward your daily intake. Don't let that stop you from reaching for a refillable bottle, though, because you need far more than what everyday foods can provide.

Understanding How Your Body Uses Water

Between 50 and 60 percent of your body is made from water, and without it, every system that keeps you alive would shut down. You need water to

» Form saliva

» Keep your mucosal membranes damp

>> Allow your cells to grow and reproduce (and survive)

>> Flush out waste

>> Lubricate your joints

>> Deliver oxygen throughout your body

>> Convert food to energy

>> Regulate your body temperature

>> Absorb shocks for your brain and spinal cord

>> Make hormones and neurotransmitters

Water is everywhere in your body — even your bones, which are about 31 percent water — and without it, you'll die fairly quickly. You lose water when you breathe, sweat, and digest food, so you have to replenish it to keep things running smoothly.

Water Is a Necessity, Not a Crutch: Avoiding Dehydration

If you're in the military, you probably experienced your share of dehydration (and don't get me started about those plastic water bottles stored on pallets in the sun downrange). *Dehydration* occurs when you're losing water faster than you're replacing it. An adult male needs about 3.2 quarts (102.4 ounces) of water every day, and an average adult female needs 2.3 quarts (73.6 ounces). Those figures can vary based on how much you sweat, how active you are, and a variety of other factors, including stress, high altitude, whether you're sunburned, and how much alcohol you consume.

TIP

Try this: Divide your body weight in half and aim to drink that many ounces of water each day. That's your *bare minimum*.

Recognizing the warning signs of dehydration

By the time you're thirsty, you're probably already dehydrated. One of the best ways to figure out whether you're dehydrated is to pay attention to your urine output. If you urinate every 2 to 4 hours and your output is light-colored, you're probably doing just fine. But if you can go several hours without urinating and then the urine is darker-colored when you do, you're likely dehydrated.

A handful of warning signs signal dehydration, and some are more serious than others are. Watch yourself (and your soldiers) for the following:

>> Decreased urine output

>> Dry mouth, with or without a swollen tongue

>> Sluggishness or fatigue

>> Headache

>> Sugar cravings

>> Bad breath not attributable to food or hygiene

>> Confusion

>> Dizziness

>> Fainting

>> Heart palpitations

WARNING

The last four — confusion, dizziness, fainting, and heart palpitations — are medical emergencies.

WHY IS THIRST SO LATE TO THE GAME?

Humans' thirst mechanism doesn't kick in before dehydration hits — that is, you don't become thirsty until your body tells your brain you're headed for trouble, and by that point a few dominoes have already fallen. When you lose water without replacing it, your blood becomes more concentrated. That tells your kidneys to start retaining water, which makes you urinate less. Your blood continues to get thicker, so your heart has to start working harder to pump it; your heart rate increases to maintain your blood pressure. Your cells start to shrink when your bloodstream starts to borrow water from them, and that's what finally puts your brain on notice that you need to drink.

TIP

Here's the Army's nifty trick to help you determine how dehydrated you are after exercise: Stand on the scale before and after you exercise. Your percentage of weight loss roughly equals your level of dehydration. For example, if you weigh 200 pounds and lose 2 pounds during exercise, you're about 1 percent dehydrated. Usually, that level is no big deal; you can replace that water easily. When your dehydration level exceeds 2 percent of your body weight, however, you're putting your body under a lot of strain. So if you lose 6 of your 200 pounds, you're 3 percent dehydrated, which *is* a big deal.

Looking at the effects of dehydration

In the short term, dehydration is tied closely to increased cardiovascular strain, lower sweat rate, lower skin blood flow, and reduced performance, which means being hydrated is especially important when you're training for the ACFT, rucking with your squad, or standing in Friday afternoon formation at Fort Bliss for your new first sergeant's first safety brief. Data from the U.S. Army Research Institute of Environmental Medicine shows that about 17 percent of heat stroke cases are associated with dehydration, and many cases of heat cramps and heat exhaustion tie into it as well.

Water performs so many important functions in your body that any (or all) of your systems can suffer when you're not getting enough over the long term. You may become easily fatigued because you have lower blood volume, which makes your heart work harder to deliver oxygen and nutrients around your body. Maybe you suffer frequent illnesses because you don't have enough water to flush toxins, waste, and germs from your body. Your skin may lose its elasticity and become flaky, dry, or prematurely wrinkled or saggy. Your brain may send you irresistible sugar cravings because you can't access your body's glucose stores for energy.

But even worse, your body can try to compensate for your dehydration by taking water from inside your cells and putting it into your bloodstream. If that keeps up, your tissues start to dry up and your cells become shriveled. That's when they start to malfunction, and you become more susceptible to conditions like kidney stones and urinary tract infections, kidney disease, high blood pressure, intestinal failure, and even dementia.

Eyeing Electrolytes

Electrolytes are essential minerals, like calcium, potassium, and sodium. They have an electric charge, and they're found all over your body. Electrolytes help you get the most use out of the water you consume by balancing how much water you retain, maintaining a healthy pH level in your body, moving nutrients in and waste out at the cellular level, and keeping all your systems operating properly. (Head to Chapter 21 for more about the minerals your body needs to function properly.)

You can get all the electrolytes you need through a healthy diet in most cases. However, you lose them through sweat and urine. If you're training hard for the ACFT, working outdoors in hot weather, or otherwise losing a lot of fluid, you may be powering through your body's electrolyte stores faster than usual. If you have dried salt on your skin after working out, a sports drink with electrolytes or a kids' drink designed for rehydration shouldn't hurt, as long as you pay attention to its sugar content and electrolyte content.

REMEMBER

You're unlikely to overdose on electrolytes through a regular diet (although you may have a higher risk of doing so if your kidneys aren't working properly). However, if you take supplements, be aware that you may be flooding your system with unnecessary electrolytes, which can cause negative effects like kidney stones and low blood pressure.

IN THIS CHAPTER

» **Discovering how metabolic equivalents relate to your exercise**

» **Shedding weight healthfully**

» **Reading up on cholesterol and fats**

» **Weighing the effects of fast food and popular beverages**

» **Recognizing the potential harm in protein and pre-workout supplements**

Chapter **23**

Making Sure Everything You Take In Counts

The U.S. Army has a recruiting problem, and it's not because people can't pass the ASVAB or because the military doesn't offer great benefits. (There's an amazing *For Dummies* book for the first one, and the military has some of the best benefits in the country for entry-level jobs.) The recruiting problem actually stems from enlistment-aged people's eating patterns. Military data shows that about 30 percent of people who want to join the military are ineligible, and the main reason is that they weigh too much. The average American consumes as many as 3,600 calories a day (that's 1,600 more calories than the across-the-board recommendation of 2,000 per day). According to the U.S. Department of Health and Human Services, about 75 percent of the population eats too few vegetables, fruits, dairy, and oils. And per person, Americans consume nearly 57 pounds of added sugar every year, which is way too much.

In order to break those stats down — and to break the cycle if you're also stuck in it — is to get to understand metabolic equivalents and how to make your calories count. In this chapter, I explain consuming and burning calories, how fat factors into a healthy diet, and the effects supplements, alcohol, and energy drinks can have on your body so you can make ACFT-smart choices.

Understanding Metabolic Equivalents

A *metabolic equivalent,* or MET, represents how many calories a person burns during a certain physical activity. This measurement is important because muscle cells use oxygen to help them produce energy to fuel contractions. The more oxygen your body uses during exercise (and even when you're not exercising), the more calories you burn. If you use a fitness tracker, you've probably noticed that you burn more calories with more intense exercises, like running, than you do with less intense exercises, like walking.

TECHNICAL STUFF

The human body expends about 5 calories of energy to consume a liter of oxygen. That's why you burn more calories when you're doing more intense activity. The harder your body has to work to cope with the stressors you're putting on it, the more calories you burn.

One MET is a person's *resting metabolic rate,* or RMR. Reading this book, you're probably expending one MET. An activity that's four METs requires you to use about four times as much oxygen as you're using right now, so it requires more energy and burns more calories. (Sneaky tip: Prop this book on the treadmill at the gym so you can kill two birds with one stone.)

Table 23-1 shows MET values for common exercises.

TABLE 23-1

MET Values for Common Exercises

Activity	METs
Jumping rope	12.3
Running at 6 miles per hour	9.8
Circuit training	8.0
Bicycling with moderate effort	8.0
Ruck marching over hills with a 10-to-20-pound load	7.3
Weight training with things like squats and explosive effort	5.0
Yardwork, like pushing a lawn mower	5.0
Golfing while walking and carrying clubs	4.3
Cleaning the house with moderate effort	3.5
Weight training with barbells and dumbbells, performing multiple exercises	3.5
Standing	1.8
Sitting	1.3

You can calculate how many calories (Kcal) you should burn for a given activity by using this formula, provided that you know the MET value of a physical activity:

$$\frac{\text{METs} \times 3.5 \times \text{body weight in kilograms}}{200} = \text{Kcal per minute}$$

If you weigh 180 pounds (that's about 81.6 kilograms), here's how many calories you should burn after jumping rope for one minute (based on Table 23-1):

$$\frac{12.3 \times 3.5 \times 81.6}{200} = 17.56$$

Jumping rope burns a lot of calories. In a minute, you burn almost 18 calories; that means in just 10 minutes, you can burn nearly 180.

TIP

Weight training is tricky (in a good way). Although weight training for an hour torches only a handful of calories compared to jumping rope, your body continues burning calories for a few hours after you leave the gym. That's because your body's repair mechanisms kick into high gear after weight training. Even better, the more muscle tissue you develop, the more calories your body burns to keep fueling those muscles.

Examining How Dietary Changes Can and Can't Help You Drop Weight

Here's some great news: You spend about 10 percent of the calories you consume just by digesting them. That means if you eat 2,000 calories in a day, your body uses about 200 of them just to break them down and put them to work, a process called *thermic effect*. Different foods require different amounts of energy to process, though. Fats are easiest to digest, so you burn only about 3 percent of those calories as they move through your system. Fibrous veggies and fruits have a thermic effect of around 20 percent, and protein is the toughest with a thermic effect of about 30 percent. (I loosely interpret that to mean that if you have a banana split with nuts on top, you're actually doing your body a huge favor.)

Every part of your digestive system helps move foods and liquids through your GI tract, which comprises a series of organs you can see in Figure 23-1.

Your food's journey starts in your mouth, where your saliva starts to break the food down as you chew. When you swallow your food, your tongue pushes it back into your throat. After that, the whole process is automatic. Here's how it happens:

1. Your esophagus starts *peristalsis,* which is the fancy name for the movement of organ walls in your gastrointestinal tract.

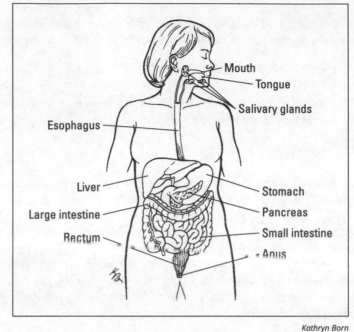

FIGURE 23-1:
The digestive
system.

Mouth
Tongue
Salivary glands
Esophagus
Liver
Large intestine
Rectum
Stomach
Pancreas
Small intestine
Anus

Kathryn Born

2. The food reaches the lower esophageal sphincter at the end of your esophagus. The *esophageal sphincter,* a ring-like muscle, relaxes to let the food into your stomach. (It usually stays closed to keep your stomach's contents from coming back up.)

3. Food enters your stomach, where the muscles mix the food and digestive fluids. The substance left is called *chyme,* and it moves on to your small intestine.

4. The muscles in your small intestine mix the chyme with digestive fluids from your pancreas, liver, and intestine. They keep pushing the mixture forward to continue digestion; at the same time, the walls of the small intestine absorb water (and digested nutrients) so they can enter your bloodstream.

5. At the end of the line in the small intestine, undigested food, fluid, and old cells from your GI tract's lining make their way into the large intestine. The large intestine absorbs water and turns the waste into stool.

6. Stool stays in your rectum until you have a bowel movement, and the rest is history.

The nutrients and water from the foods you eat follow different paths. Your circulatory system uses special cells to help them cross your intestinal lining, and then your bloodstream carries them where they need to go. Hormones and nerves make it all possible.

Safely slashing calories to lose weight

Weight loss happens in the kitchen. If you're trying to shed a few pounds so you don't have to squeak by on height and weight, combining dietary changes with exercises is a good way to do it. Losing a pound or two a week, which requires you to burn 500 to 1,000 more calories than you take in each day, is usually safe. That's why changing your eating habits while exercising works so well; you take in fewer calories and burn a larger percentage of them, which contributes to weight loss.

REMEMBER

Naturally, everyone's body is different, so you have to carefully evaluate your plan and find what works for you. You can always make an appointment at an Army Wellness Center to get dietary guidance that's tailored to your body and activity level, too.

Most people aren't aware of how many calories they're bringing in every day. "It's just one bag of chips," "I only had one soda with lunch," and "A few pieces of candy? Sure!" can really add up quickly. Plus, some bags of chips, large soda bottles, and candy bars actually contain more than one serving in a package; the labeling can be confusing. Check out Figure 23-2 for a nutrition label breakdown from an extremely popular candy.

This nutrition label shows that the container holds six servings, but like most labels, it doesn't show you how many calories you'd consume if you ate the whole box. And like most candies, it's not divided into portions inside the box. (I don't know about you, but I don't bring a measuring cup everywhere I go.) If you were to eat the entire box, you'd ingest 1,320 calories — more than half of the standard 2,000-calorie-per-day recommendation that many people go by! Even if you ate *half* the box, that's 660 calories. For perspective, you could eat all of the following for fewer calories than you'd get from half of that box of candy:

>> 3 eggs (234 calories)

>> 2 slices of wheat toast (150 calories) with strawberry jam (56 calories)

>> 10 strawberries (40 calories)

>> An 8-ounce glass of reduced fat (1 percent) milk (103 calories)

That healthy breakfast would take you a lot farther, too. Think about that the next time you smuggle candy into the movie theater.

Nutrition Facts

Serving Size 1.5 oz
  (42g/about 1/4 cup)
Servings Per Container about 6

Amount Per Serving

Calories 220 Calories from Fat 110

	% Daily Value**
Total Fat 12g	**18%**
Saturated Fat 4.5g	**23%**
Trans Fat 0g	
Cholesterol 5mg	**2%**
Sodium 25mg	**1%**
Total Carbohydrate 25g	**8%**
Dietary Fiber 2g	**8%**
Sugars 22g	
Protein 4g	

Vitamin A * • Vitamin C *
Calcium 4% • Iron 4%

*Contains less than 2% of the Daily Value of these nutrients.
**Percent Daily Values are based on a 2,000 calorie diet. Your daily values may be higher or lower depending on your calorie needs:

	Calories:	2,000	2,500
Total Fat	Less than	65g	80g
Sat. Fat	Less than	20g	25g
Cholesterol	Less than	300mg	300mg
Sodium	Less than	2,400mg	2,400mg
Total Carbohydrate		300g	375g
Dietary Fiber		25g	30g

FIGURE 23-2: Nutrition label from a popular candy.

© John Wiley & Sons, Inc.

REMEMBER

The first step in cutting calories is to actually keep track of what you eat. You can use any of several free food tracking apps. If you have a wearable fitness tracker, its app likely also has a calorie counter you can use on your phone. Keeping track of what you eat is absolutely necessary if you want to dive into an effective weight-loss program — or even if you just want to make sure you're giving your body what it needs to stay in prime condition. When you know how many calories you bring in, you know how many calories you need to burn to lose, gain, or maintain your current weight.

Ignoring the crowd following popular diets

You can't check out at the grocery store without seeing a rack full of magazines promising to help you "Lose 10 Pounds in One Month" or begging you to read "How This Man Lost 400+ Pounds and Is Now a Man-kini Model." But are any of them truthful?

WARNING

Some of these diets can work in the short-term. The problem with diets, which I discuss in Chapter 20, is that they're not sustainable, at least not if you want to keep providing your body with the right kinds of fuels and avoid hurting your health. The same is true for detoxes, cleanses, and other "quick fixes" that require you to fast, drink only liquids or eat only certain foods, use dietary supplements, or buy other commercial products. If your body is working properly, you don't need to detox or cleanse it; your kidneys and liver are all over it.

Some people swear by several popular diets, so if you want to try one, just make sure you know about the long-term effects it can have on your health. Remember, too, that you don't need to take on a complicated diet in order to improve your health. You just need to make dietary changes that stick.

Getting the Skinny on Cholesterol and Unhealthy Fats

Despite their bad raps, your body actually needs some cholesterol and fat to function properly. But too much (and/or the wrong kind) of a good thing can create problems, as I explain in the following sections.

Cholesterol

Cholesterol is a waxy substance that's a lot like fat. Your body uses some cholesterol to make hormones and substances that help you digest foods and produce vitamin D when you're exposed to sunlight. Your body makes its own cholesterol, and when things are running properly, it produces enough to meet its own needs. However, cholesterol is also found in foods that come from animal sources, such as meat, egg yolks, and cheese, so your body takes in additional cholesterol if you eat such items.

When you have too much cholesterol in your blood, it can combine with other substances and create *plaque.* Plaque is sticky, and it adheres itself to the walls of your arteries. The buildup is called *atherosclerosis,* which can lead to coronary artery disease. LDL, or *low-density lipoprotein,* is the cholesterol that causes atherosclerosis. HDL, or *high-density lipoprotein,* is sometimes referred to as "good" cholesterol because it picks up and carries cholesterol from other parts of your body to your liver for elimination. VLDL (that stands for *very low-density lipoprotein*) also contributes to atherosclerosis, but it mainly carries triglycerides while regular LDL mainly carries cholesterol.

Some people are genetically predisposed to high cholesterol, and some people get it from other medical conditions or certain medications. Hands-down, though, the most common cause of high cholesterol is an unhealthy lifestyle. Eating a lot of bad fats (saturated and trans fats, to be specific; see the following section) puts cholesterol into your body, and a lack of physical activity lowers your HDL cholesterol. Smoking lowers your HDL cholesterol levels and raises your LDL, especially in women. (As if you needed another good reason to quit.)

High cholesterol can cause many bad outcomes. For example, large deposits of plaque in your arteries can rupture; if that happens, a blood clot can form on the plaque's surface and block blood flow. When the flow of oxygen-rich blood coming into your heart is reduced or blocked, you can experience chest pain or a heart attack. Plaque can build up in other arteries, too, including those that bring oxygenated blood to your brain. That leads to medical emergencies like stroke and to chronic conditions like carotid artery disease and peripheral arterial disease. The good news is that you can lower your cholesterol, and the sooner you do it, the less likely you are to suffer permanent damage. If lifestyle changes aren't enough to sufficiently lower your cholesterol, your doctor may prescribe medication to help you.

Are you a good fat or a bad fat?

Dietary fats give your body energy and support cell growth, protect your organs, and help you stay warm while helping your body produce certain hormones. However, some types of fats are more helpful (or more harmful) than others are.

Unsaturated fats can help lower your LDL ("bad") cholesterol. Most vegetable oils — those that are liquid at room temperature — have unsaturated fats in them. *Saturated fats,* on the other hand, raise your LDL cholesterol. (You can read more about LDL and its effects in the preceding section.) Saturated fat is in things like

>> Fatty red meat

>> Chicken skin

>> Dark chicken meat

>> Whole-fat dairy products

>> Butter

>> Ice cream

>> Tropical oils, like coconut and palm

» Processed meat, like sausage, bacon, and burgers

» Pastries

You should avoid — or strictly limit — your consumption of foods that are high in saturated fats. Ideally, you want to keep saturated fats to less than 6 percent of your total daily caloric intake. Saturated fat causes cholesterol to build up in your arteries. Because it's a soft, waxy substance that eventually hardens, it often causes your blood's pathways to become clogged or completely blocked.

Trans fatty acids (or *trans fats*) are unhealthy fats you should completely avoid. They form when vegetable oil hardens in a process called *hydrogenation*. Manufacturers often use these hydrogenated fats to keep foods fresh for a long time; they're also used in some restaurants. Like saturated fats, they can raise your LDL cholesterol levels — and they can also actively lower your HDL (good) cholesterol levels.

Look at the nutrition label in Figure 23-2 earlier in the chapter. That candy has a total of 12 grams of fat in it, which accounts for 18 percent of the total value that a person on a 2,000-calorie-per-day diet should consume. It also has 23 percent of the saturated fat you're supposed to consume in a day. Although it's not as bad as many foods are, it's still probably not the best choice.

Taking a Drive through Fast Food

The key to losing weight is to maintain a calorie deficit; that is, you have to take in fewer calories than you burn in a day. But to stay healthy, you have to look at the nutritional value of all the foods you eat, including fast food and other restaurant meals.

REMEMBER

Technically, you could eat fast food every day and still lose weight, but it wouldn't make you any healthier. Too much fast food can cause life-altering problems like high cholesterol, sodium overload, and nutrient deficiency, so although you *can* eat it, you should only do so in moderation. The quality of the calories you consume matters; it affects things like how full you feel, how your metabolism works, and how your body responds to the stresses of everyday life.

Nutritional composition of fast foods

Choosing a salad at the drive-through is a better choice than a burger, at least from a health standpoint. Most fast-food menus contain calorie information, but you can see a quick breakdown of some popular fast foods in Table 23-2.

TABLE 23-2 ## Calories and Fat Content of Popular Fast Foods

Food	Calories	Fat Content
Domino's cheese pizza, 1 slice	210	8 grams
Papa John's pepperoni pizza, 1 slice	220	9.5 grams
MOD cheese pizza, 1 slice	97.5	3.1 grams
Burger King Whopper with cheese	770	48 grams
Five Guys burger with cheese	610	34 grams
McDonald's Quarter Pounder with Cheese	510	26 grams
Wendy's quarter-pound single hamburger	470	29 grams
Burger King 8-Piece Chicken Tenders	360	21 grams
McDonald's Chicken Selects, 5 pieces	660	40 grams
Burger King medium fries	440	22 grams
Five Guys fries	310	15 grams
McDonald's medium fries	380	19 grams
Taco Bell Burrito XXL Grilled Stuft Burrito, beef	860	39 grams
Taco Bell Soft Taco Supreme	210	10 grams
Baja Fresh Chicken Burrito Ultimo	880	36 grams
Chipotle steak burrito with white rice, pinto beans, and cheese	920	28.5 grams
Dunkin' Donuts glazed donut	220	9 grams
Krispy Kreme glazed donut	200	12 grams
Starbucks plain bagel	300	1 gram
McDonald's Sausage McMuffin with Egg	450	27 grams
Burger King Sausage, Egg, and Cheese Biscuit	550	37 grams

This table is just a small sample of the calorie and fat content of popular fast foods. Most restaurants have nutrition information on their websites, so if you don't see your favorites here, check them out online. You may be surprised at what kind of a punch these types of foods can pack.

In all fairness, you shouldn't deny yourself your favorite foods all the time. Just make sure you're keeping track of your calories to get an overall picture.

WARNING

One cheat day can put a damper on all your hard work. If you're careful about what you eat all week but on one day you go ape and eat fast food for breakfast, lunch, and dinner (and sprinkle in candy and soda throughout the day), you're going to consume all the calories, fat, sugar, and other ingredients you cut. Having some unhealthy foods periodically is better than packing them all into one day.

Eating smart while dining out

Most restaurants have healthy options, but you may have to ask your server to make some adjustments for you. For example, a piece of chicken marked "heart smart" may come with a large order of fries and glazed vegetables. Likewise, a simple steak loaded up with fried onions that comes with baked potato skins dripping with cheese may not be the healthiest choice. Look for words on the menu that tell you what to avoid, like *pan-fried, crispy, dipped, breaded, cream,* and *alfredo.* Then look for more encouraging words like *grilled, steamed, baked, braised, broiled,* or *seared.*

You can also use these tips:

>> Ask for a double serving of vegetables in place of bread or potatoes.

>> Ask whether the vegetables are cooked in butter (and, if so, whether you can substitute them with a better choice).

>> Think about skipping dessert until you get home, where you can make good choices.

>> Eat half of what's on your plate and take the rest home. Most restaurants give you far more than a standard serving!

When you're in a restaurant (or even at the grocery store), don't let the *health halo* effect get to you. That's the act of overestimating a food's healthfulness based on a single claim. Some of the health halos the food industry capitalizes on include the following:

>> **Gluten-free:** Sure, some people can't eat gluten, but that doesn't mean these foods are any healthier than their gluten-laden counterparts. A gluten-free cookie is still a cookie!

>> **Natural:** *Natural* means only that something exists in nature. Plenty of things in nature are bad for you. (Arsenic is one of them.)

>> **Organic:** Organic farmers definitely use different practices than other farmers do, but that doesn't have an effect on the nutritional quality of the food.

Organic simply means that the foods haven't been treated with certain types of chemicals. (Note that many organic farmers still use other types of chemicals, such as pyrethrin.)

>> **Flax, honey, kale, and other healthy-sounding ingredients:** Check the ingredients list to see what else is in the food before you decide whether it's a good choice.

Considering Coffee, Energy Drinks, and Alcohol

If you're like many people, you've had your fair share of coffee, energy drinks, and alcoholic beverages (you may have even had Wild Tiger or Rip-Its). About 64 percent of Americans drink at least one cup of coffee every day, and energy drinks are the most popular dietary supplement that young adults consume. About 55 percent of Americans drink alcohol in any given month, with some drinking much more frequently than others; the median number of drinks per week is three. (One recent study suggested that about 12.7 percent of the U.S. population — that's one in eight adults — meets the diagnostic criteria for an alcohol use disorder, but that's another story for another book.)

The best part of waking up (and the rest of the day): Savoring coffee's benefits

Scientists have identified a number of health benefits associated with drinking coffee. Its active ingredient, caffeine, is a staple in many fat-burning supplements and energy drinks because studies have shown that it can boost your metabolic rate by between 3 and 11 percent. What may surprise you, though, is that coffee beans have plenty of nutrients that make their way into the finished product. One cup has 11 percent of the riboflavin, 6 percent of the pantothenic acid, 3 percent of the manganese and potassium, and 2 percent of the magnesium and niacin you need in a day. It's high in antioxidants, too.

But like anything else, coffee is best in moderation. Most people can safely consume up to 400 milligrams of caffeine in a day (one brewed eight-ounce cup has about 95 milligrams), but overdoing it has uncomfortable side effects, like the jitters, irritability, sleeplessness, and anxiety. If you're an espresso drinker (or enjoy it in your mixed coffee drinks on the way to work), you should know that a standard one-ounce shot of espresso contains 64 milligrams of caffeine.

Loading up on caffeine through energy drinks

Science says that energy drinks can be harmful to your health, but despite that, you can almost hear them cracking open across the Army every morning at 0900. Researchers have determined that energy drinks are associated with a wide range of health problems, ranging from sleep troubles to weight gain. They can send your blood pressure through the roof, and they've been linked to mental health problems, risk of diabetes, tooth decay, and kidney damage. Some of that is likely attributable to added sugar, high-fructose corn syrup, and artificial sweeteners; on average, a 16.9-ounce can of an energy drink contains about 54 grams of sugar — more than you're supposed to get in a whole day.

Some two-ounce servings of energy drinks contain as much as 207 milligrams of caffeine. With multiple servings, that can cause some serious health issues, especially if you're using them regularly. It's not just caffeine, though. Many of these drinks include added stimulants, like taurine (an amino acid found in animal tissue), guarana, ginseng, i-carnitine, creatine, and glucuronolactone. The problem with these stimulants is that little research on them exists, so whether they're safe in the short- or long-term is anyone's guess. Stimulants can also dehydrate you, cause an upset stomach, make you anxious and shaky, give you headaches, or even kill you from overdose.

Thinking before you drink: Alcohol's effects on your system

A little bit of alcohol consumption, researchers say, may provide a few health benefits. There are no definitive answers, but moderate consumption may reduce your risk of developing and dying from heart disease, your risk of stroke, and your risk of diabetes. However, researchers still maintain that nothing can replace a healthy diet and being physically active.

But even moderate alcohol use isn't risk-free. Using alcohol regularly (even in moderation) increases your risk for some cancers, like esophageal cancer. Heavy alcohol use, which is defined as more than three drinks on any day, more than seven drinks a week for women, or more than 14 drinks a week for men, is like walking through a minefield. It dehydrates your body, fills you with calories you can't really burn easily, and increases your risk for

>> Cancer (including breast cancer, oral cancers, throat cancer, and liver cancer)

>> Pancreatitis

>> Heart muscle damage

- » Stroke

- » Liver disease

- » High blood pressure

- » Accidental serious injury or death

- » Suicide

WARNING

Your risk of being involved in an alcohol-related crash increases exponentially when you drink and get behind the wheel. Never, ever drink and drive.

For most people who drink moderate amounts (and do so responsibly), alcohol doesn't typically pose any significant problems. Your body should be able to process it normally. However, alcohol still introduces calories into your diet. Figure 23-3 shows the calorie counts of some common alcoholic drinks.

BEER
12 ounces
153 calories
(103 calories for
light beer)

RED WINE
5 ounces
125 calories

WHITE WINE
5 ounces
121 calories

**80-PROOF
SPIRITS**
(gin, rum, vodka,
whiskey, tequila)
1.5 ounces
97 calories

CHAMPAGNE
4 ounces
84 calories

MARTINI
2.25 ounces
124 calories

COSMO
2.75 ounces
146 calories

MARGARITA
4 ounces
168 calories

MANHATTAN
3.5 ounces
164 calories

PIÑA COLADA
9 ounces
490 calories

FIGURE 23-3:
Calories in
common
alcoholic drinks.

© John Wiley & Sons, Inc.

Cracking Down on Supplements

A 2017 study by the Pew Research Center shows that about 70 percent of military personnel use dietary supplements, with 22 percent using three or more every week. The most common reasons soldiers and other service members cite involve increasing energy, building muscle, and enhancing performance. These supplements are readily available, too; just head to your installation's PX or mini-mall, and you'll most likely find a major supplement store inside.

But the Army Public Health Center says that before you take any type of supplement, whether it's a tablet, capsule, powder, energy bar, or liquid, you should ask yourself whether it's safe, whether it works, and whether you actually need it. As many as 10 percent of U.S. military personnel use at least one dietary supplement *every day* that may pose a risk to the heart or liver or that may cause significant adverse reactions.

REMEMBER

The U.S. Food and Drug Administration doesn't evaluate whether supplements are safe or properly labeled. Instead, the agency leaves that task up to the manufacturers themselves.

Protein pow(d)er: Scrutinizing protein supplements

If you're like many people, adding a scoop of protein powder to a smoothie, picking up a protein shake after a workout at the gym, or taking other protein supplements seems like a fast, easy way to boost your health and supercharge your muscle development. And in some cases, that's true; adding protein to your diet can be a good idea, especially if you're not getting enough to meet your body's needs.

Protein powders can come from plants, like soybeans, rice, potatoes, peas, or hemp, or they can come from eggs. Casein and whey protein come from milk. However, protein powders can come with pretty significant health risks, and many doctors don't recommend them for the general public; even then, they'd rather supervise a patient who's using them than turn someone loose with a huge canister. The problem is that most powders contain added ingredients that you don't want, like added sugars (which can spike your blood sugar and your waistline), thickeners, artificial flavoring, and vitamins and minerals.

Because labeling for supplements is unregulated, you have no way of knowing whether the protein powder you buy really contains what the manufacturer says it does. A 2019 study by the Clean Label Project found many protein powders that contained heavy metals, including lead, mercury, cadmium, and arsenic.

The researchers also found products with bisphenol–A (BPA, which is used to make plastic), pesticides, and other toxins known to cause cancer and other health conditions.

Other problems with protein powders include the following:

>> **A lack of scientific data on long-term use:** Too few studies have examined the possible side effects of supplemental protein in high doses to definitively say what will happen to your body over time.

>> **Digestive distress:** If you have a dairy allergy or even just a little trouble digesting lactose, you can experience significant discomfort if you use a milk-based protein powder.

REMEMBER

Protein is really important for muscle growth because it helps repair muscle tissues, but the idea that it directly promotes muscle growth is a common myth. Only strength training and exercise can change your muscles. Even professional bodybuilders don't need a ton of extra protein.

Most people can get enough protein through diet alone. Besides, studies have shown that your body can only absorb between 20 and 30 grams of protein at a time. If you don't use all the protein you consume, your body stores it as increased body fat. It can pull water from where it needs to be, causing dehydration, and it can lead to a loss of calcium, which you need to keep your bones and teeth healthy. Finally, too much protein can put extra strain on your kidneys, which filter toxins. Before you reach for a can of protein powder, check out Chapter 20 for more on which foods can deliver the protein you need.

Shunning pre-workout supplements

Pre-workout supplement manufacturers can tell you all day that their products are safe and incredibly effective. You'll run like Usain Bolt, lift like Arnold, and perform with Herculean strength like Lasha Talakhadze.

Medical experts disagree, and for good reason.

Research on these supplements' effectiveness is very limited, and their claims aren't closely regulated. Pre-workout supplements are formulas designed to help improve your performance, and some of their ingredients, like nitric oxide precursors, caffeine, and creatine, really can boost athletic performance in appropriate doses. Many contain excess caffeine, however, and historically have included harmful substances to disastrous effect.

In early 2020, a court ruled that dimethylamylamine (DMAA) could no longer be sold as a dietary supplement because it's neither an herb nor a botanical, and it's not generally recognized as safe. That was nine years after two soldiers had heart attacks after consuming best-selling pre-workout supplements containing DMAA in 2011. One soldier, 22, collapsed and died while running in formation for about 10 minutes; the other, 32, collapsed during a PT test and passed away a month later. In 2016, a healthy 25-year-old male soldier had a hemorrhagic stroke after taking a pre-workout supplement containing phenethylamine, creatine, and caffeine. These aren't the only stories, either; you can find dozens more.

TIP

If you're going to use a pre-workout supplement, choose one that's been tested by a third party, such as NSF International or USP.

WARNING

Don't take a pre-workout supplement before you take the ACFT. It won't boost your performance; in fact, it's likely to drag you down during the run when you crash. A pre-ACFT supplement can also make you sick, especially if you've never taken one before. Ask a few of your battle buddies who have tried it; you'll get a handful of stories that tell you everything you need to know.

Chapter **24**

Eating Right

The Army asks you to be a warrior-athlete, and that's pretty reasonable — especially when your life can depend on your being physically fit, agile, and able to think on your feet. However, you can't do that if you don't have the right fuel for your body. The Army doesn't hold its soldiers to exact dietary standards, but nutrition is one component of its Army Performance Triad (P3; you can read more about that in Chapter 7).

Every soldier's body is different, which means your nutritional needs, caloric output, and response to physical stressors are different from your battle buddy's. Zeroing in on the right balance of diet and exercise can take a while. The guidelines and tips in this chapter can help you get there.

REMEMBER

Eating right isn't just about losing weight or bulking up, either; it's about developing good eating patterns that will improve your health as you age.

Dishing up Basic Dietary Guidelines for Soldiers

The Army may not have specific guidelines its soldiers are supposed to stick to, but it does offer these general nutrition tips, backed by science:

» **Eat sufficient calories so that you're lean and energetic but not so many that you gain body fat.**

» **Focus on complex carbohydrates.** Carbs are your body's first choice for energy, so you need them to power up during the day.

» **Pick healthy fats, but use them in moderation.** These fats are good for your overall health. Some sources of healthy fats include avocado; whole eggs; fish like salmon, trout, mackerel, herring, and sardines; nuts; and dark chocolate (preferably with over 70 percent cocoa solids. Watch for sugar content, too.).

» **Watch your protein intake.** Studies have shown that you can absorb only between 20 and 30 grams of protein at a time, so don't overdo it.

» **Stay hydrated.** Water isn't a crutch, so don't treat it that way!

» **Plan to eat three meals and two snacks every day.** Try to avoid long stretches where you don't eat.

» **Choose variety.** Don't get into a rut; pick a variety of foods so you can enjoy a balanced diet.

According to a handful of studies, more than 80 percent of soldiers fail to meet the Healthy People Guidelines for 2020, an Office of Disease Prevention and Health Promotion initiative. The guidelines are pretty straightforward; each day, they require you to eat

» 2 cups of fruit

» 3 to 4 cups of vegetables

» 8 to 10 ounces of grains

» 3 cups of dairy

» 6 ounces of protein

You can get specifics on which foods you need for essential vitamins and minerals in Chapter 21. Your dietary needs are different from mine, and if one of us is more active than the other, the more active person needs to eat more to maintain a healthy body weight.

Helping Yourself to Healthy Eating Patterns

An *eating pattern* is an overall look at the way you consume food. If you do it correctly, barring any medical conditions or other factors that throw off your body's natural balance, a healthy eating pattern supports a healthy body weight while reducing your risk for chronic disease. When you establish a healthy eating pattern, you can meet your nutritional needs without going over the limits for unhealthy ingredients, like saturated fats, added sugar, and sodium (which I discuss later in this section).

You should aim to meet all (or at least most of) your nutritional needs through food. All kinds of foods count, whether they're fresh, canned, dried, or frozen, as long as they're nutrient-dense.

Some professionals say you should eat every two hours to boost your metabolism, while others say you can stick to three meals a day. The fact is, though, that every soldier's body is different. Here's a good rule of thumb: You should wait between three and five hours between full meals because that's the average time your stomach takes to empty into your small intestine. One of the benefits to waiting this amount of time is that you can be sure you're eating because you're hungry — not just out of habit or as an emotional response.

BARRIERS TO GOOD NUTRITION FOR TROOPS

Nutrition is part of the Army's Performance Triad, but the fact is that many soldiers have to face barriers to optimal nutrition. A lot of soldiers don't have easy access to healthy foods for several reasons; when the Army surveyed soldiers on what affects their nutrition, the responses included cost, location, limited healthy options, and even dining facility hours. For soldiers who live in the barracks versus on- or off-post family housing, making healthier choices can be even more difficult due to a lack of kitchen appliances. And don't forget that on-post food courts are packed with unhealthy fast-food options.

Although the Department of Defense doesn't collect data on how many soldiers receive food assistance, an estimated 23,000 military families receive benefits through the Supplemental Nutrition Assistance Program, and about 65 percent of military kids qualify for free or reduced lunches at school. If you're a soldier (or civilian) dealing with food insecurity, visit USA.gov/food-help, your state's social service agency's website, or Army Emergency Relief at ArmyEmergencyRelief.org, where food counts as an emergency financial need.

REMEMBER

If you wait too long between meals, you may suffer from a lack of focus, irritation (you know it as being hangry), shakiness, low energy, and low blood sugar levels. Even worse, by the time you eat, you feel like you're starving so you're more likely to overstuff yourself.

In the Army, you can't always stick to a healthy eating pattern. Two weeks in the field with MREs and green mermites can throw off the best-laid plans, and NTC or JRTC can really knock you off the wagon. The important thing is that you hop back on as soon as you're able.

Putting the brakes on sodium, saturated and trans fats, and added sugars

Food and Drug Administration guidelines released in January 2020 say that you shouldn't get more than 2,300 milligrams per day of sodium, and that no more than 10 percent of your caloric intake should come from added sugar and saturated or trans fats. In your day-to-day diet, checking the labels of the foods you eat will give you a pretty good idea about how close you're getting to your daily limits. For example, if your daily diet consists of taking in 2,000 calories per day, no more than 200 calories of that should come from added sugar and bad fats. To put that into perspective, a 12-ounce can of cola is 180 calories. The following sections break down some places you can find these ingredients.

Sodium

Some foods are extremely high in sodium, and you really need very little of it to maintain a healthy balance. Unfortunately, that means a lot of foods — including canned vegetables — may have more sodium than you bargained for. Some of the worst offenders are processed meat (including bacon and deli-sliced sandwich meat), frozen breaded meats and dinners, canned entrees like chili, and salted nuts. Buttermilk, cheese, and cottage cheese tend to have high sodium, and so do pancake mixes, pizza, and prepackaged mixes for potatoes, rice, stuffing, and pasta. Pickled vegetables and commercially prepared pasta, salsa, canned soup, ramen noodles, and soy sauce are also no-gos if you're cutting your sodium intake.

TIP

Use sea salt in moderation. Even though sea salt is pushed as a healthier alternative, it has the same basic nutritional value as standard table salt. Sea salt can include minerals like magnesium, but it contains comparable amounts of sodium to table salt by weight.

Saturated and trans fats

When you're trimming saturated fats, try skipping foods like

>> Desserts and baked goods

>> Ice cream and other dairy-based desserts

>> Most cheeses

>> Whole milk and full-fat dairy foods

>> Sausages, hot dogs, bacon, and ribs

>> Ground beef and cuts of meat with visible fat

>> Fried chicken or chicken with the skin on

>> French fries that are fried in saturated fat or hydrogenated oil

Trans fats are always a bad idea, and they're found in many of the foods that contain saturated fats. However, they're also in nondairy coffee creamer, microwave popcorn, margarine that comes in a stick, and refrigerated dough. Eliminate foods that have hydrogenated vegetable oil listed as an ingredient from your diet wherever you can.

Added sugar

Added sugar is added to, well, almost everything. You find it in granola that's promoted as a healthy alternative to sugary cereal, lowfat yogurt, barbecue sauce and ketchup, spaghetti sauce, and most sports drinks. Protein bars, flavored waters, and canned soups also contain unusually high amounts of added sugar; some of them are right up there with candy bars. You don't have to force yourself to read every label, though, as long as you're eating whole foods (like fruits, vegetables, and meats).

Playing with portion control

Portion control simply means regulating how much of any food makes its way to your plate. You can take some of the guesswork out of it by using smaller dinnerware and visualizing a pie chart or the plate in Figure 24-1 as you fill it up. At each meal, allow only a quarter of your plate for complex carbs (starchy vegetables or whole grains), a quarter for protein (meat, poultry, fish, or eggs), and the remaining half for vegetables or salad. That breakdown is only a guide, though.

REMEMBER

Vegetables and salad are naturally low in calories, but they're high in fiber and other nutrients. The fiber in most veggies can fill you up more quickly, so focusing on eating more of them is often a good idea if you feel your portions of other foods are too small. Vegetables may not be your favorite foods, but your body needs them; when you infuse your system with all the right vitamins and minerals, your body can perform at its best.

FIGURE 24-1: Portion control in practice.

TIP

Before you eat a meal, drink an eight-ounce glass of water. Being well-hydrated helps your brain figure out whether you're hungry or thirsty, and the water takes up plenty of room in your stomach (as well as aids digestion).

Treat yo' self: Giving yourself a pass to indulge sometimes

Theoretically, if you want to be healthier or lose weight, cutting out all your favorite junk food makes sense. However, I'm going to tell you that you should still indulge yourself from time to time — and that's because I want you to be as healthy as you possibly can.

When you can still enjoy your favorite foods, you're more likely to stick to overall healthy eating patterns. You're also more likely to put in a few extra minutes on the treadmill (I know I do). Indulging from time to time can help you enjoy holidays and special events without worrying about every single calorie, too. And the best part? Your body will be fine (as long as you're indulging in moderation).

5

The Part of Tens

Avoid big mistakes that could cause you to fail the ACFT.

Discover strategies that can help you reach new heights on the ACFT scorecard.

Keep your workouts fresh and fun with change-up strategies.

Slash extra calories without suffering (too much).

Transform a blank template into a personal workout calendar.

Chapter **25**

Ten Surefire Ways to Fail the ACFT

Your career hinges on the Army Combat Fitness Test, so steering clear of big pitfalls that can cause you to fail makes sense. The worst part is that if you miss the mark on one event, you still have to complete the test, so if you drop the ball on the 3 Repetition Maximum Deadlift, for example, you're in for five more events with that one hanging over your head. If that's your goal, you're in luck — the following sections show you ten ways to tank your ACFT score.

Choosing Not to Work Out

Like any test, the ACFT requires you to study, but in this case, studying means hitting the pavement and carving out time at the gym. Sure, some people can wing it and count on Monday through Friday Physical Readiness Training to carry them through, but that doesn't work for most people. You have to put in the work to get the results you want, and that means using the exercises in Chapter 8, the stretches in Chapter 9, and the workout calendar in the Appendix.

Failing to Know How to Do Each Event

Every event on the test has specific instructions, and the test administrators don't read them to you on-site. Instead, you're supposed to read the instructions on your own at least 48 hours before the test. You get an opportunity to ask questions on test day, right before you start the Preparation Drill. That's when the OIC or NCOIC says, "It is your responsibility to complete proper preparation and know the event standards prior to taking the ACFT. What are your questions about the event standards?"

You shouldn't have questions at that point, though. If you read the instructions when you're supposed to, you have plenty of time (two whole days) to get the answers you need.

Falling off the Fitness Wagon before the Test

Falling off the fitness wagon from time to time is easy, but don't let yourself get run over by scrapping your whole plan to prep for the test. Everyone makes mistakes and slips up, taking too many days (or weeks) off during preparation. Life gets in the way. However, you can't forget that your job, your health insurance, and plenty of other things rely on your performance. That means if you fall off the wagon, you need to get back on.

Practicing for the Wrong Events

If you haven't taken a diagnostic ACFT, you may not know which events you're going to struggle with and which ones you'll breeze right through. Seeing how far you can throw a medicine ball behind your head is *not* the same as performing the test events in sequence. The energy you expend on early events may drain you for the later ones.

REMEMBER

On the Army Physical Fitness Test (APFT, the ACFT's predecessor) you could get up after you finished your push-ups or sit-ups if you needed to conserve energy to pass the run. This test isn't like that. There's no easy way to skimp in one area to perform better in another, so running yourself through every event (on the Army's timetable, which I outline in Chapter 3) *long* before test day to see where you need the most work is in your best interest.

Drinking Alcohol the Night before the Test

Drinking alcohol the night before you take the ACFT poses a serious threat to your performance. Alcohol increases your stomach's acid production, and it delays stomach emptying. It can even cause your blood sugar to fall, and if you've ever hit the gym without at least eating a granola bar or banana beforehand, you know how miserable that can be. Alcohol is a diuretic, so it makes you urinate more often — and that leads to dehydration (as if there weren't already enough morning-after side effects). Put all that together with the fact that you may have to perform six strenuous events with an upset stomach, and sticking with water the night before the big day just makes sense.

Forgetting to Hydrate

When you're dehydrated, your bloodstream borrows water from your cells, and they start to malfunction. Skipping water the night before and morning of the ACFT is the best way to give yourself cramps, upset your stomach, and possibly even make you vomit during or after a strenuous event. Remember that most energy drinks don't actually hydrate you; instead, they act as diuretics, which dehydrate you further.

Forgetting to Fuel Up

Think of your body like the precision machine that it is (or that it's about to become). You need a power source, so fueling up the night before — and even the morning of — the test is pretty necessary. Your immediate power source is carbohydrates, which your body stores as glycogen in your muscles. You need enough glycogen to get you through anaerobic events, like the Sprint-Drag-Carry and the Standing Power Throw. Studies suggest that eating carbs before you exercise can help improve your performance, as well as let you work out longer and at a higher intensity. For most people, eating carbohydrate-rich foods is a good idea. You can still do that if you're minding your waistline, too, by choosing things like bananas, apples, oranges, beans, and oats.

TIP

Just do yourself a favor: If you're not used to eating things like fast-food burgers, mega-sized burritos, or huge pasta dishes (perhaps because you've spent a lot of time on Chapter 23), don't treat yourself too much the night before the ACFT.

Missing the Mark on Height and Weight

No matter how well you perform on each of the ACFT events, you still have to pass height and weight. If you don't, you're subject to the tape test, which I cover in Chapter 19. You can redeem yourself there — but if you fail the tape test, you're going to receive a counseling statement and win automatic (and completely free) enrollment in the Army Body Composition Program, which used to be called the Army Weight Control Program. If you're currently toeing the line on height and weight, working on your dietary habits as soon as possible, which you can read about in Chapter 23, is a good idea.

Taking Pre-Workout or Other Potentially Unsafe Supplements Before the Test

As far as supplements go, taking vitamin E capsules and powering through a pre-workout drink, which I discuss in Chapter 21, are completely different animals. I strongly advise you not to use a pre-workout supplement before the ACFT. You can read dozens of horror stories online about PT tests and these types of supplements, ranging from cringe-worthy embarrassments to deaths linked to DMAA (an amphetamine derivative illegal in the United States). The U.S. Food and Drug Administration says that DMAA can raise blood pressure and lead to cardio-vascular problems (including heart attack), so please steer clear of it in general — and especially before you take the ACFT.

WARNING

DMAA isn't the only potentially dangerous substance in pre-workout supplements; they can overload you on caffeine or contain other substances that can have negative effects on your health.

Committing Safety Violations or Faults

Graders on any ACFT event can call out safety violations or faults, so you have to know what can earn you a no-go at each station. For example, if you commit a safety violation during the Sprint-Drag-Carry, such as throwing the kettlebells, your grader calls you back to the start line or 25-meter turn line to correct your performance — without stopping the clock. Likewise, each time you fail to maintain a straight body alignment when you're doing push-ups, your grader doesn't count that rep. That pushes you a little farther from making the grade. You can read about some potential faults and violations in Chapter 4.

Chapter **26**

Ten Tips for Maxing Out Your Score on the ACFT

P assing the ACFT isn't optional, but going above and beyond for a perfect 600 score is. Hey, the Army always has room for another PT stud. Check out these ten tips to help you get the highest scores possible — even if you're not a professional athlete.

Putting in Extra Effort and Committing to Getting a 600

Earning the highest possible score on the ACFT definitely takes extra effort, so you have to keep the big picture in mind as you train in the months ahead of test day. One Army officer wrote "600" on the whiteboard in his office and looked at it every day until he got there; some people text each other after every workout. Still others work out with a battle buddy and provide real-time feedback on performance. The common theme here is that each of these people set the goal of achieving a 600 and committed to it.

Training As You Test

The Army's "train as you fight" motto is especially important here because what your body learns in practice is what it'll automatically do during the test. No matter how far you can throw, how many times you can touch your knees to your elbows, or how quickly you can knock out hand-release push-ups, you can't max out your ACFT score if you don't know the exact rules for each of the six events. You can read detailed instructions for every event in Chapter 4. When you practice for each event, have someone check your form and give you feedback.

Doing Cardio and Strength Training Leading Up to the Test

The best time to start preparing for the ACFT was yesterday, but if you missed the boat, it's okay. Today's fine, too. Make sure you're doing a good mix of cardio and strength training in the months and weeks leading up to your next ACFT. You can use the blank workout calendar in the Appendix to create a plan with guidance from Chapter 18. Allow each muscle group sufficient rest time, build stretching into your daily routine, and plan for recovery days to get the most out of your workout calendar.

Getting Hard-Core with Your Core

Every event on the ACFT requires you to have a strong core, so spend ample time strengthening the muscles in your abdomen and back before the test. You can work your core more frequently than you can other muscle groups; head to Chapter 17 to find exercises that target all the right muscles.

REMEMBER

It's not about having a flat stomach, though (that's just an added perk); it's about providing the rest of your body with stability and support while you move through each ACFT event.

Practicing at Least One Event Every Day

You can find dozens of exercises to improve your performance on each ACFT event, but none of them can help you on test day if you haven't practiced the events themselves. Add at least one ACFT event to your workout calendar for each active day, but don't do it at the same point in your workout each time. For example, if you're practicing hand-release pushups on Mondays, do them before the rest of your exercises this Monday; next Monday, put them in the middle of your routine, and then the following Monday, do them when you're finished with all the exercises on your plan. This approach gives you a feel for the way your body responds under different conditions, and you can zero in on better training techniques as you go.

Tracking Your Progress

Watching yourself improve is a great motivator. I'm not saying you have to set up selfie mode on your phone and practice in your garage (although a lot of people do), but I am saying you should keep track of the progress you're making — not just on ACFT events, but in other areas as well. Start tracking with your very first workout so you can see your baseline, and as you add weight, run faster, or throw farther, write it all down. That way, you can get eyes on your improvements and push yourself to improve even more.

Using High-Quality Fuel

You can't put diesel in a sport bike and expect it to run smoothly (or at all). And like your sport bike, you need the right kind of fuel to hit maximum performance. Check out the principles of proper nutrition in Chapter 21 to make sure you're giving your body all the essentials so it runs like a well-oiled machine.

Hydrating before and during the ACFT

Every cell in your body needs adequate water to operate properly. Water regulates your body temperature, transports nutrients that give your body energy, and keeps you from cramping up when you use your muscles. That means you need plenty of it before the ACFT, so 48 hours out, make sure you're filling (and refilling) your water bottle.

Make sure you're completely hydrated the day before you take the ACFT, and bring your water bottle with you on test day. You need to replenish your body's stores of water as you burn through them. Don't drink alcohol the night before the test.

TIP

The American Council on Exercise suggests that you also drink 17 to 20 ounces of water at least two hours before you start exercising, another 8 ounces of water a half-hour before you exercise, and 7 to 10 ounces during exercise. (Don't worry; the Army encourages you to bring a water bottle with you when you take the ACFT.) Then you're supposed to drink another 8 ounces of water within 30 minutes of completing your exercise. That means you should drink between 40 and 46 ounces of water in a three-hour span. Sports drinks with extra calories, potassium, and other nutrients may help you perform for a longer stretch of time, but choose wisely. Don't pick one with caffeine, which can have a diuretic effect.

Getting Enough Sleep before the Test

The Army doesn't always make it easy to catch all your Zs, but the night before you take the ACFT is arguably the most important night for getting enough down time. You need to rest and recharge for the six grueling events, especially if you expect to maximize your score. Avoid taking any sleep aids (unless your primary care provider has prescribed them, of course), which can leave you groggy in the morning.

Using All the Info You Have to Your Advantage

You can find plenty of tips and tricks for performing your very best on each ACFT event; I outline many of them in Chapter 4. You can also pick them up when you practice each event during your workout routines or get them from others who've taken the test.

Chapter **27**

Ten Ways to Change up Your Exercise Routine

Working out isn't always fun. Sometimes the same old routines get boring, even if you're switching gears every few weeks. This chapter has ten great ways to vary your workouts so that they're more interesting — and so that you're more likely to stick to the plan and improve your performance on the ACFT.

Using (Or Ditching) the Buddy System

For many people, working out with someone else makes it more enjoyable. If you're used to hitting the gym by yourself, think about taking a friend along, even if it's just for moral support. Or, if you usually work out with someone else, try flying solo once or twice. You'll probably notice a change in your focus and how you feel each workout either way.

Mixing up Your Personal Speed

Are you better-suited to fast-paced workouts that leave you breathless but get the job done, or are you more of a long-haul exerciser who doesn't mind working out for an hour or more? If you know which type of exerciser you are, try to switch gears. Give yourself a goal of getting in and out of the gym in 30 minutes without skimping on exercises, or take your time and meander from machine to machine.

Getting Creative with Exercises

Try mixing two exercise moves into one to switch things up. For example, you can do a bent over row immediately followed by a hang clean and then go right back into a bent over row to repeat the process. Maybe you want to do lunges that lead right into knee drives or to run hill repeats wearing your body armor (loosely, please).

TIP

Try to keep a good focus on your muscle groups when you're getting inventive with your exercises so you don't work out the same groups on back-to-back days.

Playing Mood Music

The gym has plenty of ambient noise, whether you go to your own club or you work out in the one on-post. And now that you can wear headphones in on-post gyms, adding some music to the mix can make a tremendous impact on your workouts. (Added bonus: When you're wearing headphones, nobody's going to judge you for what you're rocking out to.)

Going Backward Once in a While

Doing the same exercises in the same order can get a bit boring, especially if you've been on the same routine for a month. If you're not quite ready to switch out your exercises, though, try working from the bottom of your list to the top. When you usually start with chest presses and finish with flys, change things up to surprise your body and see how ingrained your patterns are. Flipping the script not only causes your muscles to react differently because they're at different levels of fatigue but also adds in a little bit of brain training as well.

Switching Locations

If you usually work out at home, hit the gym (or vice-versa). If you're on a big base, go to a different gym than the one you usually use. You can even switch your workouts from indoors to outdoors, weather-permitting, to give your routine a nudge in a different direction.

Dialing up the Intensity

Feeling bored may be a signal that you can lift more or run faster. Try pushing yourself a little harder when you just don't feel like exercising — that internal motivation can make a tremendous difference in the way your workout plays out.

Trying Group Fitness

If you haven't already tried it, sign up for a group fitness class at your local gym. Group workouts have a certain energy in the room that makes them a lot of fun, and they're nearly always accompanied by upbeat music that gets you more excited to be there. I teach group fitness classes at a local gym, and I can tell you that many of my participants wouldn't work out any other way.

Downloading an App

Dozens of great fitness apps are available for you to download, and many of them are free. You get great new ideas for workouts and are able to try things you hadn't thought of before, and you can beat workout blues by changing routines from time to time. Some of the most fun exercises I've ever done came from workout apps!

Playing Games

Your workout routine doesn't have to be rigid. Major game systems have plenty of fitness games, as well as those that require you to use balance boards to score points, dance, and otherwise move around.

REMEMBER

You don't have to go digital, either. Pick up a volleyball or basketball to get some cardio in from time to time.

Chapter **28**

Ten Ways to Cut Calories without Starving

I f you're watching your waistline, you know that the best way to trim down is through a healthy diet. But making dietary changes is a big deal, and it can be really hard, especially if you're used to eating a lot more. This chapter provides ten great ways you can reduce your calorie intake without feeling like you're starving. I won't lie and tell you that you won't feel these calorie-cutting tricks at all, but I will tell you that they're easier to implement than you think.

Don't Drink Your Calories

One can of soda can eat up 200 calories in your daily intake — and those are calories that you could've spent on something far better for your body. Instead of reaching for sugary soft drinks, juices, sports drinks, and energy drinks, grab a bottle of water. If you're the "I hate water" type, add a zero-calorie flavor packet or make your own concoctions (like tossing in a few raspberries and a sprig of mint) at home.

Fill Your Water Reserves Before You Eat

Drink a full glass of water before you sit down for each meal. The water helps fill your stomach and starts sending signals to your brain to slow down the hormones that say you're hungry. Some studies have even shown that people who drink water before eating lose weight faster than those who don't.

Switch to Lowfat Versions of Your Favorite Foods

Whole milk and foods made with it have a lot of fat in them, and that means they're packed with calories, too. Make the switch from whole milk to lowfat milk, as well as other lowfat dairy products, to cut those unnecessary calories from your diet. Just make sure you're not buying something with added sugar that cancels out your lowfat choice (yogurt is a big culprit in that area).

Don't Buy Junk Food

You can't eat a bag of chips or box of cookies if it's not in the pantry, so skip the junk food aisles at the grocery store. Instead, opt for fruits and vegetables you wouldn't mind snacking on. When you get home, wash them and put them into snack-sized bags or containers so they're easy to get to when you're craving something between meals.

Cook at Home

Restaurant food is usually loaded with calories. That's because chefs aren't really interested in your healthy eating habits; they want to make good food that you'll love so you'll come back and spend more money. When you eat at home more often, your waistline gets skinnier while your wallet gets fatter, so you win twice.

Lighten up on the Condiments

Most people use far more condiments on their food than they really need, especially high-sugar, calorie-dense dressings, sauces, and dips. Go easy on ketchup, barbecue sauce, and salad dressing; generally, these condiments contain a lot of sugar, unhealthy fats, and empty calories that you can do without.

Set the Table with Smaller Plates

Portion control is one of the simplest ways to cut calories, and you probably won't really notice it. Because many people use their plates to tell them when they're full, using a smaller dish is a great way to trick your brain into eating less.

Try Low-Cal Appetizers at Home

Low-calorie starters, like homemade soups and salads, can keep you from overeating. Multiple studies have shown that people who eat an appetizer reduce their total calorie intake by as much as 20 percent, so it's worth a shot. As an added benefit, you're getting more whole ingredients in your diet, which is good for your overall health anyway.

Never Eat out of the Container

Losing track of how much you're eating is so easy when your hand is going straight from a potato chip bag to your mouth. Before you know it, the bag is empty, and you're not feeling that great about what you just did. (I'm speaking from ample experience here.) Rather than eating out of the bag (or the cookie box, which I also have experience with), put your snacks in a bowl or on a plate. Then put the container back in the pantry, carry your snack to another room, and enjoy it.

Don't Force Yourself to Clean Your Plate

Despite what your mom used to say, the amount of food you consume at the dinner table has no direct relationship with anyone else's situation. You don't have to clean your plate, ever. If you don't want to feed the leftovers to your dog, stick them in the fridge and save them for later. You can help your own children develop healthy eating habits if you refrain from making them sit at the table until their plates are empty, too.

Appendix

Fill-in-the-Blanks Workout Calendar

Mapping out your workouts is a great way to keep focused on your goals, and this fill-in-the-blank workout calendar can help. You can set up your workouts week by week or month by month, but going one week at a time is a great start. That way, if you find that an exercise just isn't working for you, you can easily swap it out with something else the following week.

For more detailed instructions on creating your own workout plan, head to Chapter 18. In the meantime, here's a blank month-long calendar.

	Sunday	Monday	Tuesday	Wednesday	Thursday	Friday	Saturday
Week 1							

	Sunday	Monday	Tuesday	Wednesday	Thursday	Friday	Saturday
Week 2							
Week 3							
Week 4							

Index

C

caffeine, 396–397

calcium, 273, 372, 374

calculating resting heart rate, 105–106

calf raises, 202–203, 342–343

calf stretch, 221–222

CALL Publication 20-09, 18

calories

  about, 272

  calculating, 387

  cutting safely, 423–426

  in drinks, 423

  reducing safely, 389–390

calves, as antagonistic pairs with shins, 200

carbohydrates

  about, 374–375

  benefits of, 375–376

  for pre-workout, 361

  simple compared with complex, 375

cardiorespiratory fitness

  about, 416

  improving, 312–314

  reasons for measuring, 308

cardiovascular endurance, aerobic exercise for, 13

cardiovascular system

  about, 290–291

  role of in aerobic exercise, 305–308

Carry phase, of Sprint-Drag-Carry (SDC), 32

cartilage, torn, 275

cat/cow, 247–248, 330

cellulose, 367

Center for Army Lessons Learned (CALL), 52

Chabut, LaReine

  Stretching For Dummies, 207

chair dips, 341–342

charting progress, 340

Cheat Sheet (website), 3

chest, stretching, 234–236

chest flys, 174–175

chest muscles, as antagonistic pairs with back muscles, 289

chest strength, 95

child's pose

  dynamic shoulder stretch from, 246–247

  against a wall, 238

chloride, 372

cholecystokinin (CCK), 359

cholesterol, 391–392

choline, 370

circuit training, 296

circulatory system, 290–291

climbing bars/pod, 44

Climbing Drills 1 and 2, 147

cobra stretch, 237

coffee, 396

Combat Lifesaver (CLS) bags (medical kits), 44

complex carbohydrates, 375

compound exercises, 294

compression

  core muscles for, 92

  in RICE, 277–278

condiments, 425

conditioning drills (CD1/CD2/CD3), 145–146

contralateral dead bug, 190–192

conventional deadlifts, 157–160

coordination, 103

core

  about, 315, 416

  beginner exercises for strengthening, 318–322

  bodyweight exercises for strengthening, 323–326

  exercises for pregnancy profiles, 329–333

  exercises with stability ball for strengthening, 326–329

  muscles, 315–318

  strength of, 91

  stretching and toning, 333–334

crunches

  as a beginner core exercise, 320–321

  testing abdominal strength with, 299–300

cuts, 275

D

DA PAM 40-502, 254, 255

dehydration, avoiding, 380–383

delayed-onset muscle soreness (DOMS), 207–208, 296

deloading, 295

deltoids, 89, 90, 95, 96, 97, 289

density, 294

diagnostic ACFTs, 19–20

diastasis recti, 257

dietary fiber, 375

dietary guidelines, 404

Dietary Reference Intake (DRI), 366, 369–371, 374

diets, 363, 390–391

digestion, 387–388

dislocations, 275

DMAA, 414

documentation, for Physical Readiness Training (PRT), 115–116

Downward movement phase, of Repetition Maximum Deadlift (MDL), 24

downward rotation, back muscles for, 94

Drag phase, of Sprint-Drag-Carry (SDC), 31

drills. *See also* exercises

  Climbing Drills 1 and 2, 147

  conditioning drills (CD1/CD2/CD3), 145–146

  4 for the Core, 145

  Guerilla Drill, 147

  Hip Stability Drill, 147

  Military Movement Drills 1 and 2, 148

  Preparation Drill, 144–145

  Push-Up and Sit-Up Drill, 147

  Recovery Drill, 149

  Shoulder Stability Drill, 147

dynamic balance, 103

dynamic stretching, 210, 239–248

E

eating patterns, 405–408

8-count T push-up, 128–130

elbow extension, arm/shoulder muscles for, 96

elbow flexion, arm/shoulder muscles for, 96

elbow-to-elbow grip, 235

electrolytes, 383

elevated shoulder rotations, 194–197

Elevation, in RICE, 278

endurance

  muscular, 12

  training, combined with strength training, 284

energy availability, in female athlete triad, 252–253

energy drinks, 397

enlisted soldiers, Physical Demand Categories (PDCs), 67–70

equipment

  requirements for, 18–19, 43–46

  setting up, 47

erector spinae, 90, 92, 94, 95, 317

esophageal sphincter, 388

Example icon, 3

exercises. *See also* aerobic exercise; drills

  anaerobic, 14, 110–111

  bodyweight, 323–326

  changing up, 419–422

  core, for pregnancy profile, 329–333

  for core, 318–322

  creativity with, 420

  heart efficiency and, 308

  MET values for common, 386

  with stability ball, 326–329

  in Strength Training Circuit (STC), 148–149

  used in training for 3 Repetition Maximum Deadlift (MDR), 155–162

explosive power, 12

extend and flex, 213, 214

extended child's pose with sphinx stretch, 242–244

extension, core muscles for, 92

external abdominal oblique, 316

external hip rotation, leg muscles for, 93

external obliques, 89, 90, 92, 94, 95

external shoulder rotations, 194–197

F

failures, 78–79, 411–414

Farah, Mo, 197

fasciitis, 275

fast food, 393–396

fast-twitch muscles, 288

fats
about, 272–273
bad, 392–393
good, 364, 392–393
for pre-workout, 362
saturated, 367, 392–393, 407
trans fatty acids (trans fats), 393, 407
unsaturated, 392

female athlete triad, 252–253

females
about, 249–250
allowable body fat for, 352
common challenges for, 250–253
crunches for, 299
fiber requirements for, 375
menstrual cycle, 251–252
postpartum, 256–257
pregnancy and, 253–256
push-ups for, 299
squats for, 300
VO₂ max cardiorespiratory fitness
levels for, 311
water requirements for, 381
weight requirements for, 351

Feuerstein, Georg
Yoga For Dummies, 207, 333

fiber, 364, 375

Field Manual 7-22, *Holistic Health and Fitness*, 11, 18, 115

fitness components (performance basics)
about, 101
aerobic endurance, 103
agility, 103
balance, 103
coordination, 104

flexibility, 104
muscular endurance, 102
muscular strength, 101–102
power, 102
reaction time, 104
speed, 102–103

FITT principles, 108–110

flax, 396

flexibility
about, 11, 103
gender and, 250

flexion, core muscles for, 92

FM 7-22, *Army Physical Readiness Training*, 42, 255

folate, 370

follicular phase, of menstrual cycle, 251

food groups, 365–367

forced reps, 294

forearm flexor strength, 226–227

forearm planks, 182

forearm strength, 95–97

form, proper, 297

Form DD 2977 (Deliberate Risk Assessment Worksheet), 44, 46

forward lunge
about, 120–122
in Preparation Drill, 144, 145

4 for the Core drill, 145

4Q model, 86–88

fractures, 275

free radicals, 377

free weights, 302–303

frequency
about, 19–20, 294
as a FITT principle, 108

frog stretch, 217–218

front thighs, as antagonistic pairs with back thighs, 290

frontal plane, 85

full-body training, 296

fun, with working out, 282

hip extensors, 93
hip flexion, leg muscles for, 93
hip flexors
  about, 93
  as antagonistic pairs with gluteals, 290
  tight, 216
hip lifts, 318–319
hip rotation, leg muscles for, 93
Hip Stability Drill, 147
hips, stretching, 216–222
His-Purkinje network, 307
honey, 396
horizontal abduction, arm/shoulder muscles for, 96
horizontal adduction, arm/shoulder muscles for, 96
hormones
  gender and, 250
  hunger, 359
Hot yoga, 334
hunger, compared with appetite, 358–360
hunger hormones, 359
hydration, 410, 417–418
hydrogenation, 393
hypothalamus, 360

I

Ice, in RICE, 277
ice sheets, 44
icons, explained, 2–3
iliacus, 290
iliopsoas complex, 290
incline bench, 130–131
incline bench presses, 172–174
infraspinatus, 94
injuries
  about, 269
  common, 273–275
  DOMS vs., 208
  nutritional principles, 272–273
  Performance Triad (P3), 269–273
  preventing, 269–273
  RICE, 276–278
  sick call, 275–276

sleep and preventing, 270–271
taking care of, 208
types of, 274–275
instructions
  for 3 Repetition Maximum Deadlift (MDL), 52
  about, 51, 52
  for Hand Release Push-Up - Arm Extension
    (HRP), 56–57
  for Leg Tuck (LTK), 62–63
  for Sprint-Drag-Carry (SDC), 59–60
  for Standing Power Throw (SPT), 55
  for Two-Mile Run (2MR), 65
instructors, 48–50
insulin, 359
insulin-like peptide 5 (ILP 5), 359
intensity, 108–110, 294, 337–338, 421
intermediate lifter, 295
internal abdominal oblique, 316
internal obliques, 89, 92, 94, 95
internal shoulder rotations, 194–197
intervertebral disk, 266
Is, Ys, and Ts, 192–193
isolation exercises, 294
isometric hangs, 189
Iyengar yoga, 334

J

junk food, 424

K

kale, 396
kettlebell pull-throughs, 193–194
kettlebell swings, 168–169
knee extension, leg muscles for, 93
knee flexion, leg muscles for, 93
knee to chest stretch, 229–230
knees, exercises and issues with, 260–265

L

lateral flexion, core muscles for, 92
Lateral phase, of Sprint-Drag-Carry (SDC), 31

About the Author

Angie Papple Johnston joined the U.S. Army in 2006. During her second deployment as part of Operation Iraqi Freedom, Angie served as her battalion's public affairs representative, covering breaking news from Tikrit to Kirkuk. She has earned a Combat Action Badge, several Army Commendation medals and Army Achievement medals, and numerous accolades for her work in Iraq. She also served as the Lead Cadre for the Texas Army National Guard's Recruit Sustainment Program (RSP) in El Paso before becoming the CBRN noncommissioned officer-in-charge in an aviation battalion in Washington, D.C.

Angie is a certified cardio and strength training instructor who helps people all over the fitness spectrum reach their physical fitness goals. She currently resides in Asan, South Korea, with her husband (another noncommissioned officer in the U.S. Army), their son, and two dogs.

Dedication

This book is dedicated to every soldier who handed the Army that blank check (and those who are thinking about doing so) and every civilian who's pouring blood, sweat, and tears into physical fitness. It's also dedicated to Mr. Beans (the Krazy Kobra), who is seriously the coolest kid in the world, and his dad, David "Iguana Foot" Johnston, Jr.

Author's Acknowledgments

Lindsay Lefevere, thank you for all the hard work you put into everything. You're amazing, and I'm exceptionally grateful to you for believing in this book. I'm also grateful that you tolerate my sketchy math abilities, but that's another story for another book. Still waiting to see your traveling Sharpie socks in person!

Chrissy Guthrie, everything about you is so impressive. You pull together complicated stuff that's all over the place and make it seem so easy, even when you have 4.3 million other things going on. Thank you for being so awesome, for putting in so much work, and keeping things seamless.

Megan Knoll, you seriously catch everything and you're always looking 27 steps ahead (but how do you feel about hyperbole?). I can't even tell you how thankful I am to you for all your fixes, redirections, and considerations — especially that you considered inclusivity, which was brilliant. Thank you so much for all of it.

CSM Carlos Corbin, I know I tell you this from time to time, but you have always played a huge role in both my and David's careers. I am so thankful for your willingness to teach and share your expertise, starting when I was a junior soldier who stepped off a plane and into your platoon in Iraq and through today. I will never forget (or stop laughing about) the time you taught that female 2LT to stay in her lane!

Erin Betron and Alan Vonderheide, the two best fitness pros ever depicted in an ACFT book: Thank you so much for showing us all what right looks like. Your fitness expertise and dedication to showing perfect form are amazing.

Kathryn Born, thank you for your spectacular illustrations and hard work to make every detail perfect.

Zack McCrory, thanks for lending your eye (and your tremendous skill) to capturing each photo with such precision.

Publisher's Acknowledgments

Executive Editor: Lindsay Sandman Lefevere

Managing Editors: Vicki Adang, Michelle Hacker

Editorial Project Manager and Development Editor: Christina N. Guthrie

Copy Editor: Megan Knoll

Technical Editor: Command Sergeant Major Carlos D. Corbin

Production Editor: Mohammed Zafar Ali

Cinematography: Keith Toombs

Audio: Dwight Beuchler

Producer/Director: Lisa Holloway

Photographer: Zack McCrory

Assistant to the Photographer: Matthew Milson

Illustrator: Kathyrn Born

Cover Image: © mihailomilovanovic/Getty Images